MICHIGAN
Quilts

The Quilt Speaks

It takes much thought to make a quilt
Some are made of wool or cotton or silk
And every stitch should be just right
The top should be ever so bright
Materials should be of uniform design
And allow one to move freely at any time
The maker is guided by God from above
And thus the workmanship is one of love
It should give the user a sense of content
And thus one's time has been well spent.

U. Florine Plumb
Jackson, Michigan
January 17, 1979

MICHIGAN
Quilts

150 Years of a Textile Tradition

Edited by
Marsha MacDowell and Ruth D. Fitzgerald

Michigan State University Museum
East Lansing, Michigan

Copyright © 1987 by the Board of Trustees, Michigan State University

Printed in the United States of America

Library of Congress Catalog Card No.: 87-62538
ISBN, hardcover edition: 0-944311-00-8
ISBN, softcover edition: 0-944311-01-6

On the cover: *Star of Bethlehem Quilt* made by Margaret (or Anna) David, ca. 1920, Peshawbestown, Leelanau County, Michigan, MQP #86.482, owned by Elizabeth and Vernon Keye. Photograph © 1987, Peter Glendinning, courtesy of Michigan State University Museum.

Design: Cynthia Lounsbery, Senior Graphic Designer, University Publications, MSU
Editing, production supervision: Kathleen Schoonmaker, Associate Editor, University Publications, MSU
Typesetting: Superior Graphics, Lansing, Michigan
Printing and binding: Lansing Printing Co., Lansing, Michigan

Photographs: All photographs of quilts are copyright © 1987 Peter Glendinning, courtesy of Michigan State University Museum, except for the following: 10, 12, 41, 43, 62, 65, 105, courtesy of Dearborn Historical Museum; 21, courtesy of America Hurrah Antiques, New York City; 42, photograph by Sharon Risedorph, courtesy of R. K. Press/ Roderick Kiracofe, San Francisco, California; 60 and 76, courtesy of Merry and Albert J. Silber; 45, 46, 48, 49, 50, 51, and 53, photograph by Betty Boyink, courtesy of Glenna VanLente; 116 courtesy of David Pottinger; 159 courtesy of Bernice Doughty; 196 courtesy of Donna Maki, first published by Caron L. Mosey, *America's Pictorial Quilts,* American Quilter's Society; 172 courtesy of City of Birmingham, Michigan; 78 and 133 courtesy of Michigan State University Museum; 218 courtesy of Aileen Stannis; 72 courtesy of Julie Silber and Linda Reuther, Mary Strickler's Quilt; 86 courtesy of Esprit, Inc., San Francisco, California; and 4, 15, 69, 101, 120, 168, 176, 190, and 219 by Instructional Media Center, Michigan State University, courtesy of Michigan State University Museum. All other photographs are by photographers credited in accompanying captions.

Funding Sources: Michigan Council for the Arts, National Endowment for the Arts (Folk Arts Program), Michigan State University All-University Research Initiation Grant, Michigan Department of Commerce YES150 Fund, Ruth Mott Fund, East Lansing Fine Arts Commission, and contributions from private individuals.

CONTENTS

FOREWORD

As Michigan celebrates the sesquicentennial anniversary of statehood, it is especially fitting that Michigan State University, the state's land grant institution, pays tribute to the rich heritage and ongoing vitality of the state's traditional arts. It is even more appropriate that the university provides the leadership and commitment to recognize and celebrate a form of traditional art so firmly tied to the experience of Michigan women, their families, and their communities.

The Michigan Quilt Project, developed by the staff of the Michigan Traditional Arts Program at the Michigan State University Museum, has focused attention on this broad area of artistic contributions by Michigan citizens. Hundreds of volunteers across the state have worked closely with MSU Museum staff in the collection of data on Michigan quilts, quiltmakers, and quiltmaking traditions. As information about each quilt, quilter, and quilt story was recorded, our understanding of the pervasiveness and importance of this art-making activity in the life of Michigan residents has increased.

The tangible results of the Michigan Quilt Project have been the formation of a resource information center, a computerized data collection storage bank, and a growing collection of Michigan quilts. In less tangible terms, the Michigan Quilt Project has engaged hundreds of Michigan residents in the process of identifying and celebrating the contributions of their families and community members to Michigan's artistic heritage.

Through research, the Michigan Quilt Project staff has begun the process of preserving these pieces of Michigan history. Now, through this publication and the corresponding exhibition, the Michigan Quilt Project staff begins the process of sharing with others the art and history of those who have helped create and preserve it.

One of Michigan's greatest strengths, yet most under-recognized resources, is the talent of our citizens. It has given me great pleasure to be associated with the Michigan Quilt Project and its efforts to honor the work of those who have contributed so much to our state.

Carolyn E. DiBiaggio
Honorary Chairperson, Michigan Quilt Project
Cowles House
Michigan State University
August 1987

PREFACE

A quilt is a textbook of information. In every piece of fabric, completed quilt, and pattern name one or more stories are to be found. Some of these stories can be learned just by looking at a scrap of fabric, a block, or an entire quilt. Others must be learned by inquiring about the quilt and quilter. Personal or family history, art, community life, religious beliefs and practices, business and political history, and more can be gleaned from these textiles, their makers, and their owners.

As Michigan celebrates its 150th year of statehood, it is appropriate to focus attention on a body of needlework that not only is striking to view but also provides a significant cultural and historical record of its people. The quilts included in this publication were chosen to represent the variety of traditions, styles, and quiltmakers that constitute the history of quiltmaking in this state. Although a few of the quilts are from public or private textile collections, most are owned by the makers or their families and have never been previously brought to public attention. The quilts selected for inclusion here repre-

sent prized family possessions, important family and community documents, and the strength and breadth of quilting as an art activity in the state.

Some quilts are quickly accepted as visual masterpieces. Others may at first glance appear homely, but the stories associated with their makers or history are compelling. Quiltmaking has been an art that is clearly linked to both personal and community experience. One does not have to "understand art" in order to be able to grasp the role that these quiltmakers and their work have played in the formation of state history. By viewing the quilts and learning the stories associated with them, we gain a better understanding of human life as it was and is in Michigan.

Marsha MacDowell
Michigan Quilt Project Director
Michigan Traditional Arts Program
Michigan State University Museum

ACKNOWLEDGMENTS

It would be impossible to thank adequately all of the individuals who have contributed to this project. There have been literally hundreds of individuals across the state who have given their time and knowledge and skills to this project. Without their interest and support and that of the persons listed below, this project would not have been possible.

General

Cynthia Lounsbery
Kathleen Schoonmaker
Peter Glendinning
Bruce Smith
Carolyn Davis
Merry Silber
Dr. Harriet Clarke
  and George Clarke
Joe Ishikawa
Dr. Susan Bandes
Betty Boyink
Dr. Carol Fisher
Barbara Hamblett
Gwen Marston
Joe Cunningham
Lorabeth Fitzgerald
John Fitzgerald
Minn Dewhurst
Mary Schafer
Kathryn Darnell
Paul Streng
John Green

Dr. Gladys-Marie Frye
Sharon Scott
Maggie Jones
Jackie Faulkner
Betty Boone
Barbara Goldman
Tom Tenbrunsel
Sandra Mitchell
Lynn Jondahl
Frank Fitzgerald
Marit Dewhurst
Harlan MacDowell
Gene Mauch
Eva Boicourt
Dr. John Cantlon
Dr. Jake Wamhoff
Dr. Gordon Guyer
Liz Hausserman
Susan Zimmerman
Dr. Marylee Davis
Carol Davey

MSU Museum Students, Interns, and Staff

Francie Freese
Judy DeJaegher
Ruth D. Fitzgerald
Gerna Rubenstein
Dr. Yvonne Lockwood
Terry Shaffer
Val Berryman
LuAnne G. Kozma
Kathy Parker
Lynne Swanson
Carrie Willard
Pam Ferguson
Diane Vandenburg
Edwina Johnson
Kris Lund
Martha Brownscombe
Dr. Marty Hetherington

Yeon Min
Dr. Betty MacDowell
Helen Hoskins
Sue Baker
Peter Wehr
Terry Hansen-Eftaxiadis
Amy Little
Melissa Prine
Laura Ashlee
Mike Smith
Sarah Day
Bob Leland
Phil Lienhart
Margie Bryant
Rhonda Davis
Cris Ballentine

From completing and submitting Michigan Quilt Project inventory forms to coordinating local Quilt Discovery Days to helping catalogue materials, volunteers have been a key to the realization of this project. Special thanks are extended to the members of the Capitol City Quilt Guild for their contributions of a quilt top for the subscription quilt fundraising effort, the assistance in local Quilt Discovery Days, the organization of the Michigan Quilt Project Celebration and Conference, and their general enthusiasm for and encouragement of the project. Thanks are also extended to the volunteers listed below who contributed so much in so many ways.

Michigan Quilt Project Local Assistance

Jackie Beard
Cathy Newkirk
Barbara Worthington
Val Fonseca
Bonnie Bus
Carol Seamon
Daisy DeHaven
Louise Mueller
Florence Vogt
Sherlee Mauch
Betty Tesner

Ruth Dukelow
Char Ezell
Terry McKenney Person
Pat Cavanaugh
Beth Donaldson
Pepper Cory
Bernadette Nipkow
Lynne Davidson
Carolyn Solomon
Betty Votruba

Subscription Quilt

Louise Mueller
Maxine Hoffman
Donna Maki
Edna Eckert
Bonnie Mercer
Shelby Hollister
Daisy DeHaven
Lucille Slye
Bonnie Bus
Doris Kollmeyer
Beth Donaldson
Marlene Eggert
Brenda Clark
Gail Hill
Maria Lopez Thompson
Nancy Myers
Georgia Hayden

Carol Seamon
Judy Mitchell
Mary Fry
Terry McKenney Person
Sherlee Mauch
Norine Antuck
Dima Sheffield
Jeanne Nielsen
Phyllis O'Connor
Ann Snyder
Gail Oranchak
Teri Nessia
Denise Houck
Ruth Dukelow
Cindy Mielock
Beverly Zurfluh

Quilt Discovery Day Coordinators

Milton Alstin, Lansing
Marcia Bernhardt, Caspian
Janie Brooks, Muskegon
Audrey Bullett, Idlewild
Sally J. Carpenter,
    Centreville
Leona Center, Detroit
Lola Choinski, Detroit
Patricia A. Davis,
    Grand Rapids
Caroline DeMauriac,
    Traverse City
Michelle Dittmer,
    St. Clair Shores
Jim Dompier, Baraga
Ruth Dukelow, East Lansing
Colleen Esch, Houghton
Sally Eustis, Cheboygan
Mike Feyers, Muskegon
Lucille M. Fleming,
    Marlette
Liz Hausserman, Ionia
Sherrie Jaqua, Marquette
Maggie Jones, Muskegon
Mary Lee Kennedy,
    Traverse City
Leila Klaiss, Charlotte
Matt Linke, Alpena
Margaret Malanyn,
    Dearborn

Sherlee Mauch, Wyandotte
Lori S. Naples, Detroit
Julie Nordin, Stephenson
Mary Pemble, St. Ignace
Terry McKenney Person,
    East Lansing
Kathy Peters, Marquette
Nancy S. Powell,
    Grand Rapids
Laura Quackenbush, Leland
Carol Saari, Ironwood
Joyce Salisbury,
    Mt. Pleasant
Lester Schick, Muskegon
Sharon Scott, Clinton
Elaine M. Seaman,
    Kalamazoo
William J. Setterington,
    Maple Rapids
JoAnn Shelby, Marquette
Henrietta Summers,
    Idlewild
Gretchen Tatge,
    Sterling Heights
Linda Tesch, Saginaw
Andy Trembath, Marquette
Terry Trupiano, Hastings
Sue Vorpagel, Bay View
Jane Wade, Muskegon
Patricia Zander, Saranac

Quiltmaking in Michigan

by Marsha MacDowell

Beginning in 1984, the staff of the Michigan Traditional Arts Program at the Michigan State University Museum initiated a systematic collection of data on Michigan quilts and quilt-related activities as a state sesquicentennial project. Like its survey counterparts in other states, the Michigan Quilt Project, or MQP as it is called, attempted to record an area of artmaking that had been largely overlooked by previous documentation efforts. (The project methodology can be found in the appendix.) Although many exhibitions of Michigan quilts had been held, and private collectors in the state had begun assembling substantial collections of such textiles, the interest in quilts had centered largely on their design aspects and not their historical or cultural associations. The MQP attempted to expand this focus by collecting data that will contribute to the process of analyzing migration patterns, ethnic or regional variations in quiltmaking styles and patterns, variance in processes of learning quilting methods, and the influence of technological change and improved communication systems on quiltmaking.

One of the most telling outcomes of the Michigan Quilt Project to date has been the discovery of the extent to which quiltmaking existed throughout all periods of postnative settlement in Michigan and the geographically widespread nature of the activity. Information was gathered about quilts and quiltmakers in every county and every year of Michigan's statehood. At Quilt Discovery Days which were held in various communities a frequently heard comment was, "You would get a lot more quilts if you hold one in the next town," or "Why don't you hold another one next year, we know many people who just couldn't get here today." Clearly, many quilts remain as family treasures in personal collections, many quiltmakers continue to produce new textiles imbedded with personal, family or community meaning, and many quilt-related memories remain firmly connected to family histories.

Over the last three years, the Michigan Quilt Project has gathered together an impressive and extensive array of data from which the process of analysis can begin. Yet a tremendous amount of information remains to be collected, and any analysis at this point is but an assessment of trends. For example, several key trends or distinctive aspects of quiltmaking in Michigan have emerged in the early stages of data collection and continue to be substantiated by ensuing research. They include the importance of quilts as documents of personal, family, community, and national history; the growing influence of technology and communication systems on the way in which quiltmaking is learned and evaluated; the variety and prevalence of certain quiltmaking traditions that continue to flourish; the continued dominance of women in quiltmaking activities; and the important meaning that the making and sharing of quilts has had in community life. By looking more closely at these trends, it is possible to gain a clearer picture of the place these objects and their makers have had in the life of this region.

Quilts as Documents and Markers

Quilts serve as documents of personal, family, community, and national history, which is one of the most important reasons for studying them. Throughout Michigan history quilts have been commonly made to mark such significant events within families as births, graduations, weddings, anniversaries, and deaths. Quilts have also been made to mark events such as the return of a veteran from the Civil War, the departure of a minister from a pastorate, or a friend's transfer to another residence. An example is the quilt that Lucille M. Rugg registered in the inventory, which had been in her husband's family. In a letter dated May 23, 1986 she explains:

> It was made by a guild in Kalkaska and depicts all the Civil War soldiers and their regiments from Kalkaska Co. who died in the Civil War. My husband's grandfather served with [Ulysses S.] Grant at Vicksburg, but he was in a PA [Pennsylvania] regiment at the time. After the war he settled in Kalkaska where he was Sheriff and Postmaster and had a saw mill. There is still Rugg Hall and Rugg Pond on the Valley Road just outside of Kalkaska.[1]

Meaning also becomes attached to pieced or patched textiles created during particular periods of a maker's life. In the following case, the quiltmaking experience itself is central to the history of the person in that period. This account, drawn

It is unclear whether these Adrian, Michigan women are piecing quilt blocks, but it is known that Louise (Mrs. W. H.) Packard Smith (pictured far left) made several quilts. From left to right are Smith, Ida and Anna Park, Mrs. A. B. Park (their mother), and Mary Frances Packard Tippett. (Photograph taken ca. 1880, courtesy of the City of Colorado Springs Pioneer Museum.)

from a letter submitted to the *Detroit News* "Quilt Club Corner" column, echoes other Depression-era stories collected by the Michigan Quilt Project:

> The quilt I am sending to the [*Detroit News* quilt] show is from a "Log Cabin" pattern. It was started in 1933. At that time I had never seen a quilt like it and started it with only a meager description that grandmother gave me. The winter of 1933 was the most discouraging time for us. We were unable to spend money for anything but the barest necessities and I was starved for something gay and pretty and new. I started to create something to fill that need. I hate to remember now what small purchases I made in order to keep that gay piecework in existence. When I look at the finished work I see things in the stitches and gay strips that will always be there for me. . . . The blocks were gayer with each increasing problem and in that way served to balance a drab life. I have never hurried in working because sewing has rested me when nothing else seemed to help. Last year my husband made me the most beautiful quilt frames I have ever seen. They were made from a *News* plan and he added a small crank for turning the quilt as I worked. It is made of wild cherry and I could easily have it in my living room the year around it is so lovely.[2]

Clearly the activities involved in making the above quilt helped sustain the spirits of the maker through a troublesome time. In a sense, quiltmaking served many individuals as a therapeutic device, easing stress or discomfort caused by financial, emotional, or physical difficulties. Quilting was often reported as instrumental in helping to pass the time during periods of sickness. An example is recounted in the following passage from a letter the MQP staff received from Phyllis E. Miller:

> This is a picture of my mother, Ida Starr, re-quilting, in 1979, a quilt made by my father, Clinton Starr, in the mid 1930s, while recovering from a severe case of tuberculosis in American Legion Hospital, Battle Creek, Mich. . . . Dad was tired of doing some of the crafts they offered at the hospital and asked mother to send him materials to make a quilt. He would be in his mid thirties, at the time. He had spent several years in the hospital, because REST was the most suggested cure at that time. Mother bought the blue cottons out of our meager earnings and the white is home bleached feed sacks. The original quilt had a part wool batt and when Mother washed it, forgetting about the wool, the water was too hot and it shrank badly. It was used some in its shrunken condition and laid unused until about 1979. I tore it apart and Mother and I requilted it, with new batt and lining. . . . Dad and Mother are both gone, but one of my brothers has the quilt, as a memory of Dad's handiwork. . . . Mother, and her mother were quiltmakers, for as far back as I can remember. I am carrying on the tradition, making them to sell at the semi annual Amish auction, held near Clare, Mich.[3]

When fabrics associated with a specific individual, event, place, or activity were used in a quilt, the resulting textile often served as a touchstone to memories of those things. It was not uncommon for the clothing of deceased family members to be cut up and reused in a quilt. One quiltmaker, whose quilt was inventoried in Idlewild, explained how she used her deceased father's clothing to make the quilt that she used regularly on her bed. The process of quilting and the nightly cover eased her grief in a period of mourning. A similar exprience 100 years earlier was recounted in a letter dated December 6, 1880 written from Union, Boone County, Iowa by James Mills, the widower of quilter Phebe Mills, and enclosed in a package sent to his mother-in-law in Perry, Michigan:

> . . . . the package contains. . . . specimens of her handy needlework, her artificial teeth. To JCH [her brother] are pieces for a bedquilt which when quilted may be to him a matter of comfort in old age. . . . I have divided her clothing and her ingenious specimens of needlework among my daughters-in-law and Sr. Sarah and Br. JCH. . . .[4]

As a memory aid, the fabrics provide a visual link to the experiences of another time and place and serve as reminders of loved ones. Many of the quilts registered in the project were considered family heirlooms. Even when the stories associated with a quilt were few or when little was known about its maker, the quilt's lineage was clear.

Interests in other hobbies were often reflected in the choices that Michigan quiltmakers made in pattern, fabrics, or designs. Examples entered in the inventory included a quilt made out of ribbons won in 4-H events (no. 208), one made of blocks of appliquéd square dancers done in preparation to show at a National Square Dancers Convention (not included in exhibit), one incorporating the tartan plaids of a family's Scottish background (no. 246), one done with scraps of all of the aprons a quiltmaker had made (no. 200), another showing a collection of antique pottery (no. 194), and several made of blocks containing the signatures of famous people (nos. 219, 238, 239). Interests in sports were reflected not only in several inventoried quilts that included printed ribbons with local sports figures on them, but also in the one described by Edith B. Crumb in a 1937 *Detroit News* quilt column:

> . . . . Mrs. Daniel Korbe, Jr. . . . is an enthusiastic fan and last year designed a Tiger quilt. The day before the last game of the World Series she sent a disc of white cloth to each of the Detroit ball players, asking him to autograph it. The day after the final game she received the first autograph and it was from Mickey Cochrane, and from then until February these kept trailing in. Some of them traveled quite a bit, "Schoolboy" Rowe's being sent from El Dorado, Ark.; Rudolph York's from Germantown, Ga.; Umpire Klem's from Hendersonville, N.C.; and "Goose" Goslin's from Salem, N.J. . . . The background of this quilt is grass green, the diamond brown, the foul line white and the bases are white with black and orange stitching. . . . All of the autographed balls are placed just where the players are located. . . . [5]

This enthusiasm for making quilts out of autographed pieces of fabrics has been long-standing in Michigan and was well expressed in an article submitted by a Saginaw, Michigan resident that appeared in an 1889 issue of *Good Housekeeping:*

> This is a day of autograph hunters. The epidemic assumes various forms. Some have the craze for postal albums. One lady of my acquaintance has an album of several hundred postals she admits she never saw, and never expects to see. Another rage is the autograph quilt, but few people at present have the temerity to aspire to the crazy quilt. For my part I have not yet been able to decide whether I like them or not, I have seen so many witched and bewitched into what was originally intended to be a thing of beauty, but what really seemed more the production of the weakened brain of some poor aesthetic lunatic.

This photograph, taken ca. 1890, shows a young girl in North Branch, Michigan and a Crazy quilt. Women and young girls were able to showcase their knowledge of embroidery stitches on such quilts. (Photograph courtesy of E. P. Dutton and Sandra Mitchell.)

> In fact, I never see a crazy quilt without a vivid childhood remembrance of a kaleidoscopic view I once had after falling from a high swing. Autograph quilts containing a block from each state and territory in the Union are also very much in vogue. My idea of an autograph quilt is something entirely different, and as it is original with myself I will give it, as it will no doubt be something new to others. I am saving a piece of each dress and apron of my children's clothes from their babyhood up. Upon each piece I fasten a bit of paper with the date and the age of the child at the time they had the garment. After I am done collecting I shall make each a quilt of his or her own pieces, then with indelible ink mark on each block the age of the child at the time the garment was bought, also what the garment was. What think you of my idea? Try it mothers. It will be something the children can always keep, and something they will prize above gold long after that dear mother has crossed the mystic river into the great beyond. I love to piece quilts, and expect to be just that old-fashioned all my life. [6]

Evidence of events of local, state, and national historical significance have also been found in Michigan quiltmaking. The end of the Civil War prompted the production of several quilts commemorating the return of war veterans to their home communities. Because of the financial austerity of the Depression-era years, numerous quilts were made by individuals who ordinarily did not quilt but needed either to recycle materials to provide warm coverings or use quilting as a means to pass time during unemployment. The celebration of the nation's centennial and bicentennial and now Michigan's sesquicentennial also initiated widespread production of quilts with patriotic symbols, colors, and patterns. During the 1976 United States bicentennial celebration, a trend emerged in the production of community history quilts. In the blocks that make up the typical community history quilt are painted, inked, embroidered, or appliquéd representations of locally significant places, people, and events. From the city of Farmington Hills to Ionia County to the Les Cheneaux region of the Upper Peninsula, the community history quilts created in each town and region provide another interpretation and representation of local history. In the case of Autograph or Signature quilts, onto the top of which individuals have inked or embroidered their names, the textile is a signed document of those who lived in a certain area or who belonged to a particular group. In some instances, such a signed quilt may be the only existing record of these events or affiliations.

Records of Patterns of Migration and Settlement

Patterns of migration to and settlement within Michigan communities have often been reflected in quilts. For instance, it is known that quilts were used by the early French settlers. According to a paper read by Mrs. M. Carrie W. Hamlin, of Detroit, before the Wayne County Pioneer Society in 1878,

The furniture of those days was very simple, but it answered every requirement. In the bedroom a four-post bedstead on stilts, with a deep valance of dimity, an immense feather-bed on a rope network, replaced later by wooden slats, huge, round bolster, large, square pillows, a gaily colored patch-quilt which was an ingenious record of all the dresses of the female friends.[7]

Although Native Americans in the Great Lakes region participated in a variety of highly skilled textile traditions, including weaving, beadwork, and appliquéd ribbon work, it appears that they were not involved in quiltmaking before contact with non-Natives. A few photographic records of tribal members with pieced and appliquéd quilting are the scant documentary evidence of their work. Only two extant Native-American-made, early twentieth-century quilts have been registered in the inventory. However, a 1938 *Detroit News* article about the fifth annual *Detroit News* Quilt Show displayed a photograph with this caption: "Miss Alma Knudsen, Mrs. Frances Heintz and Mrs. Walter Pomeroy, judges, admired a quilt that was made by an Indian squaw. Bright colors predominate and the combination of flowers and patches is interesting."[8] The quilt pictured in the article as well as the two inventoried quilts show an intersection of typical Woodlands floral and star motifs with Euro-American quilting techniques. In more recent years quiltmaking has been continued by both individual and groups of Native-American artists, such as the women of the senior citizens center at the Isabella Reservation in Mt. Pleasant.

In the nineteenth century, when thousands of immigrants came to Michigan from the Northeast and from European countries to work as miners, lumberjacks, and farmers, they brought with them a need for both emotional and material comforts. Later, when waves of immigrants from the Upland South, Appalachia, Italy, Southeast Asia, and the Arab

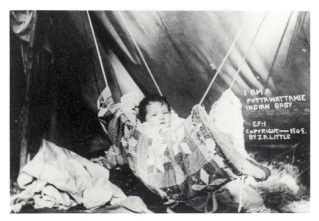

"I am a Pottawattamie [sic] Indian Baby" picture postcard, copyright © 1909 by J. A. Little. The Potawatomi baby rests in a hammock-style cradle made of patchwork. An Ottawa named Agosa who lived on Old Mission Peninsula in the mid 1840s was the first Michigan Native on record to own non-Native furniture. This fact helps to date the use of quilts as bedding among Michigan Natives. (Photograph courtesy of Michigan Department of State Archives.)

countries arrived to settle in Michigan, they too had physical and psychic needs that could be met in part by owning or making quilts. Quilts made by such settlers helped to augment physical warmth and comfort. The family quilts they brought with them helped to satisfy their need to maintain a psychical tie with the past. Many quilts that served as reminders of a homeland or loved ones left behind have been recorded in the Michigan Quilt Project. A ca. 1937 *Detroit News* article described not only the extent to which a quilt was valued by a family, but a solution to the problem of which family unit would inherit the treasure: "Mrs. Mamie Strauss is exhibiting a quarter of a treasured family quilt made in Holland many years ago, and long since, divided up among heirs."[9] The quilt was simply cut up so that its associations with a past could be shared by more than one family unit.

In each instance, the quilts brought or made by immigrants incorporated techniques, patterns, and uses that reflected the region from which they hailed. As quiltmakers came into contact with people outside of their ethnic, racial, or religious background, they began to create textiles that combined the influence of these new groups with native techniques. The process of assimilation ultimately caused traditions to be variously sharpened, celebrated, altered, merged, or eliminated. In twentieth-century Afro-American quiltmaking in Michigan an array of the variations of traditions can be seen. The extent to which Afro-American-made quilts display evidence of survivalist forms of African textiles, integration of Anglo and Afro-American techniques, or complete adaptations of Anglo-American quilt styles and practices is dependent on such factors as whether the maker lives in a rural or urban setting, is a fourth-generation descendant of a former slave who escaped to Michigan via the Underground Railroad or a citizen who came to Michigan in the 1940s from the Upland South to work in the Northern factories, or has had contact with other quilters.[10]

In 1976 Laotian-Hmong refugees began to resettle in Michigan. Female members of this new immigrant group are extremely skilled in an array of needlework traditions, including embroidered, appliquéd, and reverse appliquéd cloths called *paj ntaub* (pronounced "pan dow" and meaning, literally, flower cloth).[11] In their Laotian homeland, Hmong had created *paj ntaub* primarily for use in the production of Hmong clothes and only secondarily for sale to non-Hmong. In Michigan, the new immigrants no longer wore traditional Hmong clothes on a daily basis and had little time to devote to the intricacies of their detailed textile work. These two factors, along with other influences, prompted the needlework artists to alter and adapt the styles, colors, and types of *paj ntaub* in order to attract new audiences who would purchase their goods. As Hmong women began to have increased contact with textile techniques and forms in America, it was almost inevitable that they would begin to use their highly advanced appliqué technique in the production of quilts done in American motifs. In an effort to develop an efficient way of producing marketable Hmong-made quilts, Clarkston, Michigan, resident Jane Kennedy is coordinating a project in which women appliqué quilt tops that are then quilted by Mennonite and Amish quilters in the Lancaster, Pennsylvania and Fairview, Michigan areas.[12] The highly advanced appliqué techniques of the Hmong women have been combined with the outstanding quilting techniques of the Mennonite and Amish in this unusual marketing venture.

Quilts can be read as documents not only of those who have moved to Michigan, but also of those who have moved away. Many respondents to the Michigan Quilt Project inventory were residents who had moved, with their quilts, to other parts of the country. Because their quilts were made in or by someone from Michigan, they are "Michigan quilts." The associations of place to object remained strong even when the quilt itself no longer remained in Michigan. For some quilt owners, the "natural"

Six women and a young girl were photographed at a summer outdoor quilting party in Negaunee, Michigan, ca. 1900. It is unclear whether the women were dressed in their hats and finery for the quilting or for the photography session, but it was often reported that a "quilting" was a time to look one's best. The quilt frame shown here is of the type most often used in Michigan. It consists of four wooden boards temporarily secured to the tops of chair backs. (Photograph courtesy Michigan Department of State Archives.)

residing place of a quilt is that most strongly associated with its maker or its history. In the MQP inventory, accounts were given of quilts being sent back to their "proper or rightful" owner.

Written and oral accounts of quiltmaking associated with the experience of traveling to or from Michigan have also been noted. In a letter dated July 9, 1871 sent from Union, Boone County, Iowa, quiltmaker Phebe Homes Mills wrote to her mother and relatives who lived in Perry, Michigan, "Since I came [visited] from Michigan I have cut and piest [sic] 30 lbs of carpet rags and I have 30 blocks of the album [quilt] piest and 15 of the double T piest...."[13]

As more information is gathered on the relationship between particular quilting customs and indi-vidual native or immigrant Michigan groups, quilts will be seen as even more valuable documents of evidence of settlement patterns. Along with other forms of documentation, i.e., photographic, oral, and written, the quilts serve to substantiate the record of human history in this state.

Quilts in Community Life

Quilt-related activities have contributed in a variety of ways to the development and maintenance of cultural life within rural and urban communities. Quilting "bees" or parties, quilt exhibitions, quilt columns in local newspapers, fundraising efforts based on quilts, quiltmaking classes, and other shared quilt activities have helped to foster a sense of place among residents of local communities.

Quilting Bees or Parties

In the early years of postnative settlement in Michigan, quilting bees, like other communal work parties for sharing labor, served a crucial role in meeting the basic necessities of life, as was pointed out by A. D. P. Van Buren in *Pioneer Collections:*

> Raisings, logging-bees, husking-bees, quilting-bees and the many other occasions in which the word bee was used to indicate the gathering of the settlers to render gratuitous aids to some neighbor in need, originated in, and was confined to new settlements. It was merely the voluntary union of the individual aid and strength of an entire community to assist a settler in doing what he was unable to accomplish alone. Hence by bees the pioneers raised their houses and barns, did their logging, husked their corn, quilted their bed coverings, and enjoyed themselves in frolic and song with the girls in the evening.[14]

Equal to the importance of the work completed at these bees was the opportunity these occasions afforded quilters to meet with friends, share food and conversation, meet new neighbors, and—not the least important—meet prospective partners. One of the earliest accounts in Michigan of a quilting party is given by Elizabeth Margaret Chandler of Tecumseh, Michigan, who wrote in 1832, "I was at a quilting last week. There were about twenty girls besides myself and in the evening about the same number of men."[15] Van Buren also commented on the social aspects of these events as they occurred in Calhoun County circa 1840:

> There were no members of the early settlement who felt too indifferent or too dignified to attend the social parties that were held in the settler's log houses. But what were these parties, you ask. I will tell you. In the first place there was the quilting frolic; the girls attending in the afternoon, the boys coming in the evening. Then there was the frolic without the quilting, which the girls and boys attended in the evening. The sport in both of these parties was usually begun by the play of "snap and catch 'em," or some rhyming catch.[16]

Thus quilting parties could serve community-wide needs for sharing both labor and companionship.

However, the importance of quilting as a social activity has probably been the greatest in the context of smaller groups. Many strong and lasting friendships were formed through the hundreds of quilting clubs, guilds, and circles that have existed in Michigan. Many clubs met on a regular basis, and club members became devoted to attendance, as this *Detroit News* article describes:

About six years ago a small group of quilters organized a club which they named the Happy Day Club. It has been changed to the Rain or Shine Club, for regardless of weather, they meet every single Tuesday at the house of the member who has a top to be quilted. The group shown in the picture is finishing an Improved Nine-Patch which Mrs. Margaret Dawson has just pieced. The meeting begins at 10 a.m. and continues until 4:30 in the afternoon. The members of the Rain or Shine Club, are left to right: Mrs. Rose Bondie, Mrs. Esther Meeker, Mrs. Pearl Rhoads, Mrs. Alice Lane, Mrs. Erma Buhl, Mrs. Margaret Dawson (hostess), and Mrs. Elizabeth Kruecher.[17]

About the value of small localized quilt clubs in fostering a sense of community, another *Detroit News* column had this to say:

Nothing could be better adapted to help along the chitchat and gossip of a neighborhood party than a quilting. In many ways it surpasses bridge, since it has a worthwhile aim and requires less concentration. With good designing and skillful execution, the quilt becomes not only a work of art, but an article of lasting usefulness. If also it is a memento of a pleasant afternoon spent in companionship with friends, it has greatly added value.[18]

For many persons, memories of being present at their mother's or grandmother's quilting parties remain strong. Accounts often mention playing underneath a quilt spread out on a frame or playing with other children while mothers quilted. One Muskegon quiltmaker recalls how the female members of her family often sang spirituals as they gathered to quilt in Alabama.[19] Grace Blattert wrote about her childhood experiences with quilting parties:

In the '20s my grandmother lived only a block from our house and on her "quilting day" I would thread about fifty needles before going to school, again at lunch hour, and immediately after school. The six to eight women never lost any time from their work. The hostess of the day served lunch and a mid-afternoon snack in shifts![20]

Many quiltmakers reported memories of the food, conversation, play, and work of these occasions, and most indicated that these days were important for the friendships they helped to cement.

Quilts in Fairs and Festivals

From their initial inclusion in the "Domestics Manufacture Judging Division" of the first Michigan Agricultural Society Fair held in Detroit in 1849, displays of quilts have been a fundamental part of state, regional, and county fairs in Michigan. The importance of the place of these displays in the life of communities was clearly stated by Marie D. Webster in her 1913 publication *Quilts: Their Story and How to Make Them*:

For the women of the farm the exhibit of domestic arts and products occupies the preeminent place at the county fair. In this exhibit the display of patchwork is sure to arouse the liveliest enthusiasm. A visitor at a fair in a western state very neatly describes this appreciation shown to quilts: "We used to hear a great deal about the sad and lonely fate of the western farmer's wife, but there was little evidence of loneliness in the appearance of these women who surrounded the quilts and fancywork in the Domestic Arts Building".... There is not the least doubt concerning the beneficial influence of the local annual fair on the life of the adjacent neighborhood. At such a fair the presence of a varied and well-arranged display of needlework, which has been produced by the womenfolk, is of the greatest assistance in making the community one in which it is worthwhile to live. Not only does it serve as a stimulus to those who look forward to the fair and put into their art the very best of their ability in order that they may surpass their competitor next door, but it also serves as an inspiration to those who are denied the faculty of creating original designs, yet nevertheless take keen pleasure in the production of beautiful needlework. It is to this latter class that an exhibition of quilts is of real value, because it provides them with new patterns that can be applied to the quilts which must be made. With fresh ideas for their inspiration, work which would otherwise be tedious becomes a real pleasure.[21]

Because quilts were usually juried and ribbons were awarded as prizes at these fairs, the resulting display of ribbon-winning quilts helped to set and to validate a standard of excellence for quiltmaking within a community. In the first state fair, the jurors awarded premiums of two dollars each to three quilts and gave three discretionary premiums to six other quilts.[22] By the 100th Michigan State Fair, held in Detroit in 1949, the quilts were judged under a separate category in the "Division I—Needlework

"Rain or Shine Quilt Club," whose members met every Tuesday, regardless of the weather. (Photograph courtesy of Michigan State University Museum.)

County fair quilt show in Wolverine, Michigan, 1910. (Photograph courtesy of Michigan State University Museum.)

and Other Handicrafts, Section 14—Quilts," but the premiums had only risen to seven dollars for the top prize. An additional award of one carton of Mountain Mist Needle-Easy "Glazene" Cotton was provided by the Stearns and Foster Company for all first, second, third, and fourth prize winners in every quilt class where a cotton filling was used and quilting was done.[23]

Jury panels usually included needlework experts from the area, often from Michigan State Agricultural College (later to become Michigan State University). The importance of having qualified personnel judge the quilts was quickly realized by a set of male jurors who participated in the first Jackson County Fair held in 1853. In their report to the county agricultural society, they admitted their lack of knowledge about needle arts:

> Your Committee beg leave to state that in the articles of patch quilts, plain quilts, coverlet and bed spreads, the competition was very great. There were many exhibited, besides those that were awarded premiums, entitled to great merit—so much so that it was difficult for the committee to decide. Your committee have thought it best to give two more premiums to these articles than were specified in the list of premiums. Your Committee regret exceedingly, that there were not some one or more ladies placed on the Committee, for the purpose of examining these articles.—F. M. Foster, S. G. Strong, E. B. Fuller, E. Delamater, L. Kassick, Committee.[24]

Even with the appropriate qualified personnel, jury panels did not necessarily find their task any easier. Jurors for the 1878 Michigan State Fair commented on the problems they encountered in the adjudication process:

> Your committee has labored under great difficulties in making examinations and awarding premiums in this class. The attendance was so large as to render it extremely difficult to get around and properly examine articles, and in some cases, the persistent and unwarrantable efforts of exhibitors to bias the judgment or sway the action of the committee, have seriously hindered us in the performance of the duty assigned us. The exhibit was very large, and in most cases very creditable, and while we had considerable

difficulty in arriving at conclusions entirely satisfactory to ourselves, we have endeavored to do impartial justice. Respectfully submitted, Mrs. Roe Stephens, Mrs. D. Preston and M.C. Harr, committee.[25]

Not every jury panel appreciated the work they were asked to critique, as indicated by this excerpt from the report of the jurors in an 1853 supplement of *Michigan Farmer:*

> Flannels, rag carpets, woolen stockings, blankets, coverlets, shawls, counterpanes and quilts were piled upon the tables and filled the lines that were stretched across Manufacture's Hall. . . . While examining these things [woolens] and comparing them with some of the patchwork quilts in the same hall, we could not help thinking how far superior in real value were the former, though the work laid out on the quilts must have cost double the time and patience. It does seem a waste of time, to say nothing of the materials that might better be made into garments, and weary hands that might be more usefully employed than in putting so many stitches on a single quilt as we saw on some of those. Blankets are cheaper and warmer, and for outside bedcovering a white counterpane or simple spread is much the neatest.[26]

Quilt exhibits have also been popular components of the festivities surrounding church and civic celebrations. Events such as the centennial and bicentennial anniversaries of the founding of the nation and the sesquicentennial anniversary of the founding of the state of Michigan have included displays of quilts as part of the celebration activities. Michigan quilts were also included in displays at such national events as the 1852 International Exposition in Detroit and the 1915 Lincoln Jubilee and the Celebration of the Half-Century Anniversary of Negro Freedmen, held in Chicago. In the *Michigan Manual of Freedmen's Progress,* the handbook for the latter event, was a listing of a "fancy quilt, heirloom, age 60 yrs" entered by Fannie Anderson of Detroit and a "fancy quilt" entered by Mrs. Dennison Graine of Kalamazoo.[27]

The planning and mounting of, participation in, and attendance at quilt shows have created and enhanced opportunities for social interaction within Michigan communities. Whether a one-day display at a local church or a month-long juried exhibition at the state fair, quilt shows have provided many occasions for group activities and community involvement.

Quilts and Fundraising

The making of quilts in Michigan communities to raise funds for a variety of civic and religious causes has been well documented through information collected in this project. In the last few years, quilts have been raffled to raise funds for a wide variety of causes in Michigan: a Peace Center in Lansing, Orchestra Hall in Detroit, scholarship funds for Michigan State University students, the Lansing Symphony Orchestra, a new computer purchase for an elementary school in Rogers City, a day care center in East Lansing, a historical society in Iron

A big event in Michigan's Lower Peninsula is the annual World Relief Sale held on the first Saturday in August at the Oscoda County Fairgrounds in Mio, Michigan. In rapid succession, quilts donated by area Mennonite quilters are placed on a rotating tilted mattress and auctioned. All proceeds go toward the international emergency services provided by the Mennonite church. Similar sales are held in Indiana, Kansas, and Pennsylvania Mennonite communities. (Photograph taken in 1984 by Marsha MacDowell, courtesy Michigan State University Museum.)

River, and numerous church and mission efforts. One unusual document chronicling the making of quilts for fundraising was a card received by Alice Lane in the early 1940s and later put into her quilting scrapbook. In the card, Cecilia Rice of Troop I, Junior Catholic Daughters of America, thanks Lane for her help in quilting a top Rice's friends pieced as a fundraiser: "Dear Mrs. Lane, Troop I wishes to thank you for your assistance with our quilt. It was such a surprise when Mrs. McGrew showed it to us at our last meeting. It was beautifully quilted and a great help to us."[28]

Many Michigan quilt clubs have been associated with church women's societies that either quilt for pay or raffle their own quilts to raise funds for church-related concerns.[29] An example of such activity was provided in a recent letter from Margaret Thelen of Fowler, Michigan, who wrote:

I am fund-raising chairman of the Sr. Volunteers at Hazel I. Finley Country Manor and this year we are raffling our 5th quilt in 5 years for funds to buy needed items for the manor. 1986 netted $1340.00 which we used to buy 8 needed wheel chairs.[30]

Making quilts for the church was an accepted form of involvement by women in church affairs, and it brought much pleasure to the quilters, as evidenced in this letter from ElvaDolis McQuisten Johnson:

Mother's happiest times quilting were when she was in her seventies. She worked with a Church Group at this time. It was the third group of quilters to do this work and donate the proceeds to the Church. Some members pieced tops, others put together embroidered blocks other church members made. After the quilt was assembled and pinned to the frame the quilting began in earnest. The women met once a week during the winter months for several years (1970-1978). The most profitable work as far as church funds were concerned were the tops brought to the group to be made into completed quilts for

the person who had treasured the top for many years. This time of friendship and accomplishment was a very happy experience.[31]

Another traditional form of fundraising by means of quilts is the "subscription" quilt. For a specified sum of money, donors have their names inscribed in ink or embroidery on the top of a quilt. In line with this tradition, members of the Capitol City Quilt Guild of Lansing, Michigan donated a quilt top to the Michigan Quilt Project for the purpose of garnering funds through subscriptions.

One of the religious organizations most active in the use of quilts as fundraising tools is the Mennonite church. In 1987, the twenty-first annual Northern Michigan Relief Sale was held at the Oscoda County Fairgrounds in Fairview. Members of local Mennonite, Amish, and Brethren churches contribute time and goods, which are then sold to raise funds for the work of the Mennonite Central Committee (MCC). According to an article in a 1985 issue of *Wilderness Chronicle,*

Relief sales in the U.S. and Canada last year helped raise $9,677,243.00 for relief. Directly that aid may

Sign announcing the 1986 annual Mennonite church-sponsored Relief Auction of quilts at the Oscoda County Fairgrounds in Mio, Michigan. (Photograph by C. Kurt Dewhurst, courtesy of Michigan State University Museum.)

help provide food for the hungry and starving in Ethiopia, Chad and Mozambique, for health programs in Brazil, for assistance to El Salvadorian refugees, and for education in Nigeria.[32]

Although the sale of homemade apple, shoofly, and berry pies is extremely popular, the highlight of the event is the auctioning of quilts. Textiles are donated not only by quilters from churches in the immediate area, but by members of Mennonite churches in the Upper Peninsula, in the Thumb area of Michigan, and even from outside the state. After being displayed for view during the morning in one of the fairground buildings, the quilts are transported to a stage on which there is an elevated, tilted, and revolving bed mattress. One at a time the quilts are placed on the mattress, which is then rotated 360 degrees so that all of the audience can see them. Each quilt is usually sold within seconds of the commencement of the bidding process. Quilters scattered throughout the audience carefully keep a running tally of the prices that each quilt commands.

The *Detroit News* "Quilt Club Corner" and Exhibits

When mass-produced and widely circulated periodicals became available in the United States, information about various forms of needlework began to appear in such national magazines as *Lippincott's Monthly* and *Scribner's* and, on the state level, *Michigan Farmer*. Running regular quilt columns and printing quilt patterns in periodicals became increasingly popular. For example, *Godey's Lady's Book* carried a regular column called "Patchwork."

One of the most influential and long-lasting quilting columns in Michigan was the *Detroit News* column called the "Quilt Club Corner," founded in 1932 by Edith B. Crumb, the newspaper's interior decorations editor. Appearing in each Friday's edition for almost a decade, the "Corner" contained helpful sewing tips, quilt patterns, and news about upcoming exhibitions. More importantly, "Miss Crumb," as she was known to her readers, encouraged her followers to become members of the *Detroit News* Quilt Club and to exchange information through the column, which thus became a forum for the lively exchange of all kinds of quilting news from quilters throughout Michigan and even in some neighboring states. Crumb often reported on the events and activities of various quilt clubs. Sometimes she shared with readers humorous incidents that took place at quilting bees. For instance, she once described how, under the direction of Mrs. Marian Ridler, a group of quilters met every Thursday during the warm months on Belle Isle, an island in the Detroit River, where they gathered around eleven o'clock in the morning at the shelter near the Schiller monument. Their meeting often turned into an informal quilt exhibition. Crumb reported on the problem caused by the group's custom of placing finished quilts on top of the monument:

Newspaper advertisement for the first quilt exhibit sponsored by the Detroit News. (Photograph courtesy of Michigan State University Museum.)

Thursday was the last date for the picnic of quilters which Mrs. Marion Ridler sponsors every year.... The shelter at Belle Isle was the rendezvous and the outer sides of the shelter were lined with quilts, this being a small quilt show in itself....

A few weeks ago a great big cross policeman objected to having it on the Schiller monument and removed it with the idea of taking it away; but did he do it? I should say not! Two or three quiltmakers started to run after him and he called to his police friends in the car to open the door quickly and he dropped the quilt, jumped into the car and was rescued from these ferocious quilters![33]

During the mid 1930s, Crumb began a weekly Quilt Club radio program that was broadcast on WWJ every Wednesday evening, the theme for which was

9

"Seeing Nellie Home," a popular song that referred to "Aunt Dinah's quilting party."

In 1933, Crumb initiated the first annual *Detroit News* quilt show, which became an immediate success and had a lasting influence on many Detroit-area quiltmakers. In its first year, the three-day show attracted 10,000 visitors on opening day and was met with great enthusiasm among quilters, as this *Detroit News* article attests:

> Friendliness pervaded the show....Quilters from every part of the city, and from many outlying towns, were there, and nearly every woman, after she'd been in the building for five minutes, was comfortably chatting with a social group of women she had never seen before, but with whom, because of their mutual interest in homemaking, she was immediately on easy terms.[34]

An unusual event occurred at that first show which contributed to the personality of Crumb's "Quilt Club Corner." A Mrs. Emons Galton was reunited with her long-lost sister, Mrs. Marie Fisher, from whom she had been separated for thirty-three years, after recognizing Fisher in a newspaper photograph where she was pictured with her prize-winning quilt. Crumb immediately reported the reunion in her "Corner,"[35] and the two women, eventually known as the "Quilt Club Sisters," became regular correspondents to the column.

By 1938, Garnet Warfel reported in the *Detroit News* that more than 2,000 quilts were shown at the Detroit National Guard Armory site and that the show set a record of 18,000 visitors on a single day.[36] The show continued to be a popular annual event and lasted until the early 1940s.

The *Detroit News* Quilt Club's radio program, regular newspaper quilt columns, and quilt show provided ongoing support and encouragement for Michigan quilters. The popularity of the columns and the exhibitions prompted a renewed enthusiasm for quiltmaking that lasted until the beginning of World War II and that was not renewed until the late 1960s.

The *Detroit News* Quilt Show. (Photograph courtesy of Michigan State University Museum.)

Quiltmaker Erma Buhl of Detroit sent this photograph of herself taken ca. 1934-35 to her friends as a part of a Christmas card. (Photograph courtesy of Vivian Rybolt.)

Quiltmaking Traditions

Thus far, no single clearly identifiable style of quilt has emerged as having been initiated in Michigan, nor has any particularly distinctive quiltmaking tradition indigenous to this region been noted. However, it is evident that over the last 150 years many of the quiltmaking traditions practiced in other parts of the country were also found here, and in some instances were especially popular.

Quiltmaking as a Woman's Activity

First and foremost, quiltmaking is a textile tradition that has been firmly tied to the experience of women. Historically, quiltmaking was an artistic activity that could be done within the sphere of accepted women's roles. Because it could be picked up and put down easily, it was less disruptive to household routines than other artistic endeavors. Quiltmaking also produced an object that served a clearly defined function within the family or community. If not made as a utility spread for a household bed, a quilt was most likely made as a gift for a special occasion or to raise funds for a worthy cause. The knowledge of techniques and patterns has been passed primarily from woman to woman—from mothers to daughters, from female friends to female friends. Women have also been the primary custodians of family quilts. Time and again the ownership of a particular family quilt has passed from generation to generation through the hands of female family members.

Although men have been involved infrequently in the actual process of piecing and quilting, it has been discovered that it has not been unusual for men to be involved in such peripheral activities as building frames, cutting out templates, and developing and even marketing various quilt labor-saving devices. Several accounts have been found of Michigan men making a quilt to get through a particularly stressful period in their lives such as a time of unemployment or sickness. The involvement of men in social quiltmaking activities, such as quilting bees or quilt shows, is rare. The bias against male participation in quiltmaking was poignantly expressed in a letter sent in 1934 from Eugene Minkel of Detroit to *Detroit News* columnist Edith B. Crumb:

> As my mother is a member of your corner I am writing to ask you to please settle a little dispute in our family. (This happens to be not between mother and daughter but father and son.)....I have, with the help of my father, made a "Daddy's Bow Tie" quilt. Of course, it is not perfect; but may I enter it in the show? My father said "No" and I hope I may fool him and will if you say a big "Yes." I am only 14 years old and mother had made the Dresden Plate and Dolly Madison Star and I made a new pattern of a tulip from square blocks so I think she will make it. I have made just one block but it is nice. It is long and narrow ....Don't say I am going to be a tailor for my wish is to be a doctor, so I may take care of all those fingers jabbed with quilting needles.[37]

One can only imagine the direction quiltmaking would have taken in Michigan had men like Minkel been encouraged. Even today it is rare for men to be actively involved in quilting. Only one contemporary male quiltmaker, Joe Cunningham, is registered in the MQP inventory.

Recycling and Fabrics of the Workplace

Recycling materials in general is a traditional quiltmaking practice. In Michigan, quilts have been made from premiums found in cigarette cases or coffee cans, silk cigar ribbons, 4-H ribbons, old socks and ties, and even silk labels cut from old clothing. Some farm women in Michigan recycled feed sacks and used the wool of their own sheep for batting. Some Michigan quiltmakers who migrated from Southern farms recalled using old cotton picking

sacks for quilt linings and unginned field cotton leftover after the cotton fields were picked for batting.[38]

Another traditional practice seems to be the use by quiltmakers of materials closely connected to their occupations or hobbies or those of close family members. A number of quilts inventoried through the Michigan Quilt Project were made of fabrics from workplaces outside the home. Quiltmakers gleaned materials from a variety of workplace sources: scraps left over from tailoring or seamstress work, shoe linings from a shoe factory, fabric trimmings from a corset factory, used army nurse's uniforms, shirting fabrics from J.L. Hudson's men's department. Rella Brown, who worked in a Detroit drycleaning establishment and whose sisters Magnolia and Della are also quilters, joined with co-workers to fashion quilts out of scraps taken from clothing abandoned at the cleaners.[39]

Fabric and Pattern Swapping

The swapping of fabrics, patterns, and even completed quilt blocks has been a popular tradition in Michigan. Before the availability of printed patterns in newspaper quilting columns or in widely circulated quilter's publications, women swapped patterns both in person and by mail. Information about one interesting system of pattern exchange called a "round robin" was found in an obscure quilting publication called *Aunt Kate's Quilting Bee*. A woman interested in exchanging patterns would add her name and address to a list drawn up from a larger list printed in the magazine. She would then send the list and four or five patterns copied on onion-skin paper to the first person on the list, who would then copy any of the patterns she wanted, add four

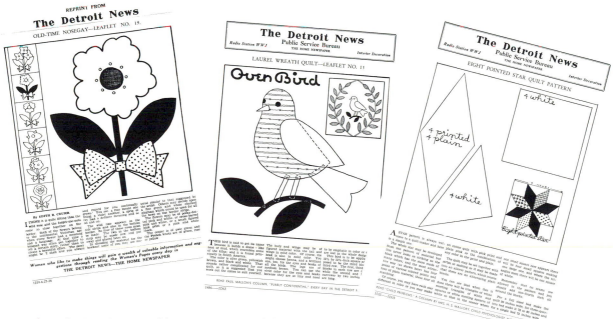

Patterns from the *Detroit News* Public Service Bureau. (Photograph courtesy of Michigan State University Museum.)

or five of her own, and send the patterns to the next person on the list. When the packet of up to as many as thirty patterns arrived back at the initiator's home, she would remove her original contributions, add new patterns, and start the circle again. Mary Schafer of Flushing, Michigan reports that at one time she was involved simultaneously in five round robins.[40]

Editor Edith B. Crumb's *Detroit News* "Quilt Club Corner" column provided another forum for the exchange of quilt information, patterns, and fabrics. Here, for example, Crumb shares one reader's letter with and solicits assistance from her column's readers: "Mrs. Joseph Blasko, Jr., writes. . . . she has "loads and loads of patches, silk, cotton and percale, all kinds to exchange. . . . even some of velvet and would like some checks and dots of any color in exchange."[41] In another column, Crumb encourages readers to help gather materials for a quiltmaker who was ill:

> If any of you have any plain pieces which you would like to send to Ruth Mary, she would certainly appreciate them. She is also looking for prints. She has had long months of illness and if she can be kept happy by having enough material for her quilt-making this summer I am sure she will be strong enough to start in school and keep up with her class.[42]

Quilt shows afforded another opportunity to swap fabric and blocks, and at some shows a special area was set aside just for this purpose. *Detroit News* columnist Garnet Warfel commented on one such area of activity at the 1937 quilt exhibit in Detroit: "In the rear of the big room is a place arranged with tables and chairs and here women sit and rest and talk—usually about quilts, and then they exchange quilt blocks."[43]

Although not a venue for swapping fabrics, department store yard goods departments were an important arena in which to learn about the availability of new fabrics and to share quilt-related talk. In such a setting, the yard goods salesperson played an important role. In an undated *Detroit News* article, a Miss Lillian Lind is paid tribute for the thirty years

(Photograph courtesy of Michigan State University Museum.)

she had spent in the percale department of a large Detroit store:

> For more than a generation she has matched colors, hunted patterns big and little and discussed percales with customers. Naturally many of them have been quiltmakers. . . . Miss Lind is not a famous quilter herself. But she has probably handled more of the gayly patterned percales that go into the quilts than any other woman in Detroit.[44]

"Made One for Everyone in My Family"

The making of a quilt for every member of a family is a traditional practice that has been frequently seen among the quilters inventoried in Michigan. Continuation of the tradition by contemporary quiltmakers was substantiated in oral accounts and news articles such as one that appeared in a recent issue of the *Lansing State Journal*:

> Flora Etta Buck, of Holt, will celebrate her 85th birthday with family and friends next Sunday. . . . Flora has six children, 23 grandchildren, and 23 great-grandchildren, said her daughter Sandra Mick of Charlotte. "And, she's made quilts for every one of them. She just can't sit still," she added.[45]

Various accounts of this practice were also recorded in interviews conducted by and letters received by the Michigan Quilt Project staff. Following are excerpts from sample letters.

> I have made quilts years back when my children were small and lately I have made 39 since my husband passed away sixteen years ago [and they have] gone to my children, grandchildren and great-grandchildren.[46]

> I am carrying on my family quilting traditions and have many quilts that are in good condition. Some have been made by my two grandmothers and are about 100 years old. Then, my mother and my aunt have done some that are about 65 years old. I have many of my own creations. Right now, I am working on getting seven baby crib quilts done so that my seven grandchildren will have one quilt for each of their "first born" or who ever wants them.[47]

> My grandmother's sister was a quilter. . . . She was born in the early 1890s. Beatrice (Jardo) Fisk from Stirling, Michigan. I'm told she had 10 children, 30 grandchildren and 50 great-grandchildren. She made quilts for each of her children and grandchildren. I have never seen any of them.[48]

> As I said, we did not keep track of the number of quilts mother [Emma Consuelo Cramton McQuiston] made but she gave one to each of her five children; to her 13 grandchildren; to her 12 great-grandchildren and to nieces and cousins and friends. She also made innumerable baby quilts that she sold at senior citizen craft fairs and she always had one ready to give to new babies among her friends and relatives.[49]

The making of a quilt for each member of a family was a way in which a woman could give something that was useful, economical, beautiful, and handmade.

Quilter as Artist/Quilt as Art

Of all of the visual art forms practiced by women in nineteenth-century America, the making of quilts was perhaps one of the most widespread, engaged in by women from all walks of life.[50] Although the use of many quilting techniques, patterns, and designs was heavily influenced by both traditional and popular culture, individual quilters often imprinted their own sense of personal design on their work. In other words, the widespread use of popular designs did not undermine the potential of an artist to express her innate artistic ability. By innovatively using color, pattern, quilting, and texture, a quiltmaker was able to produce textiles that bore her unmistakable stamp as an artist. Some women also engaged in the production of new patterns and designs. Moreover, women played active roles as astute critics and supporters of good quiltmaking. Within each community, a few quiltmakers were inevitably acknowledged by their peers as the finest because of their superb design or impeccable needle skills. In public forums, such as juried quilt shows, where quilts were judged by others, this recognition of artistic excellence was further reinforced. Whereas local-level shows relied heavily on community-based quilters to serve as judges, larger quilt shows such as those sponsored by the *Detroit News* used professional needleworkers and artists as judges, as reported in a 1938 *Detroit News* article:

> Craftsmanship as well as design and color, will be considered in the judging at *The Detroit News* Quilt Show. . . . Here are two of the three judges who will makes the awards. Mrs. Frances Heintz, instructor in Home Economics at Wayne State University, will pay special attention to the stitchery and Miss Alma Knudsen, instructor in design at the art school of the Detroit Society of Arts and Crafts, will consider the design and color in the quilts.[51]

This trend toward the use of judges from outside the community has continued and has become even more formalized in recent years. Standards for judging quilts are now set by such organizations as the National Quilting Association and tend to highly value technical proficiency and an aesthetic approach based on Euro-American art historical trends.

Newspaper accounts of outstanding quilts have also helped to underscore the general perception of what constitutes a "good" or "important" quilt, as Garnet Warfel attests:

> Probably as outstanding as any single quilt in the show is the second prize winner in the pieced quilt class, the Ann Hathaway cottage. It appears as a large picture and in fact, was copied from a tiny picture of the famous cottage at Stratford-on-Avon. It contains 18,124 hexagons and has no running seams, the material being basted over paper and whipped, in an over-and-over stitch. It has 225 different prints

and was five years in the making. Four generations, all eldest daughters of the family, fashioned the quilt, which is valued at $1,000. It will be given to a historical society when the owner is through with it.[52]

In recent years the display of quilts has moved from church and civic hall to art gallery and museum. In part this shift has been due to the emerging attention to women's art, the recent popularity of folk art among collectors, and the similarities between many pieced quilts and contemporary modern art. Quilt historian Jonathan Holstein provides this explanation of the recent phenomenon:

> Pieced quilts are the most "painterly" products of the vernacular tradition, both in appearance because of the use of geometric elements and abstract images, rectangular format, size, and flatness and in decorative technique: quiltmakers, in effect, "paint" with fabrics, choosing first a format and the ultimate look they want, then selecting colors, patterns, and textures among their available materials, their "palette," and manipulating these elements in conjunction with form to achieve the effects they wish.[53]

As quilting organizations become more highly structured and as more quilts are accepted as legitimate items to display in art museums, quiltmakers will continue to merge traditional, popular, and progressive notions of what makes a "good" quilt.

Conclusion

The Michigan Quilt Project has only begun to uncover an enormous body of information on Michigan quilting and its role in Michigan history. As the process of accumulating and analyzing data continues, we hope to expand our understanding of the role of artmaking in both traditional and progressive forms and contexts, to broaden our knowledge of the contributions of individual quiltmakers to Michigan, and to enhance our sense of place as Michigan citizens.

This volume and the accompanying exhibition are intended to share the gathered information with others. As persons view the quilts and read the stories behind them, it is hoped that they will be challenged to recognize and value the role that traditional knowledge has played in their own lives.

Quiltmaking has indeed been an important activity in the history of Michigan and continues to play a role in the lives of many individuals and communities. In 1985, 107-year-old Pontiac resident Elnora Adams declared that, until her eyesight failed her, "I used to do a lot of quilting, piecework quilting. I was quilting all the time." More likely than not, as long as there are individuals who feel as Adams does, quiltmaking will remain a strong artmaking activity in this state.

Notes

1. Michigan Quilt Project correspondence files, Michigan State University Museum, East Lansing, Michigan.

2. Mrs. Dean Parker of New Baltimore, Michigan, quoted in Edith B. Crumb, ed., "Chatty Letters Received From Quilt Club Members," *Detroit News,* Saturday, March 27, 1937. (Michigan State University Museum accession file #6268.)

3. Letter dated April 4, 1986, Beaverton, Michigan. Michigan Quilt Project correspondence files, Michigan State University Museum, East Lansing, Michigan.

4. From the collection of the Michigan State Archives and Michigan Historical Museum, Lansing, Michigan. Gratitude is extended to Barbara Hamblett for sharing this citation.

5. "It Took Four Months to Collect All the Names," *Detroit News,* April 16, 1937. (Michigan State University Museum accession file #6268.)

6. "Autograph Quilts," by Mrs. FAW, East Saginaw, Michigan, *Good Housekeeping,* October 26, 1889, p. 311, cited in Jeanette Lasansky, *In the Heart of Pennsylvania: 19th and 20th Century Quiltmaking Traditions* (Lewisburg, Pennsylvania: Oral Traditions Project of the Union County Historical Society, 1985), p. 94.

7. "Old French Traditions," *Pioneer Collections, Report of the Pioneer Society of the State of Michigan,* Vol. IV (Lansing, Michigan: W. S. George and Company Printers and Binders, 1883), p. 73.

8. October 7, 1938. Clipping found in Alice Lane's quilting scrapbook, collection of Marsha MacDowell and C. Kurt Dewhurst.

9. Undated clipping found in Alice Lane's quilting scrapbook, collection of Marsha MacDowell and C. Kurt Dewhurst.

10. For more information on Afro-American quilting, see John Michael Vlach, *The Afro-American Tradition in Decorative Arts* (Cleveland, Ohio: The Cleveland Museum of Art, 1978), pp. 44-75; also Maude Southwell Wahlman and Ella King Torrey, *Ten Afro-American Quilters* (Oxford, Mississippi: Center for the Study of Southern Culture, University of Mississippi, 1983).

11. For more information on Hmong textiles in Michigan see C. Kurt Dewhurst and Marsha MacDowell, eds., *Michigan Hmong Arts* (East Lansing, Michigan: Michigan State University Museum, 1984).

12. Michigan Quilt Project Quilt Discovery Day notes, April 1985, Michigan State University Museum, East Lansing, Michigan; and "A Star of Hope is Born for Michigan's H-Mung People," *Wilderness Chronicle,* Issue 2 (Fall, Winter), 1984, p. 49.

13. From the collection of the Michigan State Archives and Michigan Historical Museum, Lansing, Michigan.

14. "Raisings and Bees Among Early Settlers," *Pioneer Collections, Report of the Pioneer Society of the State of Michigan,* Vol. V (Lansing, Michigan: W. S. George and Company Printers and Binders, 1883), p. 296.

15. Michigan State University Special Collections, Michigan State University Library, East Lansing, Michigan. Special thanks to Barbara Hamblett for providing this reference.

16. "Frolics of Forty-Five Years Ago," *Pioneer Collections, Report of the Pioneer Society of the State of Michigan,* Vol. V (Lansing, Michigan: W. S. George and Company Printers and Binders, 1883), p. 305.

17. Clipping found in Alice Lane's quilting scrapbook, collection of Marsha MacDowell and C. Kurt Dewhurst.

18. November 5, 1933, cited in Suzanne M. Baker, unpublished manuscript, 1984. Michigan Quilt Project files, Michigan State University Museum, East Lansing, Michigan.

19. Interview with Velma Roundtree, August 1986, Michigan Quilt Project field notes, Michigan State University Museum, East Lansing, Michigan.

20. Letter dated September 9, 1984, Michigan Quilt Project correspondence files, Michigan State University Museum, East Lansing, Michigan.

21. (New York: Doubleday, Page and Company, 1915), pp. 137-38.

22. *Michigan Farmer,* October 1, 1849, p. 299.

23. The 100th Annual "Michigan State Fair and Exposition Premium List," Detroit, Michigan, 1949, p. 193.

24. *Report of County Agricultural Societies,* 1853, p. 439.

25. *Michigan Farmer,* Vol. IX, No. 43, October 24, 1878, p. 1.

26. Vol. 11, October 1853, supplement, pp. 1-6.

27. John M. Green, *Negroes in Michigan History* (Detroit, Michigan: Privately printed, 1985), pp. 37-39.

28. Undated. Collection of Marsha MacDowell and C. Kurt Dewhurst.

29. For a more complete discussion of the interrelationship of quilting and religion in women's lives, see C. Kurt Dewhurst, Betty MacDowell, and Marsha MacDowell, *Religious Folk Art in America: Reflections of Faith* (New York: E. P. Dutton, 1983).

30. Letter dated June 2, 1987, Michigan Quilt Project correspondence files, Michigan State University Museum, East Lansing, Michigan.

31. Undated letter, Michigan Quilt Project correspondence files, Michigan State University Museum, East Lansing, Michigan.

32. "August 3rd Set for 19th Annual Northern Michigan Relief Sale," *Wilderness Chronicle,* Issue 5 (Summer), 1985, p. 45.

33. "Quilters Busily Preparing for the *Detroit News* Show," undated clipping from the *Detroit News;* and "A Great Big Cross Policeman is Chased away by Quilters," undated *Detroit News* clipping, collection of Marsha MacDowell and C. Kurt Dewhurst.

34. Cited in Suzanne M. Baker, unpublished manuscript, 1984. Michigan Quilt Project files, Michigan State University Museum, East Lansing, Michigan.

35. Undated *Detroit News* clippings, collection of Marsha MacDowell and C. Kurt Dewhurst.

36. Undated *Detroit News* clipping, collection of Marsha MacDowell and C. Kurt Dewhurst.

37. In Edith B. Crumb, ed., "Here's a Chance to Get Very Interesting Patch," *Detroit News,* October 4, 1934. (Michigan State University accession file #6268.)

38. Interviews with Sina Phillips and Velma Roundtree, August 1986, Michigan Quilt Project field notes, Michigan State University Museum, East Lansing, Michigan.

39. Special thanks to Yvonne Lockwood for supplying this reference at the 1981 Worker's Culture Conference, Ann Arbor, Michigan.

40. Information on Mary Schafer's participation in round robins in Michigan is from a manuscript on Mary Schafer by Joe Cunningham and Gwen Marston soon to be published by the Michigan State University Museum, East Lansing, Michigan.

41. Mrs. Joseph Blasko, Jr., in Edith Crumb, ed., "Quilt Clubs Keep Busy; Planning for Fall Show," *Detroit News* undated clipping, collection of Marsha MacDowell and C. Kurt Dewhurst.

42. "Quilt Club Editor Receives News from Club Members," undated clipping, collection of Marsha Mac-Dowell and C. Kurt Dewhurst.

43. "Machine Age Contrast Provided at Quilt Show," *Detroit News,* April 18, 1937. (Michigan State University accession file #6119.)

44. "A Garden of Prints: Celebrate 30 Years with Percales," collection of Marsha MacDowell and C. Kurt Dewhurst.

45. September 21, 1986.

46. Frances Diamond, letter dated September 10, 1984, Michigan Quilt Project correspondence files, Michigan State University Museum, East Lansing, Michigan.

47. Zoe McKessy, letter dated September 24, 1986, Michigan Quilt Project correspondence files, Michigan State University Museum, East Lansing, Michigan.

48. Linda L. Webb, letter dated August 1, 1984, Michigan Quilt Project correspondence files, Michigan State University Museum, East Lansing, Michigan.

49. ElvaDolis McQuisten Johnson, letter dated 1986, Michigan Quilt Project correspondence files, Michigan State University Museum, East Lansing, Michigan.

50. For an extended discussion of quiltmaking in the lives of women, see C. Kurt Dewhurst, Betty MacDowell, and Marsha MacDowell, *Artists in Aprons: Folk Art by American Women* (New York: E. P. Dutton, 1979), pp. 46-55 and 125-131.

51. "News Quilt Judges," October 5.

52. "Quilt Beautiful as a Painting Wins its Skilled Maker $50," *Detroit News,* undated clipping, collection of Marsha MacDowell and C. Kurt Dewhurst.

53. Jonathan Holstein in C. Kurt Dewhurst, Betty Mac-Dowell, and Marsha MacDowell, *Artists in Aprons: Folk Art by American Women* (New York: E. P. Dutton, 1979), p. 131.

Michigan Quilts and Quiltmakers

by Ruth D. Fitzgerald, Lynne Swanson,
Gerna Rubenstein, Betty MacDowell,
Marsha MacDowell, Kathleen Parker,
and C. Kurt Dewhurst

Explanatory Note

The quilts presented here represent those documented by the Michigan Quilt Project (MQP) from 1984 to 1986. These examples portray the quiltmaking traditions evident in Michigan and give an overview of the results of the data collected by the MQP to date. The information reported here is taken from the MQP inventory forms and, in some cases, interviews with quilters or their family members. The amount of information available about the quilts varied significantly. In a few cases where a date was not provided and the interviewee could not be reached, the date of the quilt was estimated. To our knowledge, this information is accurate and complete as of the date of publication.

Information on the quilts and quilters was written by seven writers and may vary somewhat in length and descriptive content. The length of the text is not an indication of a quilt's importance or significance.

Preceding the text for each quilt is a caption identifying it, detailed in this order: quilter's name and dates, pattern name and/or title of the quilt (in italics), date the quilt was made, provenance or location where the quilt was made including county and state, lender's name, materials used, measurements in inches, and the Michigan Quilt Project (MQP) catalogue number.

Edmund Bailey , Mary Bigelow Bailey
Courtesy of Marjorie Suzanne Smith

1. Edmund Bailey (1787–1873) and **Mary Bigelow Bailey** (1795–1879). Whole cloth made ca. 1812–1813, Connecticut; brought to Michigan in 1881. Marjorie Suzanne Smith, lender. Wool and linen top, homespun wool back with wool filling, 95″ x 100″, MQP 85.1118.

This whole-cloth quilt was created in Connecticut circa 1812 or 1813 by a young couple, Edmund Bailey and Mary Bigelow, during their courtship. Together they quilted the designs that Edmund had drawn on the dark blue top. The top, filling, and backing were made from wool that was grown, spun, and woven on the family farm where the courtship took place. The top consists of two large pieces of solid-blue wool and linen fabric, often called *linsey-woolsey,* and

the backing is composed of four pieces of solid-brown wool homespun. The quilting designs include a central flower basket surrounded by scalloped feathers, tulips, daisies, and pineapples against a background of parallel diagonal lines. These motifs and the dark blue color of the top are frequently found in linsey-woolsey quilts.

Edmund and Mary Bailey, who moved from Connecticut to Racine, Wisconsin, had eight children. In 1881 their quilt was brought to Hastings, Michigan, by their granddaughter, Malvina More Lombard, who was the grandmother of the present owner, Marjorie Suzanne Smith of East Lansing, Michigan. It was displayed at the Barry County Fair in 1930.

2. Clarissa House. Whole cloth made ca. 1825–1850, provenance unknown. Collection of Detroit Historical Museum (acc. 69-117.9). Cotton with cotton filling, 88″ x 95.5″, MQP 85.2020.

Made of plain white cotton, this medallion-style quilt features a decorative hand-stitched styl-

ized flower surrounded by a wide area of small honeycomb-like design. There are pineapple motifs in each corner and the border is decorated with vines and leaves. The quilt was donated to the Detroit Historical Museum by Clarissa House's great-great-granddaughter.

3. Ann Kingsley Spalding. Sunflower made 1825, Canaan, Connecticut. Lois (Mrs. D. G.) Lance, lender. Cotton with cotton filling, 86″ x 88″, MQP 86.1507.

When Ann Kingsley Spalding made this quilt in 1825, she was living in either Canaan, Connecticut, or in Fort Ann, New York, with her husband, John Spalding, whom she had married in 1812. It is not certain whether the quilt was made in Connecticut or New York, but it is certain that it was brought to Milan, Michigan, when the family moved there in the 1830s.

Lurena (or Lovina) was one of the five children born to Ann and John and was the first inheritor of the quilt. She married David Potter in 1845, and a daughter of that marriage, Sarah, became the third-generation owner of the quilt. Sarah Potter Teall's daughter, Cora Teall Patterson, became the fourth-generation owner of the quilt, and Cora's daughter, Ruth Patterson Beals Dantzer, born in 1898, became the fifth-generation owner.

Surviving family members sold the quilt in an estate sale after Dantzer's death in late 1981. Lois Lance of Royal Oak purchased it and shared its extensive documentation with the Michigan Quilt Project. A message, written by Dantzer and dated March 8, 1968, was pinned to the quilt:

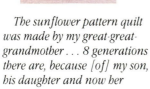

The sunflower pattern quilt was made by my great-great-grandmother . . . 8 generations there are, because [of] my son, his daughter and now her son . . . so I am a great grandma too.

In the note she adds that her maternal grandmother, Sarah Potter Teall, made an exact replica of the original Spalding quilt in 1920. She remembers that it comprised 2,325 pieces because each of the 25 sunflowers was made up of 23 small pieces in 4 sizes. Further, she states that the original Sunflower quilt had the honor of being the oldest quilt at the 1981 Royal Oak Historical Society Quilt Show.

The piecing of the red-and-white cotton patchwork sunflowers was done by hand, as was the diagonal line quilting on the white background of the top. Between the top and the two-piece white back is a thin filling of cotton with seeds, and the binding is red-print cotton cording.

4. Mary Ann Orillia Karlan Carolan. Carolina Lily made ca. 1830–1860, Wallaceburg, Ontario, Canada. Collection of Michigan State University Museum (acc. 5987.1), gift of Mary Nunneley and daughters. Cotton, 89″ x 100″, MQP 85.38.

Mary Ann Orillia Karlan Carolan is remembered by her family as the first white baby to have been born in a settlement near Wallaceburg, Ontario, Canada.

The town was subsequently named after her, and is now known as Orillia, Ontario, Canada. Carolan completed this quilt before marrying James Carolan and inscribed it with her initials, "MOK." The 21 pieced and appliquéd lily blocks are set with an equal number of plain white blocks and are framed by a winding, delicate grapevine border, which includes embroidered red tendrils.

5. Louisa Pruden Davis (1823–1894), piecer; **Virginia Newman** (b. 1918), quilter. Postage Stamp and Flying Geese made ca. 1830s, DeWitt area, Clinton County, Michigan. Family of Virginia Newman, lenders. Cotton with polyester filling, 66.5″ x 84″, MQP 87.224.

The family history of this Michigan pioneer quilt and its maker, Louisa Pruden Davis, provides a glimpse into the life of individuals in the early period of Michigan statehood. Both the Pruden (sometimes referred to as Prudden) and Davis families homesteaded in Michigan in the early decades of the nineteenth century. The Michigan town of Prudenville was named after this pioneering family. Louisa Pruden was born November 18, 1823, in Seneca County, New York, and married William Dennis Davis, who was born October 16, 1820. Together they had nine children and farmed land in Riley Township, located in Clinton County. According to Virginia Newman, the quilt owner and great-granddaughter of the piecer:

[Louisa] made this quilt by candlelight during nights when she could not sleep. . . . Her husband helped clear the land for the [Michigan] capitol building. So that would have been around 1838, I guess. He did it so he could get money to buy staples for his family. He walked home through the woods carrying a 50-pound sack of flour and a 50-pound sack of sugar. He was gone most of that winter. While he was away, she was left alone in their log cabin, which had only an animal skin for a door. At night she brought their calf and pig into the house and put firebrands out the door all night to keep the wolves away.

It is thought that Davis made many quilts, but only this one survives. When Davis gave it to her daughter, Rachel Louysa Davis, it had been pieced but not quilted. In 1972, Virginia Newman, who had inherited the quilt top from her grandmother Rachel, attached the back and quilted it.

Louisa Pruden Davis and her husband, William
Courtesy of Virginia Newman

7. Rebecca Barringer Garlock
(1824–1893). Star *(My Mother's Little Star)* made ca. 1838–1850s, Herkimer County, New York, and Clinton County, Michigan; brought to Michigan in 1856. Marilyn Maier Smith, lender. Chintz and muslin with cotton filling, 84.5″ x 86″, MQP 85.1341.

Rebecca Barringer Garlock
Courtesy of Marilyn Maier Smith

Some of the pieces in this pieced quilt date to 1838, and perhaps earlier, when the quiltmaker began to assemble the eight-pointed stars that give the quilt its name. Each of the 342 pieced star blocks consists of 17 triangular pieces of patterned cotton. The addition of 306 white cotton squares and 350 half-squares makes a total of 6,470 pieces in the quilt. Quilted diagonal lines cross the centers of the stars, which are also outlined with quilting. The quilting designs of the white blocks include hearts set into circles within squares. All of the quilting has been done by hand, with 12 to 13 stitches per inch.

Born in 1824 in Herkimer County, New York, Rebecca Barringer Garlock was still a young girl when she started this quilt, which she finished several years after her marriage in 1847 to John Garlock, a farmer. In 1856 the couple and their children moved from New York to a farm near Grand Ledge, Michigan, where their family eventually included eight children. Garlock, who completed her quilt in Michigan during the 1850s, died in 1893. The quilt has remained in the family, passing from Garlock's daughter, Elizabeth Garlock Rice, to Rice's nephew and niece, Don and Watie Garlock, then to Don and Watie's daughter, Ruth Garlock Maier, and finally to Maier's daughter, Marilyn Maier Smith, the present owner. Other quilt-makers in the family have included Rebecca Garlock's daughter, Elizabeth Garlock Rice, who lived at Wacousta, Michigan; her granddaughter, Ruth Garlock Maier; and her great-grand-daughter, Lucille Garlock Jenison of Perry, Michigan.

6. Mary Evert Tharp Bradley
(1818–1897). Christmas Cactus Swirl made 1835–1850, Farmer Township, Ohio. Ray and Alice Pengra, lenders. Cotton with cotton filling, 72″ x 84″, MQP 85.213.

Meticulous quilting, an unusual combination of border elements, and tiny appliquéd pieces are evident in this beautifully preserved whole-cloth, medallion-style quilt. The little information that is known about the maker of this quilt comes from its previous owners, Mr. and Mrs. Clifton Cox. According to a typewritten sheet they gave the Pengras, the quilt was made by Mr. Cox's great-grandmother, Mary Evert Tharp Bradley. Born on October 26, 1815, she was the oldest daughter of Isaac and Hannah Tharp, who were some of the earliest settlers in Farmer Township, Ohio. On January 2, 1838, she married Joseph Bradley of Liverpool, Ohio, and they had nine children. Mary Bradley died in December of 1887. Her quilt was passed through the family to the Coxes. A few years ago the quilt won a Blue Ribbon when the Coxes displayed it in a quilt fair at the Sauder Museum Farm and Craft Village in Ohio. The Pengras, Michigan residents, acquired it from the Coxes.

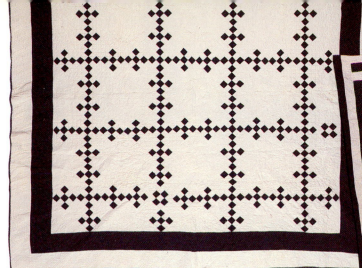

8. "Great-Grandma Bartley." ▲
Nine-Patch or Single Irish Chain
made 1838–1839, Pittsburgh,
Pennsylvania; brought to Michigan ca. 1945. Mrs. Eleanor Bartley
Vollwiler, lender. Cotton with cotton filling, 78″ x 80.75″, MQP
86.552.

This arrangement of navy-blue
and white Nine-Patch blocks,
known to its maker's family as "9-
patch within a 9-patch," has what
its owner calls "an interesting
history":

*It was given to my grand-
father when he was born on
January 10, 1840. (He was sup-
posed to have been a girl.) I pre-*
*sume it was made by one of his
grandmothers. He never used
it, and when his daughter,
Zetta, was born, he gave it to
her. She never used it either
and in the 1940s she gave it to
me to make sure it remained
in the Bartley family. My Aunt
Zetta was the only girl in dad's
family and I was the only girl
in the following generation so
that explains my getting it.*

The colors have been reversed
in two of the pieced Nine-Patch
blocks, breaking the chain pattern and providing what must
have been an intentional error.

9. "Great-Grandma Bartley." ▲
Drunkard's Path made 1838–
1839, Pittsburgh, Pennsylvania;
brought to Michigan ca. 1945.
Mrs. Eleanor Bartley Vollwiler,
lender. Cotton with cotton filling,
78″ x 80″, MQP 87.212.

Little is known in the Bartley
family about the maker of this
quilt, except that she was probably the family's only quilter. If
her two extant quilts are any indication, "Great-Grandma Bartley"
favored pieced rather than appliquéd quilts, and she liked the
combination of navy blue and
white.

Just as Bartley reversed the
colors in portions of her Nine-
Patch quilt, she also reversed the
colors in the border of this quilt.
On two sides, the border consists
of two white strips separated by a
blue strip. On the other two sides
the order is reversed, with two
blue strips enclosing a white
strip.

◀ **10. Rynearson Sisters.** Rose of
Sharon made ca. 1840, Buchanan,
Berrien County, Michigan. Collection of Dearborn Historical Museum (acc. 80-2.2). Cotton with
cotton filling, 82″ x 82″, MQP
85.1331.

Very little is known about the
makers of this appliquéd Rose of
Sharon quilt except their family
name. The Rynearson sisters of
Buchanan, Michigan, created it
circa 1840, perhaps as part of a
bride's dowry. Esther Meeker,
who donated the quilt to the
Dearborn Historical Museum,
said that it had been passed
through her husband's family and
that she had "cared for it for over
60 years without ever using it herself." Four cotton blocks, each
one-yard square, are joined together to form the top on which
the designs are appliquéd. The
Rynearson sisters gave special attention to details in making their
quilt. They dyed the green fabric
twice to obtain its deep hue and
used a buttonhole stitch to appliqué the flowers in the border.
The excellent condition of the
quilt indicates that it was seldom,
if ever, used.

11. Elmira Fazer Kibler (1851–1921). Four-Square Rose made ca. 1840–1860, Hillsdale, Hillsdale County, Michigan. Ray and Alice Pengra, lenders. Cotton with cotton filling, 72″ x 84″, MQP 85.214.

Four oversized appliquéd and reverse appliquéd roses with buds dominate the center of this quilt, which the current owners acquired in a 1974 auction of the Nellie Kibler estate. The Pengras then traced the history of the quilter through correspondence with Arlene Sanford, a friend of the Kibler family. In a letter of September 15, 1976, Sanford wrote:

Nellie told me her mother had made this quilt and that it was over 100 years old. This was probably 7 or 8 years ago. . . . Nellie was born at Leslie, Mich., and later lived in or around Reading, Mich. before moving to Hillsdale with her parents and brother, at the age of 12. She lived at that same address for 72 years. She and her brother never married. They and their parents lived at 35 Short St., and after their parents died, they continued living there the rest of their lives. Nellie's mother's name was Elmira (Frazer) Kibler, born 1851 and died 1921.

Sanford went on to say that Nellie had wanted her to have the quilt, but since she doesn't have room to store things in her Florida home, she "was glad someone has the quilt that will appreciate it."

12. Lura Williams Uhl. Rolling Star made ca. 1850, probably Charlotte, Eaton County, Michigan. Collection of Dearborn Historical Museum (acc. 74-134.2). Cotton, 52″ x 96″, MQP 85.1327.

The 50 eight-inch square blocks in this pieced top include plain white blocks alternating with pieced blocks in two different star designs to create the Rolling Star pattern. The hand quilting has been done in a half-inch diamond design.

The primary piecer of this parlor quilt, which dates from circa 1850, was Lura Williams Uhl, the wife of a circuit preacher. The Uhls lived in Charlotte, Michigan.

In her later years, Lura Uhl resided in the Dearborn, Michigan, area. Her granddaughter, Mrs. G. Trowbridge, recalls that her own mother and two aunts completed the quilt, which was always in the parlor bedroom used by her grandmother after her move to Dearborn. The parlor quilt was donated to the Dearborn Historical Museum by Trowbridge, its former owner.

13. Anna Lathrop Pettibone. Album *(Signature Quilt)* made ca. 1850s, Armada, Macomb County, Michigan. Mrs. Richard N. Kieppe, lender. Cotton, 78″ x 80″, MQP 85.1346.

Triangles, squares, and rectangles of plain and patterned cotton have been pieced together to form the 49 square blocks in the top of the *Signature Quilt,* made at Armada, Michigan. Separated and bordered by strips of patterned pink cotton, the blocks contain the autographs, written in ink, of various friends and members of the quiltmaker's family. Each block is also dated, probably with the year of the signer's birth, since the years range from 1794 through 1837. Begun in the early 1800s and completed in the 1850s, the top is also signed by the quiltmaker, Anne E. Lathrop, whose married name was Anna Lathrop Pettibone. The hand quilting follows vertical and diagonal lines to produce diamond designs throughout the pieces. This type of quilt, sometimes called an Album or Friendship quilt, was often made as a going-away gift for a departing friend or minister or, as in this case, as a textile record of one's closest associates.

The *Signature Quilt* has been handed down to successive generations of the Pettibone family: daughter-in-law Nora Pettibone, granddaughter Lois Pettibone Simmons, and great-granddaughter Shirley Simmons Kieppe, its present owner. The quilting tradition is carried on today by Pettibone's great-great-granddaughter, Karen Kieppe Duncan of DeWitt, Michigan.

14. Maker unknown. Log Cabin made ca. 1850–1875, northern Michigan. Natalie Hopson, lender. Wool, 68″ x 72″, MQP 86.1992.

This Log Cabin pattern variation is called "light and dark." The unusual pieced-strip border and misshapen corner block make the quilt unique. The corner block may have been an intentional mistake by the maker, supporting the tradition of some quilters of marring the perfection of their work because "only God can make a perfect thing." The piece is not quilted, but rather tied with wool yarn. Although its maker is unknown, this quilt has been in the Hubbard-Hopson family of Harbor Beach, Michigan, for more than 100 years.

26

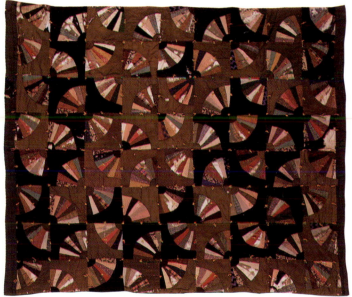

15. Mrs. Karl Schlegel. North Carolina Lily and Flying Geese made ca. 1850–1875, Detroit or Lapeer, Michigan. Collection of Detroit Historical Museum (acc. 43-177.1). Cotton with cotton filling, 39″ x 40″, MQP 85.1999.

This pieced quilt was donated to the Detroit Historical Museum by Mrs. Karl Schlegel, whose son, Henry, was the mayor of Lapeer for three terms. It is the only known quilt made by Schlegel.

16. Susan Wagner Churchill (1834–1918). Grandmother's Fan (*Fannie's Fan Quilt*) made 1850–1900, Three Oaks, Berrien County, Michigan. David and Diane Savage, lenders. Wool, 67″ x 81″, MQP 85.528.

David Savage, great-grandson of the quiltmaker, has preserved the history of the 16 quilt tops, the complete quilt, the 2 sets of blocks, the pillow top, and the set of miscellaneous blocks he inherited in 1974 from his aunt, Fanny Angeline Savage Sparling. According to Savage,

Susan Wagner Churchill was born on Feb. 23, 1834 in Dayton, Michigan . . . [and] lived in Three Oaks from 1870 until her death in 1918. Susan Churchill ran a boarding house [and a photography studio] in Three Oaks. . . . It was my understanding that while Susan Churchill ran the boarding house, quilts were used extensively. Both of Susan's daughters, Mary Florentine (Tina) Churchill (1856–1917) and

Sara Ida Churchill Savage (1858–1928), lived in Three Oaks from 1870–1875 until their deaths. . . . They helped with the quilts at times.

Savage made note of his great-grandmother's thriftiness in recycling the utility quilts: "As the tops became worn, a new top was attached to the existng quilt, saving the need for more filler and back."

One of the Churchill quilt tops is a Crazy that incorporates a candidate's ribbon from the campaign of Benjamin Harrison, who became president in 1888; two John Deere Plow trademark ribbons from Moline, Illinois; and a ribbon from the Warren Featherbone Company founded in Three Oaks in 1888.

This particular tied quilt, called *Fannie's Fan Quilt,* comprises 72 pieced 9″ x 9″ blocks. Usually such patterns contain six or eight blades in the fan; this one contains seven. Although mostly sewn by hand, it does include some machine stitching.

*Susan Wagner Churchill
(in middle)*
Courtesy of David and Diane Savage

27

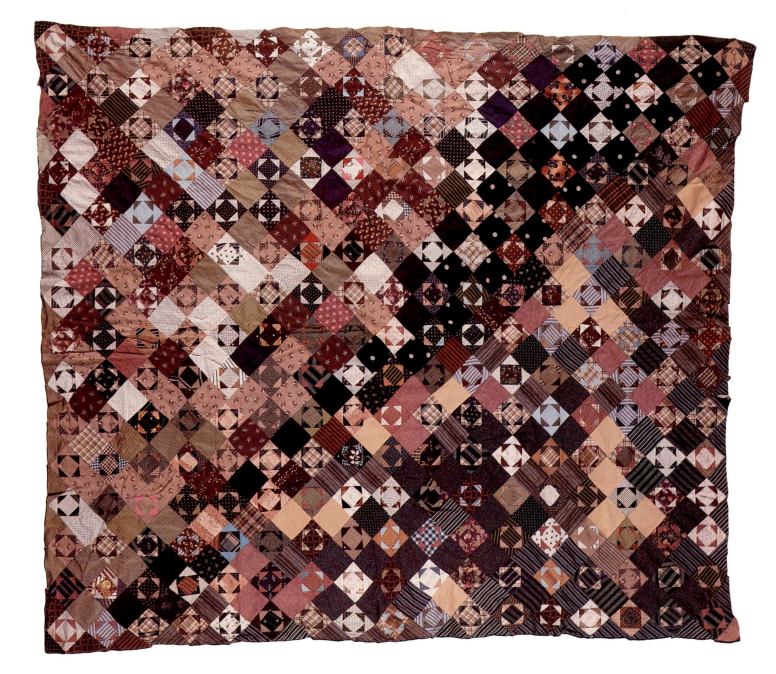

17. Susan Wagner Churchill (1834–1918) and **daughters.** Untitled design made 1850–1900, Three Oaks, Berrien County, Michigan. David and Diane Savage, lenders. Cotton, 68″ x 80″, MQP 85.537.

More than 2,500 pieces of fabric form the blocks set in diamonds that make up this quilt top. There are 255 blocks with triangles and rectangles, 224 blocks of plain cloth, 224 triangles, and 4 triangles at the corners. Other patterns made by this family include Necktie, Nine-Patch Star, Barbara Fritchie Rose, Basket of Scraps, Swastika, Jacob's Ladder, Chained Square, Snowball, and Crazy.

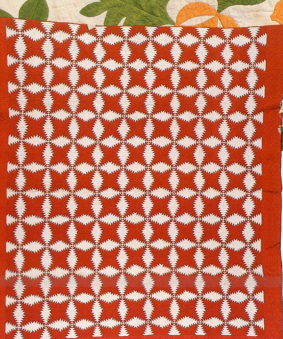

18. Maker unknown. Pumpkin ▲
Flower made ca. 1850, northern
Michigan. Joyce Hopson, lender.
Cotton, 78″ x 78″, MQP 87.203.

Although its maker is un-
known, this beautiful appliquéd
quilt has been in the Hubbard-
Hopson family of Harbor Beach,

Michigan, for more than 100
years. The quilt was found in the
family's cabin in northern Michigan. A small, yellowed, cloth tag
attached to the quilt reads,
"Pumpkin Flower 150 years old,"
adding to the mystery.

19. Katherine B. Austin ▲
Davis. Church Steps made 1852,
Roxand Township, Eaton County,
Michigan. Florentine Baril,
lender. Cotton with cotton filling,
69″ x 78″, MQP 85.1112.

A small scrap of fabric attached
to the front of this quilt carries an
inked inscription:

*Cotton Pieced Quilt—Colo-
nial Pattern—Church Steps—
Pieced about 1852 by Katherine B. Austin Davis at her
home in Roxand Township,
Eaton Co. in the early Michigan
Days when the country was
sparsely settled during winter
evenings when the country doc-*

*tor was making distant calls on
horseback. This work was done
by candlelight as was her spin-
ning, knitting and the rough
homespun garment making of
the 1850s.*
—*The Women's International
Exposition Exhibit.*

This turkey-red and white
quilt, made up of 120 blocks, is
done in a variation of the Pineapple pattern. Unfortunately, little
is known about the quiltmaker or
the exposition exhibit to which
the tag refers. The quilt's current
owner successfully bid for it at an
Eaton County farm auction in the
early 1960s.

20. Lydia Margaret Chaffin
(1825–1899). Original design
made 1853, Hancock County,
Ohio; brought to Michigan in
1854. Glee Chaffin, lender. Cotton, 72″ x 86″, MQP 85.1391.

The bold designs in this colorful quilt have been appliquéd
with red, orange, and green cotton fabrics onto 12 18-inch
square white blocks that are
joined together to form an un-
broken background. On the 7-
inch white border, a curvilinear
green vine with red tulips and
green foliage encircles the central motifs. The entire quilt is
edged with orange binding. Outline quilting and quilted designs
that repeat the appliquéd shapes
join the top to the white cotton
back.

The quilt's central designs,
tulip border, and color scheme
suggest the Pennsylvania origins
of its maker. Lydia Margaret Chaf-

fin was born in 1825 at Wilks-
burg, in Luzerne County, Pennsylvania, to Jacob E. and Margaret
Foust. In 1849 she married Solomon Asbury Chaffin, a farmer,
and with her husband moved to
Hancock County, Ohio. Eight
children were born to the couple
during the next several years.
Chaffin made her appliquéd quilt
in 1853 while she awaited the
birth of their third child, Oliver.
After it was completed, she used
it only as a bedspread. By 1854
the Chaffins were living in Michigan, first at North Star and then at
rural Perrinton. Since Chaffin's
death in 1899, the quilt has been
owned by her son and daughter-
in-law, Oliver and Loelda Chaffin;
her granddaughter, Kuthe Chaffin; and her great-grandson, Glee
Chaffin, the present owner. The
last two owners have never used
the quilt, which is kept as a family heirloom. ▶

21. Martha Hewitt (b. ca. 1799). Original Medallion made 1855, Michigan. Private collection. Cotton, 87.5″ x 76″, MQP 87.160.

This extraordinary quilt, made in Michigan by Martha Hewitt, uses patriotic and Masonic symbols together with other traditional motifs in a spectacular and cohesive design. Vivid and contrasting colors heighten the visual impact of the quilt. The brilliant central star, which resembles a hex sign, is surrounded by a Flying Geese border. The use of Pennsylvania-Dutch-style floral motifs surrounding the quilt on four sides suggests that the maker may have been of German or Pennsylvania-Dutch stock. Each of the flags, which seem to be waving in the breeze, has a different number of stars on it.

On the top of the quilt, Hewitt left this embroidered inscription: "Martha Hewitt   Age 56 Michigan   1855."

Although nothing is known about the maker except her age at the time that she made the quilt, one thing is certain: she left behind an unusually complex and colorful appliquéd creation. Her work combines technical proficiency with artistic innovation.

22. Ann E. Reeder Fowler
(1822–1896). Spider Web with Points made 1855, Sumner Township, Gratiot County, Michigan. Mary Ellen Ruark and Charlotte L. Sulen, lenders. Cotton with cotton filling, 74″ x 85″, MQP 85.75.

Ann Reeder Fowler, born in England on September 29, 1822, emigrated first to Ohio with her husband, Benjamin Fowler, and eventually settled in Sumner Township, Gratiot County, Michigan. Five generations of the Fowler family have saved this quilt as it was passed from Fowler to her daughter Clara Fowler Mulford, grandson Murle Benjamin Mulford, and great-granddaughter Laura LaVerne Mulford Baker. It is now owned by her great-great-granddaughters, Mary Ellen Baker Ruark and Charlotte Sulen.

The quilt is made in the Spider Web pattern and incorporates fabrics from housedresses Fowler brought from England. The webs in other Spider Web quilts may contain alternating pieced and plain wedges, but each segment in this quilt is pieced of several fabrics.

23. Unknown maker. Delectable Mountains made 1859, West Virginia. Linda M. Bujold Hoemke, lender. Cotton with cotton filling, 76″ x 85″, MQP 87.202.

Although the maker of this unusual pieced and appliquéd quilt signed her work in four places and dated it twice, its history remains a mystery. The initials "S M I" or "S M J" appear in four places with the dates "May the 18th, 1859" and "June 16th, 1859." The traditional Delectable Mountains pattern is complemented by an original medallion of four appliquéd fish made with hand-dyed cotton fabric. The back and top are made with handmade cotton muslin. Each of the fish has a tiny appliquéd eye. A single leaf is appliquéd onto one corner of the center medallion. Quilted into the medallion are wavy lines, probably meant to resemble water and fish scales.

Owner Linda Hoemke purchased the quilt at a farm sale near Grand Rapids, Michigan. The quilt won The Museum's Choice award at the West Michigan Quilt Guild Show in 1986.

24. Family of Anne Rosemary Calhoon. Flying Geese made 1859, Branch County, Michigan. Marion Coward VanderVeen, lender. Chintz and cotton, 72″ x 79″, MQP 84.5.

Family history describes this pieced quilt as "a memorial to Anne Rosemary Calhoon," who died unexpectedly in 1859 at the age of 11. Probably made by her mother, Patience Leach Calhoon, and sisters Sophia and Elizabeth, the quilt was made from Anne's "new dress." By arranging the triangular shapes into strips for the simple Flying Geese pattern, the quiltmakers made economical use of the dress fabrics. Today the family continues to "save" rather than use the quilt, in remembrance of Anne.

25. Mary Jane Carpenter Clark (1835–1910). Mariner's Compass *(Christmas Star)* made 1859–1910, Belleville, Wayne County, Michigan. Katherine Kay Vielmetti Peters, lender. Cotton with wool filling, 73″ x 84.25″, MQP 86.969.

In 1842, when Mary Jane Carpenter was seven years old, she and her family moved from their home in New York to Michigan and settled in Wayne County. In 1859 she married Woodbury Clark, who had also moved from New York via the Erie Canal to Michigan in 1838.

By the time she married, Clark had made 15 quilts for her hope chest and at least one quilt for the hope chest of another. As her family grew—the Clarks had three children—she continued quilting, working alone on one quilt per year for the family and working with a group on one quilt per year for the church. Her granddaughter, Gail Clark, remembered groups quilting in Mary Jane's Belleville home. Several people would sit together around a large frame set up in the front room. The materials used were usually purchased at Potter's General Store in Belleville, but once Mary Jane included a piece of her wedding dress—a dark-maroon silk taffeta—in a Crazy quilt. Because of her selection of colors and her use of even quilting stitches, her sisters thought she was the best quilter in the community. Gail saved many of the better quilts in a cedar chest so they wouldn't become worn. Because of her foresight, the family now has eight or nine well-preserved quilts.

Clark's *Christmas Star* quilt, shown here, is thought to have been made as a dowry quilt, which means it would have been made before her wedding on December 22, 1859. The top is made of solid red and solid green cotton blocks that have been pieced and quilted by hand. A saw-tooth border accents the three sides. Solid khaki material has been used for the seven-piece back. Clark combines diagonal lines of quilting on the border and in the star center with clamshell designs from the edge of each block up to the 11 concentric circles that pass through the arms of each of the stars.

The few worn spots on this quilt are in the red fabric on the border and in the stars. As a treasured family heirloom, it has been in the protective hands of four generations: Kate Crysler Clark, married to Mary Jane Clark's son, Ralph; Gail Clark, daughter of Kate and granddaughter of Mary Jane; and Katherine K. Peters, niece of Gail and great-granddaughter of Mary Jane. Peters, the present owner, is a quilter herself. See no. 255 for a quilt by Katherine K. Peters.

Mary Jane Carpenter Clark
Courtesy of Dr. Richard Kay

26. Eveline Green Seager. Basket variation made ca. 1860, Newaygo County, Michigan. Marilyn Swanson, lender. Cotton tobacco sacks with cotton filling, 66.75″ x 62″, MQP 86.2020.

This simple pieced and appliquéd Basket quilt, constructed by Eveline Green Seager from her husband's tobacco sacks, reflects the utilitarian nature of quilts in mid-nineteenth-century rural Michigan. The Basket pattern, which became popular about 1850, spawned many variations. Eveline Seager's version of this commonly used motif incorporates one brown basket among the blue ones.

The quilt's current owner, Marilyn Swanson, recounts family history about her great-grandmother:

Gramma Seager was a very capable woman. She was a born nurse, an exceptional needlewoman, and housekeeper extraordinaire. She was said to have been a beautiful creature, and although she bore many children she never weighed more than 100 pounds. The log house that she moved into upon her marriage at age 17 had cracks in the roof so the snow could get in. Gramma [Seager's daughter] remembers Eveline getting up to shake the snow off the quilts before the warmth of the fire could melt it. . . . The little quilt was made to use, and it was very much used. It covered and comforted many sick children. My mother remembers it from her childhood, and she's 96.

27. Unknown maker. Log Cabin made ca. 1860, Canada. Bethea Monroe Berg, lender. Wool, 73″ x 78″, MQP 86.2006.

This variation of the Log Cabin pattern, called Barn Raising, is composed entirely of wool and boasts an off-center design that is sometimes found in Log Cabin quilts. The unknown maker of the quilt gave it to John and Mary Ann Hurst in exchange for a kettle of soap that was too heavy to take with them when they moved from Canada to Ohio in 1854. The quilt, along with the family legend, was later passed down to the Hurst's daughter, Margaret Hurst McKinley, who gave it to her daughter, Pearl McKinley Monroe, who, in turn, gave it to her daughter, Bethea Monroe Berg, of Muskegon, Michigan.

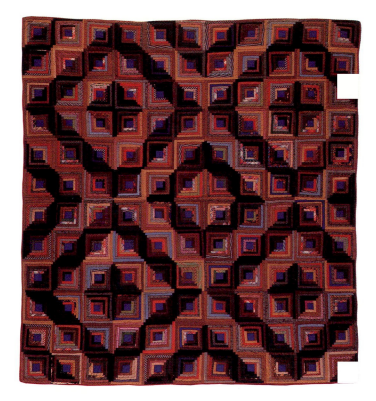

28. Edna Freshour. Crazy Pinwheel variation made 1860–1870, Hillsdale County, Michigan. William R. Freshour, lender. Cotton and silk, 70″ x 72″, MQP 86.490.

Quilter Edna Freshour's Crazy Pinwheel pattern quilt is now in the possession of her great-grandson, William R. Freshour, who inherited it from the quilter's son, William J. Freshour. Only two facts about this quilt have been documented. Edna Freshour was a resident of Hillsdale County, Michigan, when she made this quilt, and she used scraps of silk lining material from a women's high-button shoe factory to construct the pinwheels. Freshour sewed the pinwheel blades together, making a total of 16 large blocks. The use of a variety of shapes and colors throughout the blocks gives the impression that the pinwheels are in motion.

29. Cornelia Driggs Small

(1844–1903). Shoofly in a Frame made ca. 1860–1880, Reading, Hillsdale County, Michigan. Stanley C. and Nancy M. Surratt, lenders. Cotton with cotton filling, 64″ x 84″, MQP 85.176.

Biographical information provided by the family of the quiltmaker reveals that:

Cornelia Driggs Small was born 26 March 1844 at the Elyria, Ohio farm home of her parents, Joseph and Cornelia Pierson Driggs. . . . Cornelia was their eighth child.

In 1865 they . . . moved to Rome in Lenawee County, Michigan. . . . Cornelia met Henry Small at the Rome Grange, and after a courtship of three years, they were married at the home

of her parents the 20th of February 1869.

Henry and Cornelia Small purchased a farm three miles south of Reading, Michigan in Camden Township where they erected a log house from timbers on their property.

Cornelia was an accomplished homemaker, and an excellent seamstress who took great pride in her work and family. . . . Shortly after they were established on their farm Cornelia . . . purchased a weight-driven Seth Thomas clock. . . . Family history has it that this clock was the first in their area. It still keeps accurate time in the home of her great-grandson.

Henry and Cornelia had only one child, Charles Driggs Small who was born 2nd, January 1870. . . .

Cornelia Small died 19th June 1903, and was buried alongside her husband at the Berg Cemetery near Camden, Michigan.

Family history further records that this Shoofly in a Frame quilt was made by Cornelia Driggs Small while living on the farm south of Reading, Michigan. Of alternating pieced and plain blocks, it was made for family use to "equip the . . . beds." Upon Small's death, her daughter-in-law, Effie Luticia Small, inherited the quilt. It was then passed to the quilter's granddaughter, Florence Amelia Surratt, and finally to Stanley Charles Surratt, the quilter's great-grandson.

*Cornelia Driggs Small
Courtesy of Stanley C. and
Nancy M. Surratt*

30. Nancy Brown Brougher.

Rose Wreath (*Nancy Elizabeth Brown's Quilt*) made 1861, Washington County, Pennsylvania. Penny Dick, lender. Cotton, 75.25″ x 78.5″, MQP 86.224.

Although Nancy Elizabeth Brown Brougher's age at the time she sewed and quilted this work is not documented, it seems reasonable to assume that she had not yet married Albin Brougher since she uses her maiden name to identify the quilt. Velena Brougher Hainer inherited the quilt from her mother, and she in turn gave *Nancy Elizabeth Brown's Quilt* to her daughter, Mildred Harper. Harper's daughter, Penny Dick, is the present owner of this 126-year-old textile.

The color scheme used in *Nancy Elizabeth Brown's Quilt* is simple. Yellow-centered red flowers and green leaves and stems make up both the wreaths of roses and the sinuous flowered-vine border that Brougher appliquéd onto a white background. The same colors are repeated in the letters, which spell out the quilter's name and the year she finished her quilt.

Each appliquéd piece is outlined with quilting, and a quilted circle within a circle, possibly a stylized flower, appears in the center of each wreath of roses.

31. Phoebe Eugenia Shell-hammer Meacham (1848–1932). Log Cabin made 1864–1865, Union, Cass County, Michigan. Grace Evelena Field, lender. Wool, 72″ x 80″, MQP 85.548.

Known as either "Eugenia" or "Genia," Meacham learned quilting from her mother and was also known to be proficient in tatting, crocheting, and other sewing skills. Her niece, Grace Field, tells how she acquired this quilt and the Ocean Wave quilt (no. 33) from her aunt in 1915:

We were all members of the Baldwin Prairie Baptist Church in Union and attended faithfully. My Aunt Genia was president of the Union Ladies Aid and wanted to give to a special project they were wanting to raise for the church. One day Mrs. Kadish, a Chicago woman, who was living at her family's cottage at Baldwin Lake for the summer and bought milk here regularly from my mother, saw Aunt Genia's Ocean Wave quilt and admired it greatly. Aunt Genia said she'd sell it for $15 and give the money to the Ladies Aid for the church. Mrs. Kadish was delighted but said that she did not have $15 with her right then and she would buy it later when she came for

milk again. I heard this conversation and went in distress to my mother in the kitchen and told her that I wanted the quilt, and it should be kept in the family. I had $15 in my own purse and Aunt Genia would not be out anything. My saintly mother agreed and took on herself the task of going into the parlor, where Aunt Genia usually sat, and telling her that I wanted the quilt and could pay for it myself and it should be kept in the family. So within seconds it was mine. . . . On the next day, probably being a little

Phoebe Eugenia
Shellhammer Meacham
Courtesy of Grace Evelena Field

ashamed of herself for not having given the quilt to me, her young niece, she did give me, free of charge, her much older and thus more valuable "Log Cabin" throw.

Attached to the back of the "throw" to which Field refers is a piece of paper that states:

She pieced this quilt at the age of sixteen during the Civil War of the United States of America. She and her friend Amelia Rinehart, who is buried in the Rinehart Cemetery east

of Union, would make trips to the store together and would buy identical pieces of goods (or rather they bought one and divided it). At the end of their work they had identical quilts. The red and black plaid alpaca was from the material used for dresses worn by Eugenia's two younger sisters . . . they often were dressed alike, being close in age and great pals.

Quilts no. 31-34 were made by members of the same family.

32. Mary Maria (Polly) Dibble Shellhammer (1827–1885) and **daughters Eugenia, Eva,** and **Etta.** Hour Glass made before 1885, Union, Cass County, Michigan. Grace Evelena Field, lender. Cotton with cotton filling, 69″ x 84″, MQP 85.545.

Mary Maria Dibble, known as Polly, was born on February 9, 1827, and brought to Michigan in 1834 by her parents, Anson and Lydia O'Dell Dibble. At one time she lived in a log cabin on Mason Street at the foot of Ward Hill in Union. Her marriage to Aaron Shellhammer resulted in three boys and six girls, but only four of their children survived past the age of 40. According to Field, granddaughter of the quilter, Shellhammer not only was proficient in quilting but also spun and wove. Field reports that Shellhammer used "dress goods of the 1860s–80s in making this Hour Glass quilt."

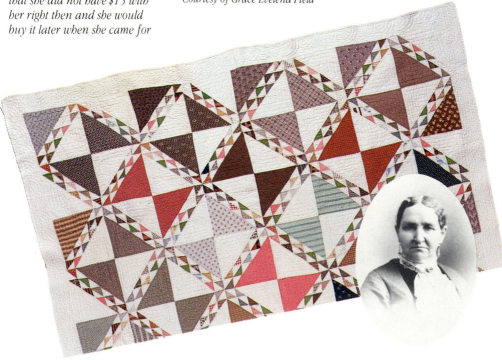

Mary Maria Dibble Shellhammer
Courtesy of Grace Evelena Field

33. Phoebe Eugenia Shellhammer Meacham (1848–1932) and **Mary Bailey,** piecers; **A. Ward,** quilter. Ocean Wave made 1900, Union, Cass County, Michigan. Grace Evelena Field, lender. Muslin and cotton dress fabrics with cotton filling, 74.5″ x 86″, MQP 85.549.

Mary Bailey was employed by Phoebe Eugenia Shellhammer Meacham at the time this top was pieced. In an interview, Grace Field said,

> *This quilt was quilted by a professional quilter at the top of Ward Hill. She quilted for*

hire, let's put it that way; I wouldn't say she was any more than an ordinary farm woman. But she quilted for hire.

Known only as "A. Ward," this woman was also known as a coverlet weaver.

This pieced quilt comprises blocks set in diamonds, and each of the white squares is quilted with wreath and heart designs.

Mary Bailey and her husband Vern Schofield, taken by F. L. Goff, Elkhart, Indiana
Courtesy of Grace Evelena Field

34. Edna Isophene Sherman Yohn (b. 1871–?) and members of Polly Edna Shellhammer's **Sunday school class at Union Baptist Church.** Untitled design made 1892, Union, Cass County, Michigan. Grace Evelena Field, lender. Muslin with cotton filling, 68″ x 80″, MQP 85.550.

Polly Edna Shellhammer received this pieced and embroidered Friendship quilt when she was 23 years old as a Christmas present from her Sunday school class at Union Baptist Church. According to Grace Field, her granddaughter,

> *the members of the class wrote their names in their own handwriting and the embroidery came over that. The girls probably embroidered the boys' names. . . . The quilter was said to be a 15-year-old girl, Edna Sherman, who later married Charles Yohn. . . . Edna Yohn and Edna [Shellhammer] Field*

Edna Isophene Sherman Yohn taken before 1898 by F. L. Goff, Elkhart, Indiana
Courtesy of Grace Evelena Field

lived as next-door neighbors in Union, Cass Co., Michigan during most of their married lives.

In an interview, Field provided a short description of each person who signed a block, and in doing so provided a glimpse of community social life in Union at the turn of the century.

35. Susan Chambers Burt
(1849–1928). *The Cactus Quilt*
made ca. 1865, Kensington, Oakland County, Michigan. Betty J.
Gillespie, lender. Cotton with cotton filling, 81.75″ x 84″, MQP
86.657.

It is thought that Susan Burt
made this quilt entirely by hand
for her son Jud B. and his wife,

Cora Childs Burt. According to information provided by Betty J.
Burt Gillespie, the owner of the
quilt,

*about 1865 [Susan] traveled
to New York to visit relatives
and saw a quilt she liked—
after returning home she made
this one—it is not known if it
was an exact copy.*

The materials used in this textile are cotton solids appliquéd
onto a pieced, unbleached muslin back. The quilting includes
cross-hatching on the border and
outline quilting of the appliqués.
The quilt was once on public display in a jewelry shop window
for the Brighton, Michigan centennial in 1967.

Burt, her husband Vine, and
other family members were buried in Kensington Cemetery.
Their home stood on property
that is now part of Kensington
Metropolitan Park outside of
Detroit.

and Night variation of the Log Cabin pattern. The unusual pieced diamond border, however, distinguishes it from other Log Cabin quilts. The quilt top is made of a variety of interesting printed cotton and wool fabrics, and the back is made of a striking red, black, and white mid-century printed fabric. The quilter may have intended that the curious asymmetrical row of half blocks at one end of the quilt be hidden by pillows.

36. Unknown maker. Log Cabin made ca. 1865, Michigan. Coralie Miller and Rita Miller, lenders. Cotton with cotton filling, 68″ x 77.5″, MQP 86.2023.

Purchased at an auction near Muskegon, Michigan, by Rita and Coralie Miller, this stunning quilt has no known previous history. It is a beautiful example of the Day

Rebecca Brickley and her husband, Jacob
Courtesy of William J. Brickley

37. Rebecca Brickley (1820–1866). LeMoyne Star made 1866, Ionia, Ionia County, Michigan. William J. Brickley, lender. Cotton, 68″ x 78″, MQP 85.596.

William J. Brickley, the current owner of this pieced quilt, provided the following information about Rebecca Brickley, who was born in Pennsylvania on May 3, 1820:

This quilt was made by my great-grandmother Rebecca Brickley, wife of Jacob Brickley, who died of cancer of the breast October 18, 1866, at the age of 46 years, 6 mos., and 15 days.

In 1865 my great-grandmother discovered that she had cancer of the breast. She told the family, "You all want to go to Michigan, so we will go this year so I won't be left behind."

In the fall of 1865 they had harvested the crops and sold the farm in Niagara County, New York. Then they started for Michigan with their possessions in wagons and with cows tied behind the wagons. They left Lockport, New York, in the late fall and traveled all winter to reach Ionia, Michigan, in the spring of 1866.

Great-grandmother made the quilt for my grandfather while she was dying. Grandfather was very choice of this quilt and refused to have it used. His daughter and then I have respected his wishes, and the quilt has not been used. That is why it is 120 years old and in the original condition.

Comprised of 42 blocks made in the eight-pointed LeMoyne Star pattern, the quilt is made of predominantly red, pink, and green fabrics.

38. Chloe A. Barnum Kimball
(1822–1873). *An Ornithological Quilt* made 1869, Bennington, Shiawassee County, Michigan. Kathleen Common Schmidt, lender. Cotton, 74" x 79", MQP 86.91.

In this quilt, 42 square white blocks, separated by orange sashes, provide the backgrounds for the appliquéd and embroidered designs. A different bird is pictured and identified in each of 40 blocks. The remaining 2 blocks contain the signature of the quiltmaker, the place where

the quilt was made, the date, and the quilt's title, *An Ornithological Quilt*. The quilting has been done in diamond, diagonal, fan, and straight-line designs. According to oral tradition, the quilt won a prize at the Michigan State Fair and was probably exhibited at the Genesee County Fairs.

The quilt was made in 1869 by Chloe A. Barnum Kimball of Bennington, Michigan. Kimball was born in 1833 at Pompey, New York, to Thomas and Huldah Barnum. She came to Michigan with her family sometime before 1853, when she married Martin C. Kim-

ball, by whom she had two daughters. In addition to her quiltmaking, Kimball enjoyed reading, drawing, singing, and playing the piano. Fond of nature, she made at least two other quilts containing birds and flowers, in addition to other types of quilts, some of which were given as wedding gifts. This quilt remains in the family, having passed first to Kimball's daughter, Leora Kimball Rinehard, and then to her great-granddaughter, Kathleen Common Schmidt of Swartz Creek, Michigan.

Chloe A. Barnum Kimball
Courtesy of Kathleen Common Schmidt

39. Rovilla Kittredge. Log Cabin made ca. 1870, Kalamazoo, Kalamazoo County, Michigan. Merilee Lawson, lender. Cotton with cotton filling, 52″ x 60″, MQP 86.241.

This striking Log Cabin quilt remained in Rovilla Kittredge's family until her granddaughter sold the quilt to its present owner. The quilt's most arresting characteristic is the complexity of its construction: 10,960 separate pieces of printed and plain-colored cotton calico fabric make up the 780 two-inch blocks that Rovilla sewed together to make this variation of the Log Cabin pattern called Barn Raising. Her careful attention to the placement of dark and light colors within each block and to the subsequent arrangement of the blocks themselves makes this brightly colored quilt appear to display alternating light and dark concentric diamonds.

40. Charity Goold. President's Wreath made ca. 1870, Dryden, New York. Edith Brower, lender. Cotton with cotton filling, 85″ x 95″, MQP 86.462.

All that is known about the creator of this quilt is her name, Charity Goold. She appliquéd pink flowers and green leaves onto white fabric to make this President's Wreath quilt, owned by Edith Brower of Leland, Michigan. Nine complete blocks and three half-blocks are surrounded on three sides by a bud-and-vine border. Outline quilting accents the designs of the border and the blocks. Goold also used diagonal, shell, and floral quilting patterns. The hand quilting shows ten stitches per inch.

41. Elizabeth Wilson McFadden Ross (d. 1900). Rocky Road to Kansas made ca. 1870, Dearborn, Wayne County, Michigan. Collection of Dearborn Historical Museum (acc. RB-8). Fabrics from men's shirts and women's dresses, 72.5″ x 79″, MQP 85.1261.

This quilt consists of 30 pieced blocks separated by sashes, in a pattern known as Rocky Road to Kansas. The blocks have been put together by hand and are made of leftover scraps of fabric from men's shirts and women's dresses. An interesting feature is the "whisker guard" at the head of the quilt.

Elizabeth Wilson McFadden Ross, a native of Ireland who came to Dearborn, Michigan, when she was 17, made this quilt circa 1870 in Dearborn. Married to Nathaniel Ross in 1859, she had seven children, of whom only three lived to adulthood. One daughter, Ellen Ramsay Ross, also made quilts before she

Elizabeth Wilson McFadden Ross
Courtesy of Dearborn
Historical Museum

died of tuberculosis at the age of 15. In 1883 the Rosses moved to new living quarters made from the former powder magazine of the Dearborn Arsenal. Their daughter, Mary Elizabeth Ross, left the family home, its contents, and land to the city of Dearborn in 1950.

42. Nancy Viola Ganong (b. 1852–?). Rising Sun or Sunflower made ca. 1870–1880, Irontown, Michigan. From the collection of the late Edwin Binney III and Gail Binney-Winslow. Cotton, 72.5″ x 99″, MQP 87.147.

Patriotism became very popular as a theme in decorative arts around the time of the U.S. centennial in 1876 and is reflected in this pieced quilt attributed to Nancy Ganong of Irontown, Michigan. In an unusual combination of motifs, the quilter paired the eagle, a commonly used patriotic symbol of the time, with the traditional Sunflower or Rising Sun pattern. The result, a striking quilt of blue and white, resembles a woven Jacquard coverlet in many ways. The repeated circular sunflower motif, the pictorial border, and the color scheme suggest that Ganong may have been influenced by design aspects of woven coverlets in her quilt making. The exceptionally fine quilting and the skillful overall design together make this an extraordinary example of a Michigan-made patriotic quilt.

*Amanda Canfield Haight and her
husband, John*
*Courtesy of Dearborn
Historical Museum*

43. Amanda Canfield Haight
(b. 1848–?). Log Cabin or Courthouse Steps made 1870, Hillsdale
County, Michigan. Collection of
Dearborn Historical Museum
(acc. 69.119.7). Silk, 43″ x 57″,
MQP 85.1312.

The Log Cabin pattern of this
crib quilt may have had special
meaning for the quiltmaker,
Amanda Canfield Haight. The
daughter of pioneer Solomon
Canfield and his wife, she was
born in a log cabin in 1848, after
her parents moved from Sodus,

New York, to Hillsdale County,
Michigan. In 1869 she married
James Haight. Their first child
was born in 1870, the year this
quilt was made. The top, pieced
out of silk fabrics to form the Log
Cabin or Courthouse Steps pattern, is tied to the rose-colored
silk crepe back with rose-colored
thread. All of the sewing except
for the border has been done by
hand. The crib quilt was given to
the Dearborn Historical Museum
by the quiltmaker's grandson,
Floyd Haight.

44. Elizabeth Kramer (1838–
1923?). President's Wreath made
1870, Stephenson County, Illinois. Gladys Chalmers, lender.
Cotton with cotton filling, 91″ x
92″, MQP 85.1051.

Wayne County resident Gladys
Chalmers, who inherited her
great-great aunt's quilt, writes,

*As far as I can determine . . .
Elizabeth came from Pennsylvania to settle in rural Illinois before 1850 . . . and [this pat-*

*tern] was rather popular
after President Lincoln's
assassination.*

An original bud design was
used with this pattern, and the
quiltmaker quilted in a particularly close and heavy pattern with
acorn designs in the border.

The pieced and appliquéd
quilt has been shown at the 1983
Vermont Quilt Festival and at the
1984 Dearborn Historical Museum Quilt Show.

*Mary Strock Zumbrun and her
husband, Joel*
Courtesy of Carolyn Oberman

45. Mary Strock Zumbrun
(1849-1914) and **her daughters.** Sawtooth made 1870-1880, Union City, Ohio. Glenna Van Lente, lender. Cotton with cotton filling, 75.5" x 85.5", MQP 86.1743.

The Zumbrun Family quilts, 13 in all, represent the rare occurrence of the documentation of four generations of family quilters and their work. The quilts, produced by Mary Strock Zumbrun, her daughter Olive Zumbrun Blocher, granddaughter Mary Blocher Hershberger, and great-granddaughter Carolyn Oberman, have been carefully recorded and preserved by Carolyn Oberman and her family. Although the quilts are different from each other in color and design, all of them show a high degree of technical proficiency and represent a love of quilting that has been passed from generation to generation. Oberman reflects on her family's tradition:

Mary Strock Zumbrun made quilts and comforters strictly for her family's use. They were a farm family in Ohio during the last half of the nineteenth century when she and her husband were raising a family of eight girls and two boys. A lot of bed coverings were needed. Making quilts was an almost

continuous year-around work with another quilt going in the quilting frame as soon as one was finished and came out. All the daughters as well as their mother quilted every day as farm work and chores permitted. But as the daughters grew into their teens and the mother's health was poor—no doubt from child-bearing—she more and more did most of the quilting. This I know from reading . . . [my grandmother's] 1893 journal which tells much about their daily life.

I know for a fact that all the women in this thrifty and hard-working German family were assiduous sewers, making all their clothing, including bonnets and men's clothing. When a quilt or comforter was in progress, everyone worked on it in their spare time. Very often neighboring women went to each other's homes to help quilt. In my grandmother's 1893 journal which I have, she writes of these quilting get-togethers.

This pieced Sawtooth quilt was made in circa 1870 by Mary Strock Zumbrun with the help of her daughters. The quilt employs a variation of the Sawtooth pattern in which the "saws" are placed in an unusual block style.

Quilts no. 45-58 were made by members of the same family.

46. Mary Strock Zumbrun
(1849-1914) and **her daughters.** Triple Irish Chain made 1880, Union City, Ohio. Barbara Corl, lender. Cotton with cotton filling, 82" x 87", MQP 86.1749.

Most of the quilting on this Triple Irish Chain quilt was done by Mary Strock Zumbrun in the 1880s. Carolyn Oberman writes:

[Because] she was either pregnant or recovering from a birth for nearly 20 years, and in ill health, she sat and quilted, or did other sewing a lot of the time. This quilt was made in Ohio but was given to a daughter when she married and moved to Michigan in 1896. Because it was made by her mother and sisters, the daughter (Olive Blocher), far from home and often homesick, did not use it for everyday, only on special occasions, hence its still good condition. It was a poignant reminder of her loved ones back in Ohio.

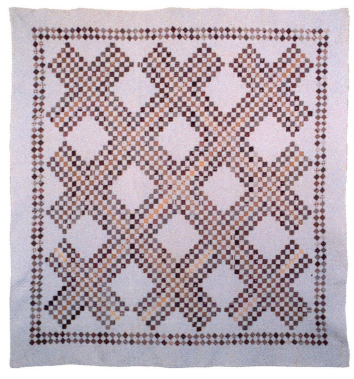

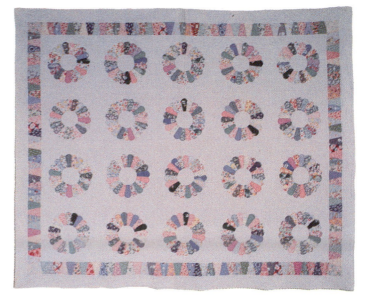

47. Mary Strock Zumbrun

(1849–1914). Caesar's Crown made ca. 1880, Union City, Ohio. Carolyn Oberman, lender. Cotton and muslin with cotton filling, 84″ x 86″, MQP 87.201.

Constructed of white cotton muslin, turkey-red fabric, and a now-faded green cotton fabric, this family heirloom made circa 1880 is kept in near-perfect condition by the quilter's great-granddaughter, Carolyn Oberman. Because it was made for use only as a summer spread, it endured less wear. An example of the meticulous piecing and quilting of Mary Strock Zumbrun, the quilt won Third Prize in the 1984 Tulip Festival Quilt Show in Holland, Michigan, 104 years after it was made.

48. Olive Zumbrun Blocher

(1870–1952). Dresden Plate made early 1920s, Woodland, Barry County, Michigan. Glenna Van Lente, lender. Cotton with cotton filling, 82.5″ x 97.5″, MQP 86.1739.

Carolyn Oberman related this information about her grandmother:

I think that the one thing that gave this quilter [Olive Zumbrun Blocher], my grandmother, the most pleasure and satisfaction during her busy life as a farm wife was the making of quilts. Most of those she made were for her own family's use, but she was also very active helping in her church Aid Society to make quilts for missions. When making her own quilts she used the traditional old patterns, but was creative in designing and making her own quilting templates. Her work, piecing the blocks and her small quilting stitches, is beautiful. This ability and competence to make a thing of beauty, in spite of hard daily work and rough hands, satisfied a creative urge and gave her much to be proud of.

The quilter, Olive Zumbrun Blocher, gave this Dresden Plate summer quilt to her daughter, Glenna Van Lente of Spring Lake, Michigan. Blocher, who gave quilts or comforters to all her daughters when they married, also made many quilts and woven rag rugs to raise funds for the Church of the Brethren Aid Society.

Olive Zumbrun Blocher
Courtesy of Carolyn Oberman

49. Olive Zumbrun Blocher
(1870–1952). Grandmother's
Flower Garden made early 1920s,
Woodland, Barry County, Michigan. Glenna Van Lente, lender.
Cotton with cotton filling, 90″ x
92.5″, MQP 86.1740.

This Grandmother's Flower
Garden quilt was made as a gift
for Glenna Van Lente by her
mother, Olive Zumbrun Blocher.
It features 49 hexagonal blocks in
various pastel colors, joined with
green diamond-shaped pieces. ▶

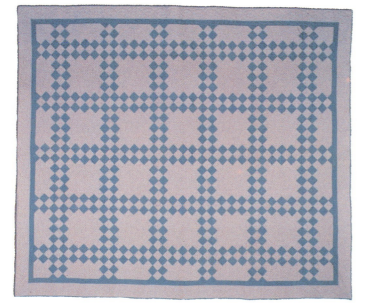

50. Olive Zumbrun Blocher
(1870–1952). Double Irish Chain
made 1935, Woodland, Barry
County, Michigan. Glenna Van
Lente, lender. Cotton fabric from
nurse training uniforms with cotton filling, 84″ x 98″, MQP
86.1742.

Olive Zumbrun Blocher made
this Double Irish Chain quilt in
1935. According to Carolyn
Oberman,

*The medium green squares
are from the uniforms of the
present owner [Glenna Van-*

*Lente] when she was in nurses'
training at Blodgett Hospital,
Grand Rapids, Michigan, during the late 1920s. The maker,
her mother, ripped the uniforms apart, and cut the material in two-inch squares to
make the quilt. Both borders
are quilted in a cable design to
fill the space. The white blocks
are quilted in a double feather
circle with square cross-hatching in center. The patches
in the pieced blocks are quilted
diagonally from corner to
corner.* ▼

51. Olive Zumbrun Blocher ▲
(1870–1952). Sawtooth made
1935, Woodland, Barry County,
Michigan. Glenna Van Lente,
lender. Cotton with cotton filling,
85.5″ x 88″, MQP 86.1738.

This Sawtooth quilt, made by
Blocher in 1935, was patterned
after a quilt made by her mother
60 years earlier. The quilter used
wavy feather and concentric diamond quilting designs. Her granddaughter Carolyn Oberman relates that,

*when buying cotton material to
make housedresses or aprons,
the quilter usually bought a little extra to use later in a quilt.
Several of the prints used in
this quilt are familiar from
years back, and one block especially I remember was a dress I
wore when quite young.*

52. Olive Zumbrun Blocher (1870–1952), quilter; **Wilma Blocher Dittmann** (1901–?), appliquér. Original design *(Potted Buds and Blooms)* made 1938–1940, Woodland, Barry County, Michigan. Mrs. Marianne Fuerst, lender. Cotton with cotton filling, 86″ x 88″, MQP 86.1746.

Wilma Dittman appliquéd the blocks of this quilt in 1938. Her mother, Olive Blocher, joined and quilted the blocks, and, in turn, presented the finished product to her daughter. The quilt has since been passed down to Dittman's niece, Marianne Fuerst, who has named it *Potted Buds and Blooms.*

The quilted cable design in the border contrasts with the quilted double-feather wreaths and one-inch cross-hatching, setting off the delicately pieced potted blossoms. The quilt pattern is thought by the current owner to be an original design by the makers.

53. Olive Zumbrun Blocher ▶ (1870–1952). Broken Star made 1940–1945, Woodland, Barry County, Michigan. Glenna Van Lente, lender. Cotton with cotton filling, 93″ x 93″, MQP 86.1741.

This Broken Star quilt was thought to have been made from a kit in 1940. It encompasses five different quilting designs, including cable, feathered pineapple, feathered wreaths, cross-hatching, and outline stitching.

54. Olive Zumbrun Blocher
(1870–1952). Double Wedding Ring made 1940–1941, Woodland, Barry County, Michigan. Carolyn Oberman, lender. Cotton with cotton filling, 86″ x 102″, MQP 86.1737.

This Double Wedding Ring quilt made in 1940 was used as a bedspread on the guest bed in the Blocher home. According to Carolyn Oberman,

Many of the wedge-shaped patches in this quilt were cut from leftover cotton material used originally to make a housedress or apron. So for me, these patches are a memory of my grandmother when she wore that certain dress or apron.

48

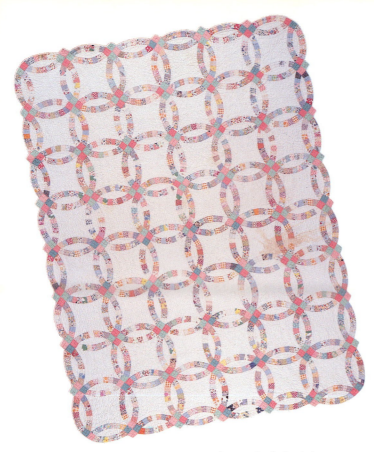

55. Mary Blocher Hershberger (1897–1973). Double Wedding Ring made 1966, Woodland, Barry County, Michigan. Barbara Scott, lender. Cotton with cotton filling, 76.5″ x l02″, MQP 86.1744.

Carolyn Oberman provided this information about the quilter:

My mother [Mary Blocher Hershberger] was a very good seamstress who made most of her children's clothes and other items for household use. However, even though she liked quilts and quilted in her church group, she did not make her first quilt until she was about 65 years old. The two quilts she made then were wedding gifts for her two oldest granddaughters. She intended to continue to make quilts for her other grandchildren but passed away before she could

do so. I think she didn't start making quilts earlier in her life because she liked better to sit and tat or crochet at which she was expert, rather than to sit and quilt.

Mary Blocher Hershberger learned to quilt from her mother, Olive Blocher. She made this quilt, a Double Wedding Ring, in 1966 as a wedding gift for her granddaughter Barbara Oberman Scott. The quilter used a variety of cotton pastel prints and added an original heart-shaped quilting design.

Mary Blocher Hershberger and her husband, Loren
Courtesy of Carolyn Oberman

56. Mary Blocher Hershberger (1897–1973). Original design *(Leafy Lanes)* made 1966, Woodland, Barry County, Michigan. Mrs. Marianne Fuerst, lender. Cotton with cotton filling, 90″ x 97″, MQP 86.1745.

Mary Hershberger made this quilt in 1966 as a wedding gift for her granddaughter Marianne Oberman Fuerst. The appliquéd cotton-print leaves on the white cotton background came from the making of family clothing. Fuerst gave the pattern the name *Leafy Lanes*. It is thought to be an original design by the maker.

57. Carolyn Oberman (b. 1921). Star of Bethlehem made 1939–1965, Fennville, Allegan County, Michigan. Carolyn Oberman, lender. Cotton with cotton filling, 82″ x 95″, MQP 86.1747.

Carolyn Oberman writes:

Although my grandmother made quite a few quilts, and my mother quilted some, [I] did not really become interested in quilting until about 1965. That was when I finally finished piecing a Star of Bethlehem, which I had started in 1939, put it in my grandmother's frame, and quilted it. After that was done I started making patchwork items to sell, such as pillows, crib quilts, and wallhangings. I discovered I loved designing and working with color, and I liked the idea of creating beautiful things that would last long after I am gone.

The first summer after I graduated from high school I saw this pattern in a newspaper, decided I would like to make a quilt, so sent for the instructions, purchased materials, and started piecing. However, because of raising a family and working full time, the piecing dragged along for the next 26 years.

The fabric used for the top of this quilt was purchased in 1939 from a department store in Manchester, Indiana, for a grand total of $1.39. In 1965 the completed top was finally quilted by Carolyn Oberman and her mother, Mary Hershberger, whose meticulous work produced this beautiful result.

Carolyn Oberman
Courtesy of Carolyn Oberman

58. Carolyn Oberman (b. 1921). *Colorama* made 1984–1985, Fennville, Allegan County, Michigan. Susan Scott, lender. Cotton/polyester with polyester filling, 62″ x 90″, MQP 86.1748.

Carolyn Oberman was awarded a First-Prize Blue Ribbon in the appliqué category at the Ottawa County Fair in 1985 for this unique quilt entitled *Colorama*. The quilt was made as a graduation gift for her granddaughter Susan Scott. Oberman, a self-described traditionalist who likes "old-time patterns," chose this bright contemporary quilt design because her granddaughter likes rainbows.

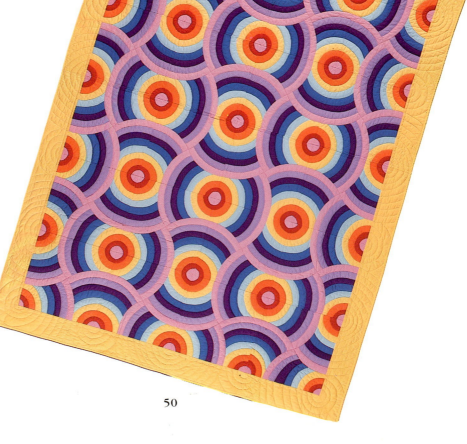

59. Susannah Johnson Justice

(ca. 1813–1887). Original design made 1875, Campbell Township, Ionia County, Michigan. Mildred E. Sussell, lender. Cotton, 68″ x 70″, MQP 85.180.

This pieced quilt has been passed through four generations of Susannah Johnson Justice's family, treasured first by her daughter Nancy Cummins, then passed to J. Elizabeth Cummins Potter, Maude Potter Shores, and Mildred E. Sussell, the current owner. Justice fashioned the quilt in 1875 to commemorate her country's centennial and as a memorial to her late husband, Jeremiah Justice. Family history records that

Susannah Johnson Justice
Courtesy of Mildred E. Sussell

Susannah Johnson was born somewhere in Pennsylvania ca. 1813. Before 1820 her parents had moved to Tuscarawas Co., OH. She was married in Holmes Co., OH 6 March 1834 to John Justice, who died 11 January 1849 in Wood Co., OH. She then married his younger brother, Jeremiah, who was several years younger than she, and moved to Fulton Co., OH. There Jeremiah enlisted in the Civil War along with his nephews/stepsons. None of the families today know what happened to Jeremiah after he was mustered out at Louisville, KY,

in August 1865, exactly 3 years after he entered service, but he had been in ill health much of that time and it is assumed that he soon died.

About 1867 Susannah and all her children, married and unmarried, moved to Campbell Twp., Ionia Co., MI.

Susannah had a large handkerchief, reported to have been carried by her husband in the Civil War. In 1875 she decided to use it to make a centennial quilt in honor of the centennial which would be celebrated the following year.

Susannah died in Ionia Co., MI, 28 April 1887.

60. Maria Louise Lyon.

Brick Wall made 1876, Hillsdale, Hillsdale County, Michigan. Collection of Al and Merry Silber. Cotton, 78.5″ x 88″, MQP 86.1718.

Made by Maria Louise Lyon of Hillsdale, Michigan, this Brick Wall quilt appears to have been pieced in several sections. The diagonal chevron pattern shifts, producing an interesting fluctuating effect. A large variety of cotton fabrics dating from the mid nineteenth century are found in the 1876 quilt.

61. Unknown maker. Ocean Waves made 1877, provenance unknown. Elaine Saxton, lender. Cotton with cotton filling, 32.5″ x 32.5″, MQP 85.179.

It is not known who made this pieced baby quilt for John Willard Brodock, born April 26, 1877. It was passed to Brodock's only child, Doris Marie Bryan, and is now owned by Elaine Saxton of Britton, Michigan.

Sarah Gardner and William Leslie, 1882
Courtesy of Dearborn Historical Museum

62. Sarah Gardner Leslie (1850–?). Flower Basket made ca. 1880, near Dearborn, Michigan. Collection of Dearborn Historical Museum (acc. 55-19.12). Wool and silk, 63″ x 79″, MQP 85.1274.

The flower-basket design on this quilt has been appliquéd and stuffed to create a three-dimensional effect. The top is made of solid-colored wool and silk, and the straight edges of the quilt are bound in wool tape. The quilting is in a diamond pattern. All of the sewing has been done by hand, except for the machined seams.

The Flower Basket quilt was made circa 1880 in the Dearborn, Michigan area by Sarah Gardner before her marriage to William Leslie in 1882. Her mother, Elizabeth Gould Gardner, also was a quiltmaker. The photograph taken of the young couple when they were married shows Leslie in her wedding dress, which was purchased by selling the family cow. Inherited by the Leslies' daughter, Mahala Gardner Brown, the quilt is now in the collection of the Dearborn Historical Museum.

63. Elizabeth Lahr (1862–1950) and **Jenny Strawser.** Tulip variation made ca. 1880, Deshler, Ohio. Theodore and Barbara Webster, lenders. Cotton, 72″ x 72″, MQP 86.323.

Family history records that the makers of this quilt were Pennsylvania-born Mennonite women who had settled in Ohio. After Elizabeth Lahr and her sister Jenny Strawser completed the quilt, Lahr kept it for family use. On her death, Lahr's adopted daughter, Grace, inherited the quilt. Grace gave it to her brother, Frank Lahr, who in turn gave it to his daughter, Helen Webster. Today the quilt is owned by Theodore and Barbara Webster.

64. Unknown maker. Cottage Tulips made ca. 1880, provenance unknown. Kay Mertz, lender. Cotton with cotton filling, 69″ x 86″, MQP 86.175.

A family heirloom with a scantily recorded history, this quilt passed through the Mertz family to its present owner. Circles of green-stemmed red tulips are widely spaced across the white cotton top, leaving large expanses of white space for the feather, feather swag, diagonal cross-hatch, and diagonal channel-quilting stitches. The three green borders are also quilted with feather stitching. The limited color scheme of green and turkey red on white is typical of the period. It accentuates both the stitching and, in a pattern of alternating areas of color and background, the quality of the appliqué work. The alternation of circles of appliquéd tulips and curved criss-crosses of feather stitching against the cross-hatched background displays the quiltmaker's interest in combining intricate needlework with attractive piecing.

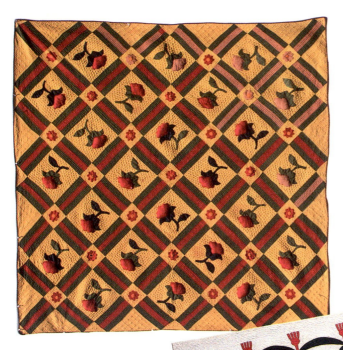

65. Mary Ann Thurber (1836–1889). Tulip Appliqué made ca. 1880s, Michigan. Collection of Dearborn Historical Museum (acc. 61.63.1). Cotton, 80" x 81", MQP 85.1292.

Separated by green and red sashes, 24 diamond-shaped blocks and 16 half blocks provide the backgrounds for the appliquéd and stuffed tulip designs of this quilt, made in the 1880s by Mary Ann Thurber. Her quilting designs, done by hand in colored thread to match the colors of the cotton fabrics, include closely spaced, parallel lines in some areas. In other places, Thurber used her thimble to trace the quilting pattern. A color change in the fabric in one area suggests that Thurber may have been following the tradition of incorporating an intentional error in her quilt, to acknowledge that "perfection can come only from God." Born in England, Thurber made this quilt in Michigan during the last decade of her life. It was donated to the Dearborn Historical Museum by Phoebe Lapham Brown.

Mary Aylesbury Randall
Courtesy of Mary D. Zehner

66. Mary Aylesbury Randall (1844–1914). Original design *(Randall Quilt)* made 1880, Tamaqua, Pennsylvania. Mary D. Zehner, lender. Cotton with cotton filling, 94" x 95.5", MQP 85.1889.

Nine square blocks of bleached white muslin furnish the background for the appliquéd floral wreaths that dominate the top of this quilt made in 1880. Red flowers and dark blue-green foliage form the original wreath designs. The same colors are found in the swags and tassels of the appliquéd border design. The top has been quilted to the cotton filling and muslin back with cross-hatching, clam-shell stitching, and outlining.

The maker of this quilt was Mary Randall of Tamaqua, Pennsylvania. Born at St. Clair, Pennsylvania, to Robert and Dorothy Aylesbury, she was married in 1863 to Walter Randall and had two daughters, Emma and Irene. Used only occasionally, her quilt has remained in the family, having been owned by Emma Randall Zehner, Louis Zehner, and its present owner, Mary Zehner of East Lansing, Michigan.

Mary Gardner Crawford taken about 1888 by Mrs. M. E. Leigh, artist, Ionia, Michigan
Courtesy of Coralane McLeod Boyes

67. Mary Gardner Crawford

(1793–1885). Old Maid's Puzzle pieced 1880, quilted 1984, Ionia, Ionia County, Michigan. Coralane McLeod Boyes, lender. Cotton with cotton outting flannel filling, 79″ x 89″, MQP 85.521.

In 1879, the Presbyterian Church of Ionia presented the following proclamation to Mary Gardner Crawford:

At a Meeting of the Ladies Missionary Society of the First Presbyterian Church of Ionia Mich. held the 16th day of May 1879, the following Preamble and Resolution were unanimously adopted.

Whereas Mrs. Mary Crawford, one of the oldest members of this church has, during the past eight years or more, made with her own hands and presented to our Society upwards of eighteen bed quilts to be sold for the benefit of its treasury, therefore

Resolved, that we hereby express, not only our high appreciation of Mrs. Crawford's remarkable industry at her advanced age, but, also, our deepest gratitude in view of that large-hearted generosity which has prompted our sister to make these offerings to the cause of Home Missions. And we most sincerely pray that the richest blessings of Him whose grace led her to bestow these gifts and who always rewards the benevolent deeds of his children may descend upon her. By order of the Society.

Family tradition says that this native of Ireland enjoyed making quilts and that several family members have examples of her quilts. Crawford left this quilt top to her granddaughter Lana Marsh McLeod, who in turn gave it to her daughter Mary McLeod Weed. In the 1960s the top was then passed on to Weed's niece and present owner, Coralane Boyes, who finished quilting it during the winter of 1984–85. Boyes is an active participant in the family quilting tradition carried on by her great-grandmother, grandmother, and mother. In a letter dated April 17, 1985 she says:

I have pieced and quilted since the mid 1930s. I still do this type of thing. Presently I have on my quilting frames a quilt with the blocks hand-painted (probably in the 1950s). . . . We have a family tradition of piecing blocks for a quilt for the bride, as a wedding gift. The blocks were made by sisters, cousins, grandmothers, aunts, god-mothers, mother and then I finished the quilt. Some of these were tied but the last two I quilted . . . . Most of the work I have done has been of a practical nature as we used them on the beds daily. So you can see they were not fancy, as some of the ones I see today. Over the period of years I have quilted about twenty quilts and tied more than that.

68. Hattie Kelley (1865–1931). Crazy made 1885, Kelley's Corners (later Cement City), Jackson County, Michigan. Collection of Michigan State University Museum, gift of Lura Jean Harbaugh (acc. 6030). Velvet and silk, 64″ x 73″, MQP 85.216.

According to information provided by Lura Jean Harbaugh, the quiltmaker's granddaughter,

this quilt was made by Hattie Kelley in the year 1885 and was to be used in her future home. She lived at Kelley's Corners (Cement City), Colum-
bia Township, Jackson County, Michigan. She was married to Hazael Choate in 1886, and lived in Liberty Township. She got her quilting experience from Mary Reed Hill, a well-known quilter in the 1880s.

The quilt, done in the Crazy-block style that was popular in the late nineteenth century, incorporates a blue letter *H*, which might have stood for either Hattie or Hazael. "H   K   Jan. 20 1885" is stamped in ink on the quilt. (See no. 69 for quilt made by Kelley's daughter.)

69. Mercie Bell Choate (1894–1981). Nine-Patch variation and Crazy made 1914, Cement City, Jackson County, Michigan. Collection of Michigan State University Museum, gift of Lura Jean Harbaugh. Wool and velvet, 72″ x 85″, MQP 85.217.

Mercie Bell Choate received help on this quilt, which was made as part of her wedding trousseau, from Hattie Kelley Choate, her mother, and Mary Reed Hill, her future husband's grandmother. According to a 1926 *Jackson Citizen Patriot* article entitled "Jackson Woman, 90 Years Old Today, Is Believed to Be The Champion Quilter of Michigan,"

The honor of being the champion quilter of Michigan, if not of the United States, is probably held by Mrs. Mary Reed Hill, 231 Rockwell Street, who is quietly celebrating her ninetieth birthday today.

During the past eight years
Mrs. Hill has completed 306 quilts, 32 of this number having been finished since last September.

If a record had been kept of the work previously accomplished, the total would indeed be a large one, as Mrs. Hill has been quilting ever since she can remember. In fact, it was as a girl in her early home in Erie County, N.Y., that she learned the art of quilting from her mother, but it was not until about 20 years ago, when she was past the allotted three score and ten years, that Mrs. Hill's industry assumed such large proportions.

It was the exquisite workmanship on a quilt given as a wedding present, at a large and fashionable wedding in Detroit, that launched her on this form of needle work.

(See no. 68 for quilt made by Choate's mother.)

70. Roe G. Van Deusen, designer; **Lois Van Deusen Darcus** (1865-1926), piecer. Crazy designed 1885-1887, pieced and finished 1887, Elsie, Clinton County, Michigan. Mr. and Mrs. Clarence Husted, lenders. Velvet and silk, 65″ x 74″, MQP 85.1093.

According to family history, this pieced quilt was made by teenager Lois Van Deusen for her father, Roe G. Van Deusen, whose initial is in the lower left-hand corner. The father designed the stitches, which he drew in a notebook entitled "Fancy Stitches for Crazy Work." In that book he also made floral drawings in watercolor and pen and ink, which he asked his daughter to duplicate

in embroidered form. If her needlework did not perfectly copy his drawings, he reportedly made her take out the stitches and start over. Roe Van Deusen also was a contributor to the *Elsie Sun,* in which he had a regular column called "Old Saws." Very little is known about his daughter except that she married James B. Darcus on April 27, 1891 and spent most of her married life in Ithaca, Michigan.

The quilt and sketchbooks have been passed down from Darcus to her daughter Ruth Darcus Husted and in turn to her son and present owner Clarence Husted.

Lois Darcus and her husband, James
Courtesy of Mr. and Mrs. Clarence Husted

72. Helen Mary Rounsville.

Crazy made ca. 1887, Fowlerville, Livingston County, Michigan. Collection of Mary Strickler's Quilt. Satin and silk, 50″ x 64″, MQP 87.146.

This beautiful Crazy quilt, constructed of irregularly shaped satin and silk blocks, was made by Helen Mary Rounsville circa 1887. Rounsville grew up on a large horse farm in Fowlerville, Michigan. Her fondness for horses is expressed through her careful appliqué and embroidery work around the border of the quilt. Center blocks feature a variety of detailed, embroidered flow-

ers and leaves. Rounsville's initials are displayed prominently in the center of the quilt.

Rounsville was born Helen Mary Glenn, the daughter of Nelson A. and Ann E. Torrey Glenn. Her grandfather Seth B. Torrey came to Michigan in 1846, where he worked as a contractor, road commissioner, and township clerk. Rounsville's father was employed as a pump peddler. ▶

◀ 71. Unknown maker. Greek

Key made 1885–1900, provenance unknown. Florence Clute, lender. Cotton and silk, 81″ x 92″, MQP 86.816.

The Greek Key quilt combines an unusual collection of colors. The back is of a dark red-and-blue print, chosen presumably to complement the top and not compete with it. The rectangles and strips in the top are hand-pieced

and the quilting, also done by hand, consists of literally thousands of stitched rectangles.

Although the names of the quilters are not known, owner Florence Clute believes her aunts designed and constructed the quilt between 1890 and 1900. They made it for their sister, Hilma Lindgren, who then passed the quilt to her daughter, Florence Lindgren Clute.

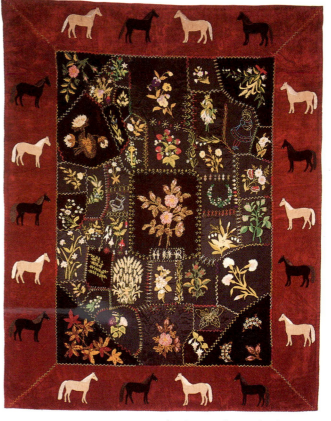

◀ 73. Martha Wade Sherwood,

piecer; **Mary Vida Schafer** (b. 1910), quilter. Drunkard's Path pieced 1887, quilted ca. 1967, Holly, Genesee County, Michigan. Mary Vida Schafer, lender. Cotton with polyester filling, 91" x 97″, MQP 85.1626. The top was completed in 1887 at Holly, Michigan, by Martha Wade Sherwood, who signed her name and date in embroidery. In about 1967 Mary Schafer of Flushing, Michigan, added a white border to the top and quilted it to a polyester filling and cotton back, using diagonal, straight feather, outline, and original quilting designs. The finished quilt has been exhibited at the Whaley House in Flint, Michigan.

74. Adella Penoyer, piecer; **Mary Vida Schafer** (b. 1910), quilter. Bear's Paw pieced ca. 1890–1910, quilted 1975, Flushing, Genesee County, Michigan. Mary Vida Schafer, lender. Cotton with cotton filling, 81″ x 98″, MQP 85.1621.

The 36 pieced blocks in this quilt contain Bear's Paw motifs made from patterned blue cotton and set against white backgrounds. Patterned blue sashes separate the blocks. Blue borders, one at each side and two at both the top and the bottom, complete the arrangement. Zigzag, diagonal, and outline quilting fasten the top to the white cotton backing.

Made between 1890 and 1910 by Adella Penoyer of Flushing, Michigan, the quilt was restored and quilted circa 1975 by Mary Schafer, also of Flushing. The Penoyers were one of the first farm families to settle in the Flushing area.

Mary Vida Schafer
Courtesy of Alan Zinn

75. Mary Vida Schafer (b. 1910). Nine-Patch variation *(Eisenhower Quilt)* made 1968, Flushing, Genesee County, Michigan. Mary Vida Schafer, lender. Cotton with polyester filling, 55″ x 100″, MQP 85.1629.

Made for a bed narrower than twin size, this quilt is an original design that pays tribute to U.S. President Dwight D. Eisenhower. The middle section holds 20 red-and-white pieced blocks (done in a variation of the Nine-Patch pattern), 12 plain white blocks, and 1 appliquéd center block, as well as 16 half-blocks and 4 quarter-blocks. The simple Nine-Patch blocks suggest Eisenhower's unpretentious background. The central block holds an appliquéd red eagle to symbolize the presidency and five appliquéd green stars to represent Eisenhower's rank as a five-star general. A continuous green vine, running through the wide white border, stands for the unity that existed between Eisenhower and the American people. Its appliquéd leaves symbolize the many honors he received during his lifetime. Appliquéd in red along the vine and quilted in the blocks, 48 stars represent the number of states at the time Eisenhower became president.

Other quilting designs include diagonal lines, interlocking circles, wreaths, and extensive outlining. The top is signed with the maker's name and the date of its completion.

The *Eisenhower Quilt* was made in 1967–68 by Mary Vida Schafer of Flushing, Michigan. Born in Austria, Schafer came to the United States at the age of four with her mother, who died the next year. Her father, who raised her, arranged for neighborhood women to teach his daughter how to crochet, tat, and do needlepoint. In 1929 she married Fred Schafer. Her first quilts, made from kits, were done between 1952 and 1956, while their son was in the Navy. After his return, he brought home from a beach party a battered, old, pieced quilt that someone had left behind. Through her efforts to make a similar quilt, Schafer began her serious involvement with quiltmaking, which soon became her chief interest. In addition to becoming a prize-winning quiltmaker, Schafer has amassed a major collection of antique quilts. She has also collected unfinished tops, many of which she has completed by adding original borders and quilting designs. Schafer first used a patriotic theme in the *Eisenhower Quilt.* It has been exhibited at the Whaley House in Flint, Michigan.

76. Jenny Emmons McAllister. Crazy made ca. 1888, Detroit, Wayne County, Michigan. Collection of Al and Merry Silber. Silk, 53″ x 72″, MQP 86.1727.

Incorporated into this pieced and elaborately embroidered Crazy quilt are silk ribbons commemorating union meetings and campaigns held in Detroit in the 1880s. Quilter Jenny Emmons McAllister, whose husband, William, was a conductor on the Detroit-Port Huron railway, used a variety of silks and stitches in this special quilt. William's initials, "W Mc A," appear in one of the six, pieced, Crazy blocks.

77. Rose Shilling Haskins (1869–1931). Log Cabin made ca. 1888, Mount Pleasant, Isabella County, Michigan. K. C. and Vivian Charnes, lenders. Silk and cotton, 67″ x 76″, MQP 86.1948.

This variation on the Log Cabin pattern is called Courthouse Steps. The "step" effect is achieved by the use of alternating arrangements of light- and dark-colored fabrics. The quilt, composed entirely of one-quarter-inch strips of cotton and silk fabrics, was made by Rose Shilling Haskins in 1888. Haskins was born on March 3, 1869, in Brinton, Michigan, the daughter of a Michigan lumberman. She and her husband, Fred, also a lumberman, eventually settled in Mount Pleasant, where she lived until her death in 1909. The log house where Haskins lived still stands in Isabella County.

78. Unknown maker. Crazy made 1888, provenance unknown. Collection of Detroit Historical Museum (acc. 60-51.2). Silk, ribbon, and cotton with cotton filling, 52″ x 52″, MQP 85.2017.

Although little is known about the history of this textile, referred to as a "throw," it is a fine example of the diversity of images that were included in Crazy quilts. One patch is a printed silk picture of U.S. President Grover Cleveland and his wife, Rose

Elizabeth Cleveland, printed by Thomas Stevens Company, Coventry, England. Another patch is a Richmond Straight Cut Cigarette advertising picture with a woman on a horse, also printed by the Thomas Stevens Company using a technique called a "Stevensgraph." Embroidery depicting a wide assortment of people, animals, and other decorative features decorates the various Crazy patches. Of special note is a family tree embroidered in one block.

79. Dorothea Peterson. Original design *(Flags of the Nations)* made 1889–1913, Norway, and Escanaba, Delta County, Michigan. Ann Spear, lender. Cotton and flannel, 68″ x 74″, MQP 86.989.

Dorothea Peterson began her *Flags of the Nations* quilt to help her son learn geography. The family was then living in Norway, and by the time she finished the quilt they had moved to Escanaba, Michigan. The quilt was given to her son to use as a

spread on his single-size brass bed. Peterson's son later gave the quilt to his daughter, Ann Spear, of Marquette, Michigan.

The 54 blocks, each of which depicts an embroidered national flag in use at the time the quilt was made, are machine-pieced to connecting pieced sashes. The quilt was made from a kit, and each of the printed flannel block flags originally came as a premium in a coffee can. The top was never bound or quilted.

Armenia Winchcomb
Courtesy of Bethea Monroe Berg

80. Armenia Winchcomb
(1859–1934). Lone Star made ca. 1890–1900, Traverse City, Grand Traverse County, Michigan. Bethea Monroe Berg, lender. Wool with wool filling, 71″ x 69″, MQP 86.2004.

The diamond-shaped pieces that compose the star on this Lone Star comforter have been documented by the lender as having come from the clothing of members of Armenia Winch-comb's family. For instance, the red fabric in the center came from a dress belonging to the maker's niece, Dora Monroe; the red-and-green plaid was a shirt belonging to the maker's father, John Winchcomb; and the mottled green print came from one of the maker's dresses. The background is a plaid wool blanket, which provides an interesting contrast to the colorful pieced star. The comforter is not quilted, but rather tied with red wool yarn.

Armenia Winchcomb was born in New York on April 9, 1859, one of ten children of John and Elizabeth Winchcomb. The Winchcombs emigrated from England in 1841 and eventually settled in Traverse City. Armenia, who never married, lived on 10th Street in Traverse City and worked as a seamstress for 40 years until her death in 1934.

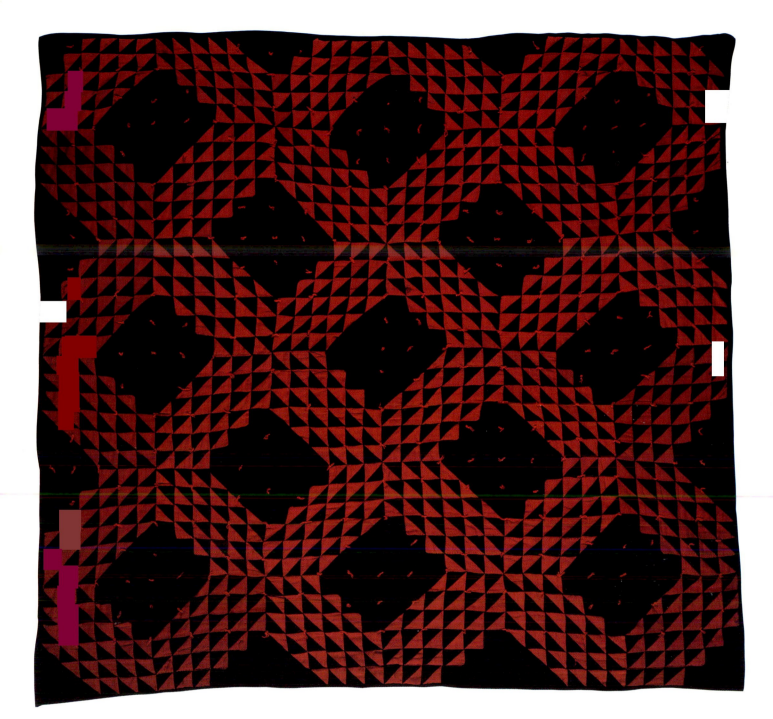

81. Unknown member of Bryant or Murphy family. Ocean Waves made ca. 1890–1910, Upper Peninsula, Michigan. Collection of Michigan State University Museum (acc. 5968). Wool with wool filling, 79″ x 81″, MQP 87.231.

According to Dorothy Murphy, who donated this pieced quilt to the Michigan State University Museum, both this quilt and one similar to it were believed to have been made by members of the Bryant or Murphy families, who were related to her husband and who hailed from Cornwall, England. Heavy, wool, tied quilts with wool filling were typical of those made in or brought to the Upper Peninsula. One correspondent to the Michigan Quilt Project related that when she was preparing to be transferred to a job in the Upper Peninsula she suddenly found herself the recipient of all of her family's wool quilts. She said that her family was worried she wouldn't be warm enough there during the winter months.

*Helen Marr Randall Carrick
taken in Charlotte, Michigan*
Courtesy of Marlene Eggert

◀ **82. Helen Marr Randall Carrick** (1842–1909) and unidentified members of **her church quilting group.** Made 1890, Fenton, Genesee County, Michigan. Marlene A. Eggert, lender. Cotton, 74″ x 77″, MQP 85.57.

Helen Marr Randall Carrick was a member of the church quilting group that made this quilt, on which they recorded their names and the names of their family members. It is not known why this quilt was made, or how Carrick came to own it, but it has been kept in her family for four generations. Carrick's daughter Mattie Jane McConnell, granddaughter Helen L. McConnell Eggert, and great-granddaughter in-law Marlene A. Eggert have all treasured this textile record of their ancestors. Dated May 3, 1890, the quilt provides a list of residents of Fenton, Michigan, which augments the official government census of the community.

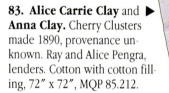

83. Alice Carrie Clay and ▶ **Anna Clay.** Cherry Clusters made 1890, provenance unknown. Ray and Alice Pengra, lenders. Cotton with cotton filling, 72″ x 72″, MQP 85.212.

A small piece of paper attached to the back of this quilt states, "This quilt was made around 1890, by the mother and grandmother of Mary Etta Cramton, Alice Carrie Clay and Anna Clay." The present owners, who purchased the quilt at an auction and brought it to Michigan, have discovered the quiltmakers were descendants of Henry Clay. It is not known where the quilt was made. It takes its name from the nine appliquéd blocks of green leaves and swirling vines topped with clusters of round, red "cherries." The quilt incorporates feather and cross-hatch patterns in intricate quilting designs.

*Minnie TenEyck Rice at
age 30-35*
Courtesy of the Dr. William Hyser
Rivers Museum

84. Minnie TenEyck Rice. Original design made 1890–1900, Grand Rapids, Kent County, Michigan. Collection of Dr. William Hyser Rivers Museum. Cotton, 72″ x 90″, MQP 86.806.

This floral appliqué quilt, of original design, was donated to the Dr. William Hyser Rivers Museum in Belmont, Michigan, by Gayle Rice, daughter of the ▲ maker, Minnie TenEyck Rice. The border design of vines, urns, and birds combined with the 12 unusual floral motifs done in solid cottons demonstrate her individuality as an artist. Unfortunately, very little is known about Minnie Rice, and it is not known whether she made other quilts.

64

Ada Miller
Courtesy of Ruth Smith and
Della McKay

85. Ada Miller (1861–1923). Heart and Hands made 1891, Merrill, Saginaw County, Michigan. Ruth Smith and Della McKay, lenders. Cotton with cotton filling, 72″ x 89.5″, MQP 85.673.

A member of the Lakefield Quilting Club, Ada Miller learned quilting at home from her mother. Working at a wooden frame held down by clamps and quilting "10 minutes at a time when time was available," Miller made more than 100 quilts in her lifetime, many of which she gave away as wedding gifts. This particular appliquéd quilt was recently returned to the Lakefield Quilters club by a great-granddaughter who had inherited it. The granddaughter had moved to California and wanted it placed in a museum.

86. Sarah Haynes. Hexagon (*The Sarah Haynes Quilt*) made 1892–1909, Gladwin, Gladwin County, Michigan. Collection of Esprit, Inc. of San Francisco, California. Silk, MQP 87.145.

This dazzling quilt, made from 33,782 tiny silk triangles, was the 17-year task of quilter Sarah Haynes. Haynes, the wife of a Civil War veteran from Gladwin, Michigan, began the quilt in 1892. She purchased the silk in half-yard lengths, and, for each of the half-inch pieces of silk, she cut a tiny paper template. The quilt was then pieced with mathematical precision in the English manner, overhand, from the back of the quilt. Haynes finished the quilt with a maroon silk ruffle and silk-covered buttons at six-inch intervals. The result has been described as a "tribute to obsession."

In 1929 Sarah Haynes won a $15 First Prize at the Women's International Exhibition at Detroit's Convention Hall. Sometime later the magnificent quilt passed from the family's hands to a Detroit attorney in lieu of a fee. The quilt is now part of the Esprit Collection of Esprit, Inc., San Francisco, California.

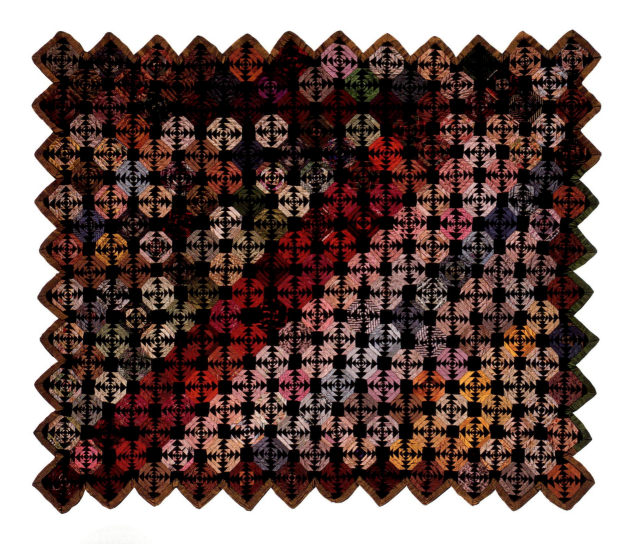

Agnes Lovering Metcalf, ca. 1894
Courtesy of Lois (Mrs. D. G.) Lance

87. Agnes Lovering Metcalf
(d. 1960). Pineapple made 1894, Detroit, Wayne County, Michigan. Lois (Mrs. D. G.) Lance, lender. Velvet and silk, 56″ x 68″, MQP 86.1516.

An asymmetric placement of vivid reds and yellows highlights the overall pattern of contrasting black and more subtle pastels in this 1894 pieced velvet Pineapple quilt. The Pineapple pattern is a variation of the Log Cabin pattern, in which patches are added in an outward direction from a center square. There is no filling in this quilt; the back is of two pieces of commercially made patterned silk.

In addition to quilting, Detroit native Agnes Lovering Metcalf collected and made lace and did water color painting. She married Dr. William Metcalf in 1897, and they had two children, son William and daughter Jessie. Jessie inherited the quilt from her mother. Current owner Lois Lance, who purchased the quilt from Jessie at a Detroit auction, refers to this textile as a "throw."

88. Women's Relief Corps, Grand Army of the Republic (G.A.R.) Post.
Eight-Pointed Star made 1894, Mancelona, Antrim County, Michigan. J. Gordon Smith in name of Winchester R. Rice, M Co. Mich. 6th Cav., lender. Cotton, 73″ x 83″, MQP 85.254.

On Thursday, May 10, 1894, the *Mancelona Herald* carried the following news item:

A G.A.R. social was held at the post rooms in this village Saturday evening at which speeches were made and a very pleasant time was had. A patchwork quilt containing the name, company and regiment of each member of post was sold at auction and W.R. Rice being the highest bidder, the same was struck off to him. The quilt netted the society about $15.

J. G. Smith, the current owner of the quilt and a great-grandson of W. R. Rice, acquired the quilt from his uncle, William F. Catlin, in about 1952 or 1953. Intrigued by the names on the quilt, Smith began to research its origins, which led him to the above clip-ping about the textile and its makers, the Mancelona Women's Relief Corps (the Women's Auxiliary of the local G.A.R. post). He discovered that each of the 56 stars carried the name, rank, and military unit of a member of the G.A.R. post at Mancelona and that the setting blocks carried the names of other famous individuals in United States history. He also learned that W. R. Rice was born in Rochester, New York, in 1831, served as a member of the Sixth Regiment Michigan Volunteer Cavalry during the Civil War, married Lucy Marsh in 1882, and died in Mancelona in 1902. The quilt is an important document of Mancelona community and Michigan military history.

89. Sylvia Idella Rathbun Menzies (1866–1954) and friends.
Sixteen-Pointed Star made 1894–1895, Caledonia, Kent County, Michigan. Doris G. Ockerman, lender. Dress fabric scraps, 71″ x 84″, MQP 85.267.

Doris G. Ockerman, a granddaughter of the quiltmaker, provided this information:

This Friendship quilt was made for the wedding of Miss Sylvia Idella Rathbun to Henry Menzies. The quilt pattern was given to her many friends and each made one of the blocks using her own dress material.

Sylvia then put the blocks together and there was a "quilting bee" held to finish the quilt.

Sylvia Idella Rathbun Menzies was born in Caledonia Township (near what is now known as 9518 Sanborn Avenue, Alto, Michigan) in a log cabin owned by her grandfather, Orsemus Rathbun, on April 6, 1866. Her father and mother were Levi and Alzina (Streeter) Rathbun. Sylvia was married to Henry Menzies on April 7, 1895. They had two children, Bertha Mryl (Sanborn) and Walter Robert Men-zies. Sylvia and Henry lived almost all of their lives on a farm in Caledonia Township (now 8172 92nd Street, Alto, Michigan). Sylvia died April 4, 1954. Henry preceded her in death on June 11, 1944.

I remember this quilt being on the bed in my grandmother's "parlor" bedroom. This room was used only for company, and for sick grandchildren. I survived the German measles in that bed.

Each of the blocks carries the embroidered name of its maker.

Sylvia Idella Rathbun Menzies
Courtesy of Doris G. Ockerman

90. Hannah Elizabeth Thursby Conquest (1849–1915?) and **the Ladies of the Auxiliary of the Relief Corps of the Grand Army of the Republic, Post 194.** *Relief Corps Quilt* made November 1895, County Line (now Clio), Genesee County, Michigan. Chris Hayden, lender. Cotton, 66″ x 86″, MQP 86.561.

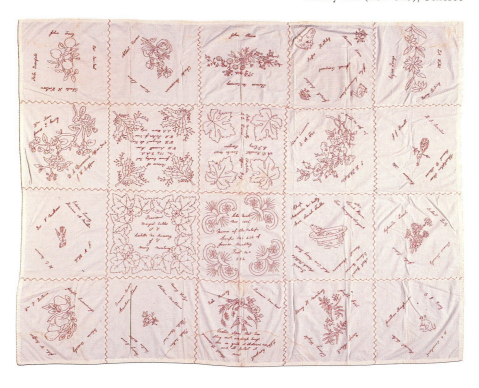

The *Relief Corps Quilt* has been in the Conquest family since it was made. The present owner, Chris Hayden, is the great-granddaughter of one of its embroiderers, Hannah Elizabeth Thursby Conquest, known as "Libbie." The quilt top came to Hayden from her father, Myron Hutchinson, whose mother, Martha Hutchinson, was Conquest's daughter. This Autograph quilt was embroidered by the wives of men who had served in the Grand Army of the Republic Relief Corps during the Civil War. Each embroidered her own design—many of them are flowers or birds—in her square, then added the names of the men who had served and her own signature. Among the women known to have worked on this community effort are: Sarah Phillips, Mary Leach, Elsina Monroe, Harriet Anderson, Sara Warn, Ermogene Sargent, Amanda McNelly, Sarah Fuller, Sarah Diamond, Kate Larvey, and Lucrecia Van West.

91. Lottie Stites (1884–1968), piecer; **Marjorie L. Faris,** quilter. Garfield's Monument pieced 1895–1900, quilted 1981, Traverse City, Grand Traverse County, Michigan. Clarence E. Stites and Marjorie L. Faris, lenders. Cotton and cotton/polyester with synthetic filling, 92″ x 105″, MQP 85.927.

Lottie Stites
Courtesy of Clarence E. Stites and Marjorie L. Faris

In recent years Berkeley resident Marjorie L. Faris has quilted several of the quilt tops made by her grandmother, Lottie Stites. She inherited them from her father (and Stites's son), Clarence E. Stites. The particular pattern used in this quilt is seldom used. Other patterns that Stites used for quilt tops include Nine Patch, Grandmother's Flower Garden, and Sunbonnet Sue.

The original portion of this quilt top is made up of two reverse prints of blue-and-white cotton material. The border material is a cotton/polyester blend purchased at Stewart's fabric store in Birmingham, Michigan.

*Mary Elizabeth Fredricks Courser
and her husband, Herbert
Courtesy of Mrs. John
(Marjorie) Benedict*

92. Mary Elizabeth Fredricks
(or Fredricks) **Courser** (ca.
1870–1937/8). Eight-Pointed Star
made 1898–1899, Portland, Ionia
County, Michigan. Mrs. John (Marjorie) Benedict, lender. Cotton
with cotton filling, 70" x 76",
MQP 85.688.

Mary Elizabeth ("Lizzie")
Courser and her husband, Herbert, were devout church goers
who took their two small children to worship in a horse-drawn
buggy one Christmas Eve, even
though Anna, age eight, had a
cold. Shortly after, the cold
turned into pneumonia, and Anna
died in 1898. Mary Elizabeth's
granddaughter, Marjorie Benedict, heard this story from her
mother:

*Grandma used pieces of her
dresses to make the star quilt.
Christmas Eve was cold and
blizzardy and they knew it was*

*hazardous. When [their]
daughter got worse and died
they were always bitter because
God could let such an awful
thing happen to "His Children."
They never went to church
again . . . Mary Elizabeth's father [a German immigrant]
homesteaded on the west end
of a swamp south of Kilmartin
School, Orange Township. He
was drafted for Civil War. Not
having the $500 to buy someone to take his place, as was
custom then, he went. Thinking
that joining Company K, Mechanics and Engineers, he
might survive, he went. He left
a pregnant, blind wife and one
two-year old girl, Mary
Elizabeth.*

Comprising plain turkey-red
squares set alternately with
pieced blocks on the diagonal,
this quilt shows much wear. The
quilt was passed by the quiltmaker to her surviving child,
Dale Courser. He, in turn, gave it
to his daughter and present
owner Marjorie Benedict.

93. Mary Scotten. Baby Blocks
or Tumbling Blocks made ca.
1900, Detroit, Wayne County,
Michigan. Collection of Michigan
State University Museum (acc.
6521), gift of Al and Merry Silber.
Silk with cotton filling, 57.5" x
76.5", MQP 86.1721.

This colorful Tumbling Blocks
quilt was made near the turn of
the century by Mary Scotten,

whose husband owned the
Scotten-Dillon Tobacco Company
on Fort Street in Detroit, Michigan. In this quilt, constructed entirely of silk, the rich colors and
careful placement of light and
dark pieces enhance the three-dimensional effect of the Tumbling Blocks pattern. The green
border was added circa 1920 to
cover the deteriorated original
border underneath.

94. Ailene McKeller (1879–1961) and **Julie Copeland.** Original design made ca. 1900, Magnolia, Arkansas. Martha Gilbert, lender. Cotton hog feed sacks with field cotton filling, 61″ x 74″, MQP 86.30.

Martha Gilbert, the owner of this quilt, recalls sitting on the lap of her grandfather, a Cherokee Indian with "a very long beard," while her grandmother, Julie Copeland, carefully bleached out hog feed sacks to be used to make quilt tops. The sacks used in this pieced quilt were hand dyed and arranged in strip fashion, then stuffed with field cotton by Copeland and Gilbert's mother, Ailene McKeller. Both were wives of Alabama farmers and were homemakers and avid quiltmakers. They passed their knowledge and love of quilting on to Martha Gilbert, who moved to Muskegon, Michigan, in 1962, and who now, at the age of 80, still spends 24 hours a week quilting in her living room.

95. Unknown maker. Crazy Stars made ca. 1900, possibly Michigan. Private collection. Silk, 66″ x 73″, MQP 86.1726.

A profusion of colors and hundreds of tiny silk pieces make up this turn-of-the-century Crazy Stars quilt. The intricate piecing and carefully designed concentric borders are not typical of the Crazy quilt style, but the overall visual effect defines the word "crazy." The quilt features six different types of stars. Of particular interest are the Danish, Swedish, American, and other flags pieced into the quilt in eight places. The letters *A, A E,* and *B* are embroidered in the Old English style in four places on the back of the quilt. These may be initials of the quilter or quilters, or of their family members.

Unfortunately, no information is available about the maker of this tribute to creativity, but her talent for design and color and her excellent needle skills speak for themselves.

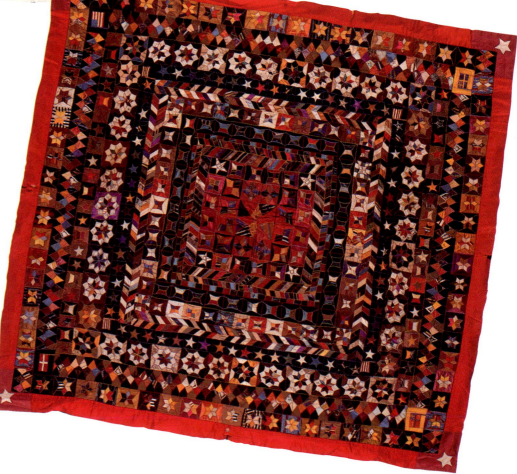

96. First Presbyterian Church Women's Association. ▶ Pictorial Block made ca. 1900–1902, Birmingham, Oakland County, Michigan. Archives, First Presbyterian Church, Birmingham, Michigan, lender. Cotton, 72″ x 88″, MQP 85.836.

In 1973 the top of this quilt was returned to the First Presbyterian Women's Association on its 100th anniversary by the heirs of Marion Clizbe Allen. Current members of the Women's Association enlisted the help of Merritt Olsen, one of Birmingham's unofficial historians, to help identify some of the names embroidered on each square. Olsen not only recalled the relationships of the relatives, neighbors, and friends whose names were inscribed, but also remembered that Signature quilts were popular as fundraisers in Birmingham during the early 1900s.

Further investigation into the Women's Association records revealed that for payment of $1.00 the names of family and friends could be embroidered on a square of plain white fabric. Records also indicate that the top was started in about 1900 and finished in 1902.

In 1986 a group of volunteers from the church took on the task of completing the quilt. Although it is unclear if this top was made as a fundraiser for a special occasion or purpose, it has special significance today as a record of those living in the Birmingham area in 1900–1902 and as a record of church history.

---

97. Lena DellAngelo (1899–1984). Moon and Star made early 1900s, Ishpeming, Marquette County, Michigan. Barbara H. Roose, lender. Cotton, 68″ x 84″, MQP 86.951.

Lena Malvasio DellAngelo was born on April 5, 1899 in France to Italian parents, Andrew and Comenica Malvasio. The family emigrated to America and settled in Michigan's Upper Peninsula,

where her father was employed ▶ as a miner and where Lena met her husband, Charles, an electrician foreman in the iron ore mines. The DellAngelos made their home in Ishpeming and had three children.

DellAngelo's Moon and Star quilt was passed to her sister, Rose H. La Parche Hamel of Michigamme, and then to the present owner, Hamel's niece, Barbara H.

Roose of Ishpeming. According to Roose, this quilt displays a pattern that was a favorite of its maker, Lena. A few small stains and one small hole are all that mar the beauty of this family heirloom of the early 1900s.

Lena DellAngelo, 1983
Courtesy of Barbara H. Roose

◀ **98. Mary Vitale** (ca. 1860–1920). Whole cloth *(Mamafina's Quilt)* made late 1890s, Terrasini, Sicily. Clement and Barbara Bommarito, lenders. Cotton with cotton filling, 80″ x 80″, MQP 86.671.

"Long ago and far away" are words that aptly describe the beginnings of this family treasure. Mary Vitale made this quilt probably during the late 1890s for her daughter Sarafina's trousseau. Sarafina brought the quilt with her in a hand-carved trunk when she and her sister arrived in Detroit around 1901 for prearranged marriages to two brothers who hailed from their same Sicilian

village. Sarafina married Franco Paulo Alongi—she was 16 at the time.

The work is hand pieced and hand quilted; the quilting includes stylized floral, leaf, and pineapple designs; concentric circles; and a floral and crown medallion in the center. Because of its extreme weight, the family has not used it in the last generation, saying "it weighs more than a mortal sin." The quilt is now owned by Clement Bommarito, great-grandson of Vitale, and his wife, Barbara. It is a symbol of a valuable family tradition and a Sicilian mother's love.

99. Alice Whitmore Reed Sweet (1879–1939). Crazy made 1900, Alanson, Emmet County, Michigan. Marlene Bradshaw Bunker and Helen Reed Bradshaw, lenders. Cotton with sugar sack backing, 62" x 82", MQP 85.1197.

This cotton Crazy quilt top was made by Alice Whitmore Reed Sweet in 1900, before she was married. It consists of 18 square blocks, each pieced together from cotton dress scraps in random Crazy quilt fashion, with blues and reds predominating among the patterned and solid-colored fabrics. Each block has been backed with a sugar sack that still bears the printed brand name. The quilt was never completed with a back and binding. The quiltmaker's thrifty use of scraps and commercial sacks stemmed from her early experience at "making do."

Alice's father followed the lumber mills for a livelihood. In 1890, while the family lived in the Gaylord area, several of its members died during an epidemic of scarlet fever, including Alice's mother, leaving 11-year-old Alice to run the household. In addition to her regular domestic duties, young Alice became skilled at needlework and made many quilts during her girlhood and throughout her life. In 1907 she married a logger, George Reed, and settled near Alanson, where the couple had three children. After Reed's death in 1913, she married Lewis Sweet in 1916 and remained near Alanson, where she was active in the Alanson Methodist Church and Alanson Benevolent Society, worked in resort hotels during the tourist season, and continued to make quilts.

Alice's granddaughter, Marlene Bunker, the present owner of the Crazy quilt top, recalls that her grandmother made quilts because

it gets cold up here in Northern Michigan! Temperatures reach well below zero each winter. . . . Most folks lived rather simply and without waste. It was also a way of life for housewives to make and do for their families and making quilts fell into that natural order of things. Rarely was new material purchased for the sole purpose of making a quilt top.

Most usually scraps and leftovers from other sewing projects were used in this way, therefore what might have been wasted was turned into something beautiful to look at as well as serving a practical use.

Although many of Sweet's quilts were used by the family, countless others were given away to those in need, sometimes after a fire had destroyed all their possessions.

Alice Sweet's other talents included gardening and cooking. On her small farm near Alanson she kept a cow and some chickens and raised vegetables and flowers, especially her prized peonies or "pineys," as she lovingly called them. She was known for her excellent meals, prepared on her old black cook stove, and even more for her generous way of providing food to her neighbors when there was sickness or need. States her granddaughter,

Likewise whenever there was a funeral in this small community, Alice could be depended upon to show up with an armful of fresh-cut garden flowers and a pair of helping hands to ease the family's sorrow.

Alice Whitmore Reed Sweet
Courtesy of Marlene
Bradshaw Bunker

Ida Benawa Matthewson and her husband, Robert
Courtesy of Kenneth and MaryLou Crumback and Gerald and Lorraine Crumback

100. Mary Hitzler Mathewson (1852–1930). Sampler *(Wedding Quilt)* made 1903–1904, Caledonia, Kent County, Michigan. Kenneth and MaryLou Crumback and Gerald and Lorraine Crumback, lenders. Cotton with cotton filling, 78″ x 90″, MQP 86.1243.

This block-style quilt of assorted patterns was made as a wedding present for the 1904 marriage of Robert E. Mathewson and Ida E. Benawa. In December of 1903, work commenced on this collaborative piece. The corner blocks were made by Mathewson's aunt and cousins, who were living in Lehigh County, Pennsylvania; the remaining blocks were made by his rela-

tives and some neighbors; and it is thought that Mathewson's mother, Mary Hetzler Mathewson, pieced the blocks and quilted the top. Each block was signed in embroidery with the name of the maker and the date. The quilt has been passed through three generations, first to Robert E. Mathewson's daughter, Nellie E. Mathewson Crumback, and then to her sons, Kenneth and Gerald. It is now jointly owned by Kenneth and MaryLou Crumback and Gerald and Lorraine Crumback of Caledonia.

The inclusion of blocks made in both Pennsylvania and Michigan had a special significance, as told by its current owners. According to them, Mary H. Mathewson's father, George Hetzler, left Pennsylvania with his six young children after his wife, Cora Schuler Hetzler, died giving birth to their eighth child. The seventh child, a little girl, stayed behind to live with her maternal aunt in Pennsylvania. It is because of this child that a geographically separated line of descendants developed in that state, and thus the four quilt corners represent that portion of the family.

Hetzler eventually settled in Michigan, where one of his daughters, Mary, became the wife of John E. W. Mathewson and went to live on the Mathewson farm in Caledonia. The Mathewson family had purchased the land for this farm from the government in 1850, and it is still owned by the family today.

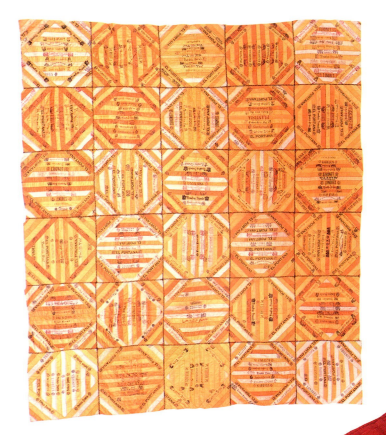

101. Julia E. Davidson. Original design made ca. 1904, Bay City, Bay County, Michigan. Collection of Detroit Historical Museum (acc. 51.194.1). Printed cotton cigar labels, 55.5″ x 64.5″, MQP 85.2029.

Made of printed cigar ribbons and backed with coarse white cotton, this quilt top includes 30 squares of machine-stitched cigar ribbons. The squares are embroidered by hand. The quilt top has never been bound. The use of printed cigar ribbons was a popular quilting fad around the turn of the century.

102. Unnamed artists. Album made ca. 1904–1910, Ingalls, Menominee County, Michigan. Daniel Deacon, lender. Cotton with cotton filling, 70.5″ x 77.5″, MQP 86.1072.

Little information is available on this Album quilt made circa 1904–1910 for a raffle by a church group of Menominee County. It is now owned by Daniel Deacon of Faithhom, Michigan, who inherited it from his grandmother. As is the case with some Album quilts, the signed top provides documentation of a group of individuals in a community who participated in a local project.

The work was pieced by hand and by machine and then tied. It was never quilted. Predominantly red cotton fabrics have been used for both the top and back.

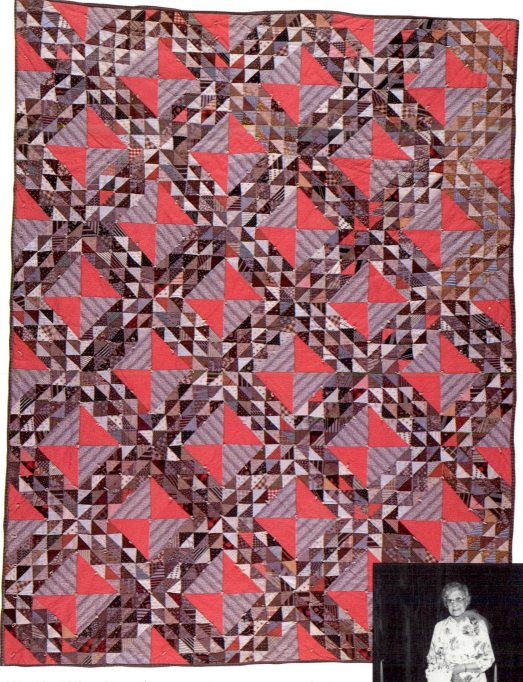

103. Edna Tickner Towns (b. 1896). Hovering Hawks made 1906, Sunfield, Eaton County, Michigan. Linda Harms, lender. Cottons, 86″ x 68″, MQP 86.1372.

This early twentieth-century creation was made by Elizabeth Tickner Towns with the help of her mother, Elizabeth Tickner.

Combining cotton prints, checks, plaids, and stripes of primarily pink and brown colors, Towns pieced the block-style quilt top and attached it to a backing made of brown- and blue-plaid cotton. Made for family use, the quilt was never displayed outside the home.

Edna Tickner Towns
Courtesy of Linda Harms

Margaret A. and Julius P. Hudson on their wedding day, November 16, 1901
Courtesy of Marguerite Alice Hudson Goerke

104. Margaret A. Hudson
(1867–1912). Crazy *(Family Names)* made 1905 or 1906, Cheboygan, Cheboygan County, Michigan. Marguerite Alice Hudson Goerke, lender. Wool, wool and silk blends with cotton filling, 77″ x 87″, MQP 85.1110.

Estimating that Margaret A. Hudson made more than 75 quilts, her daughter Marguerite Goerke also remembers that her mother made templates and patterns from cardboard or paper and worked at a wooden quilting frame set up in the parlor or liv-ing room. In a letter dated March 26, 1987, Goerke provided this information on her family:

This is the wedding picture of Julius P. and Margaret Ann Lawson Hudson, November 16, 1901. They met at a lumber camp near the Cheboygan River where she was a cook. They had each lost their spouses in 1901. She was working at the camp because she could have her three children, one girl and two boys, there with her. He had four children, three girls and one boy. His last two were born in the house that he had built on a small farm which he owned. That was also in Cheboygan County, on another part of the Cheboygan River.

Julius and Margaret and their combined family of seven children lived in that house. . . . Together they had two more children, two girls.

The quilt was probably started in 1905 or 1906. The top was finished in 1908, containing the names of the eight children, two years before the youngest was born. So her name Alice (as she was called) and date 1910 were added to a center block near the bottom.

The story is told that during a forest fire in the area the family went to a neighbor's house that was farther from the fire. The youngest child who was four or five at the time took that quilt top and carried it to safety.

I was that child, Marguerite Alice.

In previous correspondence, Goerke told how she acquired the quilt:

After my marriage, my mother made the borders to make [the quilt] larger. I helped to put it on the frames. That is when it became mine. I had always admired this quilt, possibly more so than my sisters.

In each block one of the following Hudson family names is embroidered in large letters: Julius, Margaret, Charlotte, Gladys, Susie, Morris, Albert, Rose, Leonard, Myrtle, and Alice.

◄ **105. Mrs. Henry Schroeder.** *Crazy (Crazy Buffalo Robe)* made ca. 1908, Dearborn, Wayne County, Michigan. Collection of Dearborn Historical Museum (acc. 55-82). Wool, 62″ x 74″, MQP 85.1278.

This Crazy quilt, known as the *Crazy Buffalo Robe,* was made for family use circa 1908 at Dearborn, Michigan, by Mrs. Henry Schroeder. The 16 blocks that form the top were pieced together from the selvage ends of wool remnants obtained at a local woolen mill. Two five-inch borders trim the top and bottom edges. Formerly owned by Carl Schroeder, the quilt is now in the collection of the Dearborn Historical Museum.

106. Mary Welling (1870–1950). *Detroit Buildings Quilt* made 1908, Detroit, Wayne County, Michigan. Karen Tetzlaff, lender. Cotton, 87″ x 96″, MQP 84.36.

This quilt top of 120 embroidered blocks provides a glimpse of the buildings of Detroit in 1908 and also illustrates the quilter's interest in birds and flowers.

Family history records that Mary ► Welling began this top in 1906 and completed it two years later. Her inclusion of a square embroidered with the year 1908 documents the completion date. Three successive generations of the Welling family have treasured the top, and it is now owned by her great-granddaughter Karen Tetzlaff.

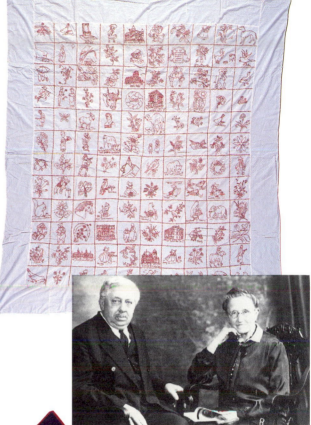

Mary Welling and her husband, Matthew
Courtesy of Karen Tetzlaff

107. Marie Herrick. Eight-Pointed Star made ca. 1910, provenance unknown. Mary Molden Karshner, lender. Cotton, 74″ x 88.5″, MQP 86.702.

One of the most notable features of this early twentieth-century quilt is the very small size of each of its 1,020 blocks. Squares of solid blue alternating with pieced eight-pointed stars on white backgrounds form the overall design of this fully hand-pieced and hand-quilted textile. The 8,160 pieces that constitute the top are quilted to a brown gingham back.

Very little is known of the history of this quilt. It was made circa 1910 by Marie Herrick for Della Nevius Shaver from dressmaking scraps of Della and Della's mother, Augusta Post Molden Nevious. Della Shaver was half-sister to the grandfather of the present owner, Mary Karshner. Karshner, who provided this information, lives in Royal Oak, Michigan. ▼

Completed circa 1910 and known as *Stripes of Triangles,* this medallion-style patchwork quilt features an original design by the quiltmaker, Anna Rolf of Flushing, Michigan. The top consists of patterned and plain cotton triangles, pieced together into strips that are set in square rows around a central block. Double borders at the top and bottom and a single border at each side complete the arrangement. Quilted diagonal lines, running in alternating directions, fasten the top to the red-and-white cotton back. Rolf sold her quilt to its present owner, Mary Schafer.

108. Anna Rolf. Original design *(Stripes of Triangles)* made ca. 1910, Flushing, Genesee County, Michigan. Mary Vida Schafer, lender. Cotton with cotton filling, 66.25″ x 78.25″, MQP 85.1648.

Martha Ernst Reichle
Courtesy of the Frankenmuth
Historical Association

109. Martha Ernst Reichle (1843–1924). Original design *(Detroit Landmarks)* made ca. 1910, Frankenmuth, Saginaw County, Michigan. Collection of Frankenmuth Historical Association of Frankenmuth, Michigan. Cotton with wool filling, 78″ x 80″, MQP 85.2067.

Martha Ernst Reichle was married to the Frankenmuth black-smith, Heinrich Reichle, a successful German-American businessman who "traveled through several states in the interests of his trade." In 1895, his business advertising noted that he

> was a Maker and Dealer in Buggies, Wagons, Cultivators, Plows, Harrows, and other farm equipment. Agent for the distinguished Jackson wagon. All articles repaired at shop, attended to promptly and durably repaired. Wheelwright shop connected. Horseshoes a specialty.

Reichle was accomplished at tatting and was known to have been "well educated and well read—and very interested in her grandchildren." According to her granddaughter, "Reichle was so impressed with the landmarks in Detroit that she worked them into the embroidered designs." The quilt includes Detroit landmarks interspersed with floral and storybook designs.

110. Edith Coty Simon (1894–1957). *Forty-Eight States' Flowers* made 1912, probably Chicago, Illinois. Dorothy Simon Totten and Carole Totten Adams, lenders. Cotton, 71″ x 80″, MQP 86.1680.

Edith Coty Simon was born in 1894 in Chicago, Illinois, to Alphonse and Josephine Coty. At age 18, her father was a member of the company that strung the first wires along the Santa Fe Trail. Buffalo Bill Cody was also a company member, hired to provide the group with meat while they worked along the trail. Edith Coty learned to quilt while still in her teens. Married in 1916, the quiltmaker and her husband, Francis O. Simon, had two children—a son killed in World War II and a daughter, Dorothy, who now resides in Colon, Michigan.

Little is known of Simon's reasons for making this quilt except

Edith Coty Simon
Courtesy of Dorothy Simon Totten

that it was to be used as a bedspread. It is known that *Forty-Eight States' Flowers* was awarded Honorable Mention in the quilt competition at the 1933 World's Fair in Chicago. Simon used sawtooth quilting on the multicolored blocks and on the green sashes and borders and white background.

111. Amelia Ferguson. *Baseball Blocks and Flags* made ca. 1914, probably Michigan. Collection of Detroit Historical Museum (acc. 67.141.1). Cotton, 54.125″ x 69.5″, MQP 85.2037.

The practice of making quilts of small, printed, square, fabric premiums collected from tobacco, flour, sugar, or tea was popular in the 1890s and early 1900s. Flags, historic personages, commemorative events, and advertising trademarks were most common; baseball heroes were also printed.

This quilt features printed cotton-flannel patches that may have been premiums from cigar packages or tobacco pouches. In addition to the four large flag patches, 32 baseball players are presented with their team and league affiliation. Four were members of the Detroit Tigers in 1914. Little is known about the quilter, Amelia Ferguson. The quilt was passed down to her grandson, Arthur Howell, who donated it to the Detroit Historical Museum.

112. Emeline Mathews (ca. 1832–1928). Grandmother's Fan made 1916, Emmet County, Michigan. Fern Nesberg, lender. Cotton, wool, and linen, 70″ x 82.5″, MQP 84.30.

This elaborate quilt top has been in Fern Nesberg's family for four generations. The quilt was passed from the quiltmaker, Emeline Mathews, to her son Ernest, then to granddaughter Emily Wilsey, and finally to Fern Nesberg, the current owner. Nesberg writes of her great-grandmother:

This quilt was made by my great-grandmother. Grandmother's Fan is the pattern with much embroidery in various patterns. It was finished in 1916 when she was about 80 years old. She did the work in her home probably using kerosene lamps for light much of the time. She and her husband were homesteaders among the very first in northern Emmet County, Michigan. Her husband died from an illness contracted while a soldier in the Civil War. She was left with eight children to raise.

Emeline Mathews and her son Ernest
Courtesy of Fern Nesberg

113. Roxanna Brazee (1851–1921). Crazy made 1918, Tecumseh, Lenawee County, Michigan. Collection of Michigan State University Museum, gift of Lucile Norelius. Velvet and satin, 66″ x 67″, MQP 85.93.

Roxanna Alverson Brazee was 67 years old in 1918 when she tried out her newly acquired skills of painting to embellish this Crazy quilt. The quilt was passed to Brazee's daughter Iva Dell Piper and then to granddaughter Lucile Norelius, who in turn donated it to the Michigan State University Museum.

80

was making a quilt and this time he said, "Mrs. Whitney do you want a new quilt pattern?" She told him "yes." He went across the road and when he came back he had a piece of brown wrapping paper. In those days meat and cheeses were always wrapped in brown paper & tied with a string for the customer. Anyway he was folding the brown paper over and over and then began tearing out pieces. We used to do this to make a snowflake in school. When he got through he handed it to Great Grandma and said "Here's your pattern." And they said when he went through the next time she had the quilt completed.

Mizer's sister, Loma Viola Darling Tippin, who quilted the *First Ladies Bi-Centennial Quilt* included in this volume (no. 219), also told the story about *Grandmother's Snow Flake Quilt.*

Sarah E. White Whitney
Courtesy of Sibyl S. Darling Mizer

114. Sarah E. White Whitney (1846–1926). Original design (*Grandmother's Snow Flake Quilt*) made 1918–1919, Breckenridge, Gratiot County, Michigan. Sibyl S. Darling Mizer, lender. Cotton with cotton filling, 75″ x 96″, MQP 85.68.

At the time of her death in 1926, Sarah E. White Whitney had made more than 100 quilts. Married in 1859 at the age of 13, and mother of eight children, she lived all of her married life on a farm five miles north of Breckenridge, Michigan.

Whitney traveled to visit a friend in Detroit in 1919, and while there she entered her prized quilt in the Michigan State Fair, where she was awarded a Blue Ribbon. Whitney later sewed that ribbon onto the center of the quilt. The quilt was given to her daughter, Caroline Whitney Herling. When "Aunt Carrie" was breaking up her household in 1951, Sybil Mizer, Whitney's great-granddaughter, purchased the quilt for $15.00.

Mizer told this story of the origin of *Grandmother's Snow Flake Quilt:*

We were always told by mother & grandmother that one day a peddler (a man who went from house to house selling items to the country folk) stopped at Gr. Grandma's house. Everytime he stopped she

Della Eley, 1943
Courtesy of Mrs. Audra Byron (Thelma) Eley

115. Della Eley. Crazy (*World War I Quilt*) made 1918–1920, Henryville, Indiana. Mrs. Audra Byron (Thelma) Eley, lender. Wool, 70.5″ x 79.5″, MQP 86.1686.

At the beginning of World War I, the United States government contracted with individual seamstresses to produce shirts for soldiers. These women worked in their homes and were issued wool material with which to sew. Della Eley was asked to make two dozen shirts by the government agency in Jeffersonville in southern Indiana. Her son, Audra Byron Eley, served with the U. S. Army's 150th Artillery, Battery B, of the Rainbow 42nd Division. Eley made her quota of shirts, then kept the scraps of khaki wool. In 1918, she used these scraps to make a Crazy quilt for her soldier son, feather stitching the pieces with red, white, and blue thread. Audra Byron Eley died in 1984, leaving the quilt to his wife, Thelma.

116. Sarah Bontrager. Nine-Patch Cross made 1919, Centreville, St. Joseph County, Michigan. David Pottinger, lender. Cotton, 64″ x 83″, MQP 87.161.

The dark, rich, solid colors that are traditionally found in quilts made by Amish women reflect the religious strictures that were placed upon them within their communities. Printed fabrics and bright colors are not missed in these quilts, however, because the exceptional and intricate quilting and the striking color combinations more than make up for their absence.

In this Michigan-made Amish quilt, the traditional Nine-Patch Cross pattern was used. It was made by Sarah Bontrager for her daughter Amanda. When the quilt was in the frame, Amanda's young cousin Jacob Bontrager was present and asked if his initials could be included; hence the inscription "J.B."

117. Irene Roe. Star or Snowball variation made ca. 1920, White Cloud, Newaygo County, Michigan. Dora Morris, lender. Cotton with cotton filling, 72″ x 76″, MQP 86.29.

Made in 1920, this Star or Snowball variation was pieced in the strip method that is typically used in Afro-American quilting. The strong verticality of the quilt and the slightly mismatched rows of pieced blocks are evidence of this technique. The stark contrast between the yellow strips and the dark blue background gives the quilt an almost three-dimensional effect, as the yellow strips seem to jump into the foreground. A loosely structured quilting design, resembling a large cable, runs diagonally across the quilt and sets off the otherwise strict verticality.

118. Margaret (or Anna) David. Star of Bethlehem made ca. 1920, Peshawbestown, Leelanau County, Michigan. Elizabeth and Vernon Keye, lenders. Cotton with cotton filling, 76″ x 91″, MQP 86.482. See 119.

119. Mrs. Ogahmahgegedo. Star of Bethlehem (*Indian Quilt*) made 1912, Ahgosatown, Leelanau County, Michigan. Florence Lackie Hanes, lender. Cotton with cotton filling, 66″ x 75″, MQP 86.489.

These two quilts of the Star of Bethlehem or Lone Star pattern are known to have been made by two Native American women from Leelanau County, Michigan. According to James M. McClurken, co-author with James A. Clifton and George L. Cornell, of *People of the Three Fires: The Ottawa, Potawatomi, and Ojibway of Michigan,* the star and floral motifs exhibited in these two quilts are typical components of Ottawa designs. Each square and triangle formed against the white background by the center star is filled with floral designs that embellish the central design and mimic designs depicted in earlier porcupine quill work and beaded pieces of the same region. It is probable that Native Americans began quilting after the Grand Traverse Mission period; the first person who was recorded to have had furniture in his home, and thus have a need for domestic furnishings such as quilts, was Agosa, who lived on Old Mission peninsula during the mid 1840s.

Little is known about the maker of quilt no. 118. She sold it to Mrs. Richard Lay, who in turn passed it on to its current owners, Elizabeth and Vernon Keye.

The owner of quilt no. 119, Florence Lackie Hanes, writes that her father, Walter Lackie, acquired it "as a trade for some farm goods. Always treasured by the family, and never used [it is] just called the *Indian Quilt.*" The quiltmaker was known to the family as Mrs. Ogahmahgegedo, but further research has revealed that she may also have been known as Catherine or Jenny Steele. She lived in a settlement known as Ahgosatown, located between Omena and Northport, Michigan.

120. Margaret Minimia Ward.
Crazy made 1921, Clinton, Lena-
wee County, Michigan. Ruth
Palmer Ward and Marilyn Ward
Hewlett, lenders. Silk, 78″ x 80″,
MQP 85.219.

Margaret Ward made this Crazy
quilt in 1921 on the occasion of
the approaching marriage of her
son Lawson Ward to Ruth Palmer.
Lawson worked in Detroit in the
"gents' furnishing" department
of Newcomb Endicott and Hudson's department stores. At each
store he had access to the silk
samples used in custom shirt
making, which he then brought
home to his mother who used
them to piece this top. The wedding date, June 24, 1921, is embroidered on the quilt, and fancy
embroidery stitches are used
over the seams connecting each
block.

*Margaret Minimia Ward and her
husband, Albert
Courtesy of Ruth Palmer Ward
and Marilyn Ward Hewlett*

121. Elsie Ella Brom Earle
(1893–1971). Triple Irish Chain
made ca. 1920-1930, Calamus
Township, Wisconsin. Donna M.
Paananen, lender. Cotton with
cotton filling, 81″ x 82″, MQP
85.1981.

According to Donna M. Paananen of East Lansing, Michigan,

*Elsie Ella Brom Earle with
her husband, Edward, and
daughter, Marjorie
Courtesy of Donna M. Paananen*

> I was given this quilt because it
> was too small for many mod-
> ern beds. It has been used only
> a few times as a bedcover. It
> won First Prize in the Heirloom
> Quilt Division at the Ingham
> County Fair (1978) and the
> Needlework Sweepstakes Prize.

Elsie Ella Brom Earle, from a German farm family, is known to
have made six quilts, all quilted
in her living room on a wooden
frame mounted on chairs.

122. Gertrude Phillips (1877–1979). Double Irish Chain variation made ca. 1920–1940, Cassopolis, Cass County, Michigan. Lena E. Wessels, lender. Cotton, 66″ x 90″, MQP 85.11.

Little is known about Gertrude ("Gertie") Phillips, the maker of this quilt. A life-long resident of southwestern Michigan, she lived to be 102 years old and was quilting until the age of 101. A newspaper article in the *Kalamazoo Gazette* written at the time of her 100th birthday reported that "Mrs. Phillips keeps busy with sewing and gardening." Her long-time friend and neighbor Lena Wessels treasures this quilt as a remembrance of Phillips.

Gertrude Phillips at age 100 in 1977
Courtesy of Lena Wessels

Vivian Rybolt and Nona Alice Ginger Lane
Courtesy of Betty and Harlan MacDowell

Nancy Fritts Ginger
Courtesy of Betty and Harlan MacDowell

123. Nancy Fritts Ginger (1860–1940), piecer; **Nona Alice Ginger Lane** (1884–1967), quilter. Lone Star made ca. 1925–1940, Detroit, Wayne County, Michigan. Marsha MacDowell and C. Kurt Dewhurst, lenders. Cotton with cotton filling, 80″ x 82″, MQP 87.217.

This Lone Star medallion-style quilt was received by Marsha MacDowell, the current owner, from her grandmother, Vivian Rybolt, as a gift for completing a master's

degree. With the gift, Rybolt passed along the textile's history:

This quilt was pieced by your great-great grandmother, cornered out and quilted by your great-grandmother, and the new binding was put on by your grandmother.

Over the years the quilt was used regularly as a bed covering, and its binding became worn. Vivian Rybolt, who repaired the binding, is now in the process of completing a quilt she began about 50 years ago. (See nos. 138

and 139 for quilts by related family members.)

An identical quilt is owned by Rybolt's daughter and MacDowell's mother, Betty MacDowell.

Nancy Fritts Ginger made the central star portion of the quilt top at her home in Hardin County, Illinois, but little else is

known about her quilting activities. Her daughter, Nona Alice Ginger Lane, of Detroit, picked up the partially completed quilt top on one of her trips back home to visit her family. Lane finished the piecing, and the quilting was probably done by members of Lane's quilting club.

Viola Larsen Kelsey
Courtesy of Carolyn Kelsey Harvey

Carolyn Kelsey Harvey
Courtesy of Carolyn Kelsey Harvey

124. Viola Larsen Kelsey
(1913–1986), and **Carolyn Kelsey Harvey** (b. 1937). *Colonial History Quilt* pieced 1927, quilted 1984, Lansing, Ingham County, Michigan and Battle Creek, Calhoun County, Michigan. Carolyn Kelsey Harvey, lender. Cotton with polyester filling, 78″ x 96″, MQP 84.9.

Viola Louise Larsen Kelsey was 14 years old and in the ninth grade at Lansing West Junior High School when she competed in a quilt contest sponsored by the *Lansing Capital News.* The newspaper announced the contest for the *Colonial History Quilt* in its February 12, 1927 issue and then published two patterns a week for 12 weeks. Instructions for a single-bed quilt called for joining 24 blocks together, 4 blocks wide and 6 blocks long. Kelsey made her quilt large enough for a double bed by alternating the embroidered pictorial blocks with nine-inch squares of plain cotton sateen.

The completed blocks were submitted to the *Lansing Capital News* for judging, and a grand prize of $25.00 was awarded by the Dancer-Brogan Company of Lansing, the forerunner of the J. W. Knapp Company. The *News* then awarded $5.00 for the winning quilt in each age group. Kelsey was given the prize for first place among the ninth and tenth graders entered in the contest.

Kelsey married Elbert Sherwood Kelsey, moved to a farm in Delta Township, and had two children, Forrest and Carolyn.

In January 1983 Kelsey and her daughter, Carolyn Kelsey Harvey, who had become interested in quilting and had enrolled in a class at Kellogg Community College in Battle Creek, Michigan, decided to finish the quilt. Harvey's husband, Robert, secured the published information about the quilt contest from microfilm files. After reviewing the articles Harvey realized that the placement of the last block, The First Flag, was incorrect. Traditionally, a quilt has one obvious error, and Harvey had ensured this by changing her mother's original placement of this block.

Harvey embellished her mother's top by adding a print border, backing, and filling, and then began to quilt it. She originally planned to complete the quilt by her parents' 50th wedding anniversary in 1983; however it was finally finished on April 29, 1984, just in time for Mother's Day.

125. First Baptist Church of Newburg Ladies Aid. Album made 1927–1929, Three Rivers, Berrien County, Michigan. Loralee Knepper and June A. Marks, lenders. Cotton, 71″ x 81″, MQP 86.1626.

The blocks for this Album quilt were pieced and signed by 30 members of a group who belonged to the First Baptist Church of Newburg, also known as Poe's Corners Baptist Church. This Three Rivers area church was organized four years after Michigan achieved statehood, so it will be celebrating its own sesquicentennial in 1991. Members of the group whose names are embroidered on the top include: Mae Rifenberg, B.E. Chappell, Maude Wheeler, Jessie Beam, Bernice Bissell, Stella Standerline, Della Harwood, Leone Butler, Carrie Burnham, Nancy Rifenberg, Cora Frank, Edith Rockwell, Carrie Poe, Helen Wheeler, Ellen Rumsey, Carrie Harwood, Margaret Jones, DeVere Warner, Jennie Poe, Helene Avery, Ella Pettit, Marion Hardy, Jennie Norton, Amanda Standerline, J. Young, Minnie Kahler, Katie Eberhard, Lois Kahler, Mary Smith, and Leola Rumsey. Hand-pieced striped, checked, and print cottons were used in the construction of the top, which was hand quilted to the white, three-piece back.

Loralee Avery Knepper, present owner of the textile, provided this information on one of the signers:

The quilt represents another way of life to my mother and me . . . both my grandmothers autographed this "Friendship"

quilt. . . . Of thirty contributors, there is only one surviving person (Leola Rumsey). She is eighty-four years old. . . . My grandmother, Edith Rockwell, the person who generated this quilt, was chosen as Michigan's "Typical Mother" in 1946.

Knepper's letter enclosed a newspaper clipping that shows Rockwell accepting this award from a representative of the Golden Rule Foundation of New York City.

Edith Rockwell
Courtesy of Loralee Knepper and June A. Marks

Leola Rumsey Welburn
Courtesy of Loralee Knepper and June A. Marks

87

126. Emma Schlenter (1879–1934). Original design *(Friendship's Park)* made 1928–1932, Detroit, Wayne County, Michigan. Joann E. Bell, lender. Cotton with flannel sheet filling, 80″ x 85″, MQP 86.670.

Friendship's Park was displayed at the Michigan State Fair, probably in the early 1930s, and was once featured in an article by quilt columnist Edith Crumb in the *Detroit News* (date of issue unknown). According to Crumb:

When Mrs. Ernest Schlenter . . . decided to make a quilt that would be "different" she thought if she pictured the homes of her friends on it she *would have a quilt that would be a real heirloom. So with the help of Mr. Schlenter, she drew, planned and laid out the quilt. She used only colored prints, plain colored wash materials and a few French knots to represent the different material used in building homes and also for the park.*

In addition to the homes of her friends, Emma Zimmerman Schlenter pictured her childhood home on Parker Avenue in Detroit and the first home she and her husband built on Somerset Avenue in Detroit. According to their granddaughter, Joann Bell, Ernest Schlenter, a cabinet maker, drafted the drawings of the homes. Emma then used them as her patterns. The finished work was hand pieced of cotton prints, checks, solids, and stripes, with cotton bias tape as the binding.

Schlenter was born in Sebewaing, Michigan, of German parents. She married in 1905, had three children, and lived her adult life in Detroit, Michigan. Quilting was a big part of her life. The Ladies Aid Society would come to her home to quilt in the dining room, where a large quilting frame was set up.

When Emma died, her unique *Friendship's Park* quilt was passed on to her daughter, Ruth Betts, and then to her granddaughter, Joann Bell.

Emma and Ernest Schlenter on their wedding day in 1905, taken by Nicholson of Toledo, Ohio
Courtesy of Joann E. Bell

127. Mary Ann Finegan Mahony (1857–1949). Double Irish Chain made ca. 1949, Brant Township, Saginaw County, Michigan. Mr. and Mrs. Thomas Haven, lenders. Cotton with cotton filling, 69.5″ x 82.5″, MQP 86.506.

Four generations of quilters are represented by quilts 127-32. The following carefully researched family and quilting history was submitted to the Michigan Quilt Project by a quilter of the fourth generation, Judith Erdmann:

Mary Ann Finegan Mahony
March, 1857–March 26, 1949

Mary Catherine Mahony
February 24, 1884–April 30, 1960

Margaret Jane Mahony Frendscho
February 20, 1887–June 3, 1945

Mary Adeline Frendscho Erdmann
April 5, 1910

Judith Ann Erdmann
April 15, 1942

The use of the Double Irish Chain pattern in quilt no. 127 reflects the interest of Mary Ann Finegan Mahony in her Irish heritage. Born in Kinkora, Ontario, Canada she was raised by Tobias and Alice Murphy after her father's death. While living with the Murphy family Mahony learned to quilt. Mahony's son recalled that his mother made many quilts for family use and for gifts throughout her lifetime.

This quilt was owned by Mahony's unmarried daughter, Mary Catherine, and later by Mahony's son, (Joseph) Stephen. After Stephen's death in 1986, his estate was divided among his 11 nieces and nephews, and the quilt now belongs to Mr. and Mrs. Thomas Haven.

Quilts no. 127-32 were made by members of the same family.

Left to right, Mary Ann Finegan Mahony, Margaret Jane Mahony Frendscho, Judith Ann Erdmann, and Mary Adeline Frendscho Erdmann
Courtesy of Judith Erdmann

128. Margaret Jane Mahony Frendscho (1887–1945). Double Irish Chain made ca. 1943–1944, Saginaw County, Michigan. Mary Adeline Erdmann, lender. Cotton with cotton filling, 85″ x 93.5″, MQP 86.158.

Margaret Jane Mahony Frendscho probably learned to quilt from her mother, Mary Ann Mahony, although Frendscho did not begin quilting until she had left the family home either to work or marry. Even so, her family estimates that she made more than 50 quilts, for use in her home and as gifts.

If she did learn to quilt from her mother, it is probable that this Double Irish Chain was copied from or made at the same time as one her mother made. Judith Erdmann said that "the red and green colors of this quilt were, at least in the Mahony family, the traditional colors for a Double Irish Chain quilt."

Margaret Jane Mahony Frendscho with her husband, Charlie, and grandson Richard Erdmann, ca. 1938
Courtesy of Judith Erdmann

129. Margaret Jane Mahony Frendscho (1887–1945). Double Wedding Ring made ca. 1930s, St. Charles, Saginaw County, Michigan. Mary Adeline Erdmann, lender. Cotton with cotton filling, 73″ x 85″, MQP 86.159.

Although it is known that Margaret Jane Mahony Frendscho made two Double Wedding Ring quilts, it is not known exactly when she made this one, which is pieced of leftover scraps from other sewing projects. After Frendscho died, the quilts remained in the family home until the death of her husband when her quilts were divided among family members. This traditional quilt is now owned by her daughter, Mary Adeline Erdmann, while its mate is owned by her son, Eugene.

130. Mary Catherine Mahony (1884–1960). *Aunt Mary's Quilt* begun 1898, finished 1942, Brant Township, Saginaw County, Michigan. Catherine J. Richards, lender. Cotton with cotton filling, 69.5″ x 81.5″, MQP 86.505.

Judith Erdmann, grandniece of the quilter, explained how this quilt was made over a number of years:

Mary started the top at age 14, using scraps from sewing-dresses & possibly shirts. She didn't have enough of the colors she was using, so she quit. In 1941 or 1942, her brother said she should finish it. She said she wouldn't be able to get the right materials to match. He said she should do the best she could, and he gave her money to buy material. She bought what she could get in war time and finished the quilt.

90

131. Mary Adeline Frendscho Erdmann (b. 1910). Trip Around the World made ca. 1943, St. Charles, Saginaw County, Michigan. Judith Ann Erdmann, lender. Cotton with polyester filling, 73″ x 89.5″, MQP 86.160.

Third-generation quilter Mary Adeline Frendscho Erdmann doesn't remember actually being taught to quilt, but recalls she always saw it done at home. Her mother and grandmother were quilters, and most probably they were Erdmann's teachers.

This Trip Around the World quilt is accompanied by a variety of stories. When Erdmann started the quilt around 1943, she pat-terned it after one that her neighbor, Mrs. Edgar Leach, was making. Erdmann didn't learn that the pattern had a special name until much later.

Erdmann assembled the top from scraps left over from her sewing, including material used to make a maternity top she wore when pregnant with her daughter Judy. All of the piecing was done by Mary Erdmann, but her husband, Frank, helped to cut the pieces used in the last four or five rows, and Judy helped to quilt it during January and February 1978.

132. Mary Adeline Frendscho Erdmann (b. 1910). Whole Cloth *(Cody's Quilt)* made 1986, St. Charles, Saginaw County, Michigan. Loretta M. Erdmann and son "Baby Cody," lenders. Cotton with polyester filling, 35.5″ x 47″, MQP 86.161.

This whole-cloth, crib-size quilt was made in anticipation of the birth of Mary Erdmann's fifth great-grandchild. Erdmann's daughter Judy designed the quilt, using animal and heart motifs that she had already used in an Irish Chain crib quilt. The quilt is made entirely of unbleached muslin, and all of the quilting is done in contrasting rose and blue thread. ▶

133. Unknown maker. *Label* ▶ *Quilt* made ca. 1930, Alexandria, Virginia. Susan M. Smith, lender. Silk clothing labels, 58.75″ x 68″, MQP 85.2199.

According to oral tradition, this quilt was made by stitching together hundreds of clothing labels from clothing collected by the quilter, her family, and friends. Some premium patches were also added into the random design of labels that make up the delicate top.

91

134. Unknown maker. *Flags, Baseball Players, Rugs* made ca. 1930, provenance unknown. A. Jean Hauser, lender. Cotton, 54" x 70", MQP 86.1354.

Jean Hauser of Hastings, Michigan, purchased this colorful pictorial at an antique shop in Grand Rapids, Michigan. Flannel premiums from packages and other printed ribbons include pictures of flags, baseball players, and Oriental designs, which are tied to a one-piece back. No filling was used between the top and back. It is unfortunate that nothing is known about the maker or circumstances of this piece.

Quilter's family homestead
Courtesy of Dearborn
Historical Museum

Esther Child Claucherty
Courtesy of Dearborn
Historical Museum

135. Esther Child Claucherty (1873–1970). Spider Web *(Spider Web Comforter)* made ca. 1930, Laingsburg, Shiawassee County, Michigan. Collection of Dearborn Historical Museum (acc. 79.65.1). Cotton with hand-carded wool filling, 69" x 83", MQP 85.1330.

Between the 20 pieced cotton squares that form the top of this comforter and the purple-and-white floral fabric of its back is a wool filling that was made entirely by the quiltmaker. Esther Child Claucherty gathered the wool fleece from her grandfather's sheep, carded it by hand, and made the wool batt that she later used for this tied comforter.

Claucherty was born in 1873 to Benjamin and Jane Child, who lived on her grandfather's home-stead near Laingsburg, Michigan, where her father tended the sheep. Married in 1893, she continued to live at Laingsburg and had one daughter, Elizabeth.

In the 1920s and 1930s, Claucherty belonged to a neighborhood quilt club. At meetings in each of their homes, club members pieced and quilted for one another. The *Spider Web Comforter* was made circa 1930.

In 1948 Claucherty moved to Dearborn to be near her daughter, who was then a teacher at Dearborn's Fordson High School. She lived in Dearborn until her death in 1970 at the age of 97. Elizabeth Claucherty gave her mother's comforter to the Dearborn Historical Museum.

136. Unknown makers. *The Sunflower Quilt* made 1930s, Kansas. Lorabeth and John Fitzgerald, lenders. Cotton with cotton filling, 70″ x 89″, MQP 87.210.

Although *The Sunflower Quilt* hardly looks like a political document, its story is based in politics. During the 1936 U.S. presidential campaign, Alf Landon was the Republican candidate for president and ran against Franklin D. Roosevelt. A group of women in Kansas, Landon's home state and "the sunflower state," made a sunflower quilt for each of the Republican governors in office at that time. Frank D. Fitzgerald, elected governor of Michigan in 1934, received one of these quilts. The quilt has remained in Fitzgerald's family and is now owned by his son, John.

137. Vera Smith (1887–1959), piecer; **Anna Shoemaker,** quilter. Appliquéd Roses made 1930s, Kalamazoo, Kalamazoo County, Michigan. Patricia Hagerman, lender. Cotton with cotton filling, 79″ x 82.5″, MQP 86.602.

A solid green 5½″ border surrounds this block-style quilt pieced by Vera Smith from a Bucilla kit. Each of the five dominant blocks features appliquéd pink roses and green vines with alternating blocks displaying appliquéd rosebuds on green stems. This design was the result of "the one and only quilt project attempted" by Vera Smith. According to her niece, Patricia Hagerman,

Smith spent many hours making the top during the Depression. . . . [the quilting was done by] Anna Shoemaker, wife of a tenant farmer near Vicksburg. She did quilting for income after the death of her husband.

Shoemaker used flower and vine, diamond, and cross-hatch quilting patterns, which further enhanced Smith's work.

Born in North Dakota the daughter of a carpenter, Smith lived in Kalamazoo, Michigan, and worked there as a teacher until she retired. Smith passed her quilt on to her niece, Patricia Hagerman.

138. Nona Alice Ginger Lane

(1884–1967). Hummingbird made ca. 1930–1940, Detroit, Wayne County, Michigan. Betty and Harlan MacDowell, lenders. Cotton with cotton filling, 76″ x 88″, MQP 87.174.

Alice Lane gave this quilt to her granddaughter Betty Rybolt on the occasion of her marriage to Harlan MacDowell on June 21, 1947. The five MacDowell children remember this quilt being used for many years on their parents' bed.

Lane gave away many of her quilts, and it is estimated that she made more than 50 in her lifetime. Much of her quilting was done with members of the "Rain or Shine" Quilt Club, which met every Tuesday, regardless of the weather, in one of the members' homes. This club was registered as a *Detroit News* Quilt Club and its members were active participants in the annual *Detroit News* quilt shows. Vivian Rybolt, the quiltmaker's daughter, also remembers that on several occasions the quilt club members met on Belle Isle (an island park on the Detroit River) for a day of quilting and conversation. When her husband died in 1940, Lane moved from the neighborhood of her quilt club friends and found work as a housekeeper. Away from her friends and without much space to call her own, she ceased most of her quiltmaking. (See nos. 123 and 139 for quilts by related family members.)

139. Metta Celeste Schroll Rybolt

(1876–1955). Variable Star made ca. 1930–1950, Lapeer, Lapeer County, Michigan. Betty and Harlan MacDowell, lenders. Cotton with cotton filling, 72″ x 80″, MQP 87.175.

Metta Schroll Rybolt became very interested in quilting when she spent time in Detroit with her son's family. According to her daughter-in-law, Vivian Rybolt,

when my mother-in-law stayed with us she spent time with my mother who was very active in quilting . . . when she went back up to Lapeer she kept quilting. . . . She liked more simple patchwork designs. Most of her quilts are made in simple block patterns set with alternating plain block squares.

Marsha MacDowell, who received several quilts from her

great-grandmother Rybolt, saw her quiltmaking relative only a few times because Rybolt died when MacDowell was young. However, MacDowell vividly recalls one of her first visits at the age of four to Rybolt's second-floor apartment in Lapeer:

I remember only two things about that trip . . . going up a very steep set of stairs and seeing the quilt frame set up in her living room . . . the frame seemed to take up a lot of space.

Another quilt, made by Rybolt for MacDowell's birth, holds a special place in the family's collection of quilts. Over the years, the red and white quilt with embroidered pictures was used constantly, and as a result, much of the red embroidery thread was worn away. As a surprise present for MacDowell's 25th birthday, her mother, Betty MacDowell, re-embroidered all but one of the squares. The last one was left unrepaired, but with a needle and thread stuck in it so that it could be finished by the owner who "would then appreciate how much work went into it."

Many other members of the Rybolt family received quilts from Metta Rybolt as gifts for special occasions. It is estimated that she made more than 50 quilts. (See nos. 123 and 138 for quilts by related family members.)

Metta Celeste Schroll Rybolt and her husband, Harry
Courtesy of Betty and Harlan MacDowell

94

140. Martha Russell Ferguson

(1898–1984). Autumn Leaf variation *(Leaves and Vines)* made ca. 1930–1940, Detroit, Wayne County, Michigan. Dr. and Mrs. Robert J. Ferguson, lenders. Cotton, 58″ x 78.5″, MQP 86.126.

The maker of this appliquéd quilt, Martha Russell Ferguson, took its Autumn Leaf pattern from a quilt that was a regional winner in a nationwide contest sponsored by Sears, Roebuck & Co. during the 1930s. The regional prize-winning quilts were sent to the Century of Progress exposition, and the winning quilt of the national contest was presented to Eleanor Roosevelt. Made between 1930 and 1940 at Detroit, Michigan, this quilt is known to Ferguson's family as *Leaves and Vines*. The central appliquéd block, containing bright green vines with leaves in varying colors and prints, is framed with pale green sashes. Encircling the central block is a vine in similar colors and fabrics, also framed by green borders. Additional vines at the head and foot of the quilt complete the arrangement of the top, which is quilted with cable, diagonal, and straight stitching to a

Martha Russell Ferguson
Courtesy of Dr. and Mrs.
Robert J. Ferguson

pale green back. *Leaves and Vines* was exhibited at the Piecemaker's Quilt Guild show, held at the Saginaw Historical Museum in 1985.

Martha Russell Ferguson was born in 1898 at Tolfree, Scotland, to a coal miner and his wife. She and her Scottish-born husband, William Ferguson, had three children. Shè also enjoyed knitting, crocheting, and doing various handcrafts. Ferguson's sister, Agnes Gordon, also was a quilter.

141. Unknown maker. *Cinderella* made 1930, provenance unknown. Needleart Guild/Mr. and Mrs. Garrett Raterink, lenders. Cotton with cotton filling, 39″ x 56.5″, MQP 86.510.

This small child's quilt, made by an unknown quilter from an artist's drawing, may be the only one of its kind. The drawing was made for the F. A. Wurzburg Company of Grand Rapids, Michigan during the 1930s. The company intended to mass produce a quilt kit from the design, but the idea was never marketed. Scenes from the fairy tale *Cinderella* are portrayed in five bands of quilted images. Reading from top to bottom, the bands depict Cinderella working while her three ugly stepsisters tell her what to do; Cinderella's Fairy Godmother at the moment of changing pumpkins into

a coach and mice into horses; the ride to the Prince's ball in the bewitched carriage; Cinderella fleeing the ball at the stroke of midnight and losing her glass slipper, which the Prince finds; and finally, the Prince trying the glass slipper on Cinderella while her three stepsisters look on. Details such as the hearth and cooking pot in the top and bottom panels and the party decorations in the fourth panel identify the location of each scene. The quilting designs for this crib quilt include outline quilting for the appliquéd figures and objects and diamond quilting for the background of each panel. The *Cinderella* quilt was exhibited in 1986 at the West Michigan Quilter's Guild Quilt Show.

Mathilda Borg Christensen, 1956
Courtesy of Phyllis Burgess Andersland

142. Mathilda Borg Christensen (1866–1967).

Rob Peter to Pay Paul made 1930, Columbus, Ohio. Phyllis Burgess Andersland, lender. Cotton, 78″ x 86.5″, MQP 85.1891.

More than 220 square blocks have been pieced together in this quilt top, made in the pattern called Rob Peter to Pay Paul. The design suggests interlocking circles with alternating color schemes in red and white. The scalloped red-and-white edge completes the effect of overlapping circles. Quilted crosshatching and circular designs join the top to a white cotton back.

The quiltmaker, Mathilda Borg Christensen, was born in Bjornakulla, Sweden, to blacksmith Per Borg and his wife, Thyra Larsdotter. The mother died when Mathilda was eight months old, and she was raised by her father and stepmother, Christina Lundberg. The family then moved to Helsingborg where Per Borg became a police constable. There, the Borgs lived with their six children in an old renovated home, furnished with fine things acquired at auctions, and the children learned to appreciate good quality and design. After her father was killed in the line of duty, Mathilda learned to be a dressmaker and clothing designer. She also met her future husband, Niels Christensen, a Danish cabinet maker.

In 1889 the Borg family moved to Chicago, where Christensen had already located, and Mathilda and Niels were married. The couple eventually had four children, though their first son died very young. While Niels worked for an interior finishing company and designed furniture, Mathilda cared for her family and continued to do needlework of all kinds, including knitting, crocheting, and dressmaking. She was in her sixties when she began to make quilts. Christensen pieced her quilts together by machine. Others did the actual quilting. Her last quilts were made when she was in her mid eighties. Although her eyesight was poor, she continued to crochet, sew, and knit until almost blind and nearly 100 years old, always stressing good design and quality.

Both Christensens were active in the Swedish Lutheran Church. After her husband's death in 1921, Mathilda lived in Champaign, Illinois, then alternately with her daughters, in whose homes she did her quilting. She was also an astute investor in the stock market. A frequent traveler, she returned to visit friends and relatives in Denmark and Sweden in 1934. At the age of 98, she went by car from Minnesota to California and, when nearly 100, from Minnesota to North Dakota. Christensen died in Moorhead, Minnesota, in 1967, two months after her 100th birthday. Her quilt is now owned by her granddaughter, Phyllis Burgess Andersland of East Lansing, Michigan.

Delphine Paulus Miller second from top with her sisters, taken in Detroit
Courtesy of Tracy and Joanne Miller

143. Delphine Paulus Miller

(b. ca. 1868–?). Original design *(Tracy Miller Family Quilt)* made 1930–1936, Detroit, Wayne County, Michigan. Collection of Michigan State University Museum, gift of Tracy and Joanne Miller. Cotton with cotton filling, 67.5″ x 81.5″, MQP 86.853.

This extraordinary one-of-a-kind quilt, made by Delphine Paulus Miller between the years 1930 and 1936, is a testimony to one woman's creative genius and ver-

satility. The quilt, made as a gift for Miller's son Tracy and his wife Margaret, is composed of intricate appliquéd designs taken from her own original drawings and from her mother's original paper cuts. Many blocks portray family members. For instance, the picture of a woman with a baby and child was meant to portray Miller's daughter-in-law Margaret and two of her children. The boy pulling the cat's tail is one of Miller's grandsons.

Miller,the granddaughter of Leland's first citizen, Antoine Menseau, was born circa 1868 in a log cabin in Leland, Michigan. She

lived most of her life in Detroit. In addition to being an accomplished quilter, Miller was proficient in painting, bead work, lace and rug making, sewing, and, according to her letters, was an avid canner. A lace piece designed and made by Miller in 1908 depicting an eagle with the American flag was given by her to the Michigan State Historical Museum in Lansing, Michigan. Much of her best work was done late in her life. This quilt, her masterpiece, was made while she was living on Pontiac Street in Detroit. Although Miller made lace and other goods to order for sale, she

never felt that she had the recognition she deserved.

In a letter dated August 13, 1935, Miller wrote:

[Detroit hasn't] found me out yet, but they're going to. I'll probably have some of my work in the "News" soon, then hope to do something worthwhile "yet" even though I am almost 67. It is never too late to try, even if I have been trying all my life.

This quilt was donated to the Michigan State University Museum by Miller's grandson Tracy and his wife, Joanne.

145. Irene E. Vasey and **Jean Wasser.** *Mexican Rose* made 1975–1976, Saginaw, Saginaw County, Michigan. Irene E. Vasey, lender. Cotton/polyester with cotton filling, 70″ x 88″, MQP 86.287.

Mexican Rose, made from a pattern Irene Vasey found in *Better Homes and Gardens* magazine, is the only quilt she made in this pattern. Vasey's sister-in-law, Jean Wasser, helped make the top.

In diamond fashion 18 complete pattern blocks and 14 partial blocks are set within an inner border of green triangles and an outer border of buds on a vine. *Mexican Rose* is predominantly red and green pieces appliquéd onto a white background, a color scheme reminiscent of the quilts of the 1880s.

144. Irene E. Vasey and **Margaret Wasser.** Garden Bouquet made 1932–1933, Coleman, Saginaw County, Michigan. Irene E. Vasey, lender. Cotton with polyester filling, 78″ x 94″, MQP 86.288.

Irene Vasey was born in 1912 in Coleman, Michigan. Vasey's mother, Margaret Wasser, taught her to quilt when she was a girl of 14. After her marriage in 1940, her husband, Ronald, made her a quilting frame, which she set up in an empty bedroom and still uses today. In the years since her introduction to quilting, Irene Vasey has made 15 quilts, many of them gifts for family and friends.

Using a pattern she found in the *Saginaw News,* Vasey appliquéd this Garden Bouquet quilt with assistance from her mother. One of three quilts that Vasey eventually made of this pattern, the quilt won a county fair prize and was chosen to be exhibited at the Chicago World's Fair of 1933, where it was awarded another ribbon, now stitched to the quilt.

Irene E. Vasey taken ca. 1980
Courtesy of Irene E. Vasey

The 20 Garden Bouquet pattern blocks are set with elaborately quilted plain white blocks. The three borders of blue and white are unified by a quilted leaf design. The Garden Bouquet blocks show a variety of flowers, from differently colored tulips to roses, and even a blooming cactus. Although the flowers all differ, the birds and the flower pots are the same in each block, providing continuity.

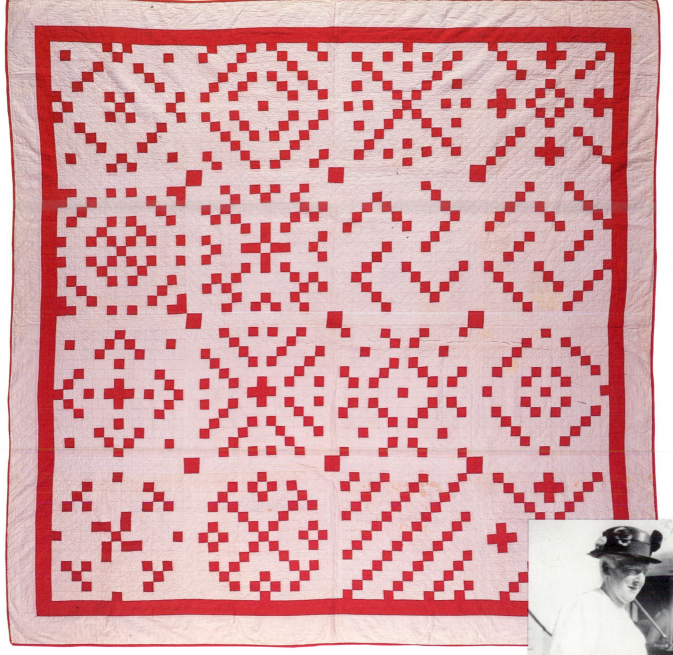

146. Emma Underwood

(1862–1942). Original design (*Crossword Puzzle Quilt*) made 1932–1935, Woodland, Barry County, Michigan. Alberta Curtis, lender. Cotton with cotton filling, 82″ x 82″, MQP 86.1285.

Emma Underwood promised this red-and-white *Crossword Puzzle Quilt* to the first grandchild to marry—and Alberta Curtis was the lucky grandchild. Curtis tells us that the quilt's very unusual design originated with her grandfather William Underwood, who did the crossword puzzles in the paper each week. He drew the designs of various weekly crossword puzzles on paper as patterns for his wife, Emma, to use in making this quilt, which she began making in 1932 and completed three years later. Sometime between 1936 and 1938 she entered it in a quilt competition at the Ionia County Free Fair, where it won a Blue Ribbon.

Curtis tells us that she thinks her grandmother began quilting at the age of 14 and continued doing it until her eyesight failed very late in life. She spent many hours quilting, at a home-built frame and drawing her own patterns.

The *Crossword Puzzle Quilt* is described as a summer quilt because of its very lightweight cotton filling. The pieces of this quilt were hand sewn together and then hand quilted to an all-white two-piece cotton back. The quilting uses criss-crossed lines stitched on the squares of the top. Curtis says she never washed

Emma Underwood
Courtesy of Alberta Curtis

the quilt because she was afraid the red fabrics would discolor the white; consequently it has only been dry-cleaned. The 50 years of special care it has received are evident.

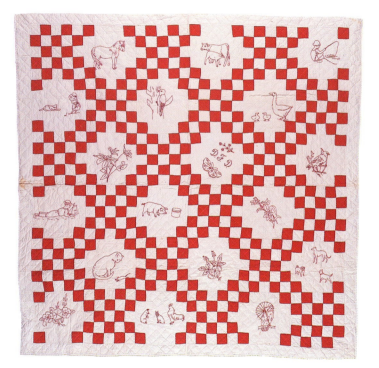

147. Mary Etta Hesburn Vanderburgh (1888–1970). Bouquet of Tulips made 1933, Farmington, Oakland County, Michigan. Stella Vanderburgh Strye, lender. Cotton with cotton filling, 72″ x 72″, MQP 85.41.

Stella and Frank Strye received this quilt as a wedding gift from Stella's parents in 1934. Her mother, Mary Etta Hesburn Vanderburgh, fashioned the Bouquet of Tulips top from flour sacks and carefully saved pieces of colored fabric. In 1932 she paid $1.00 for the *Detroit News Wonder Package of Modern Hand Needlework*, which included this pattern. Strye writes of this gift:

Mother made quilts as a necessity for our large family. She was a most practical woman. My wedding gift was very special because it was made during the Depression and materials had to be carefully saved from welfare bundles given to her to make clothing for the children. Being appliquéd it was a gift of luxury.

Vanderburgh learned to quilt as a child from her mother, Anna Jane Hewitt, and in turn taught her daughters. In addition to making quilts for her own family, Vanderburgh was part of a Ladies Aid group at the Methodist Church which met weekly to make quilts for needy parishoners during the Depression. (See also no. 186 for a quilt by Stella Strye.)

148. Laura Deacon. Irish Chain made 1933, probably Michigan. Daniel Deacon, lender. Cotton with cotton filling, 78″ x 78″, MQP 86.1073.

An Irish Chain dominates this embroidered pictorial quilt made in 1933 by Laura Deacon for her grandson Daniel F. Deacon. The animal pictures, scenes of a boy fishing, and sailing boats suggest the recipient was a young boy when it was made for him. The quilting was done in diamonds, the three-piece backing is white cotton, and the filling is made of cotton.

Laura Deacon
Courtesy of Daniel Deacon

Sarah Catherine Halladay
Courtesy of Sarah Catherine Halladay

149. Sarah C. Halladay (b. 1903) and **members of the Priscilla Class of the Congregational Church.** Eight-Pointed

Star variation *(Star Quilt)* made 1933–1940, Clinton, Lenawee County, Michigan. Sarah Catherine Halladay, lender. Cotton with cotton filling, 76″ x 97″, MQP 85.188.

Sarah Catherine Halladay provides the best description of the *Star Quilt:*

*During the "Great Depression" of the thirties many means were used to raise money for our churches. In 1933 the Priscilla Class of the Congregational Church decided that some of the class members would each make a quilt block using cloth donated by friends or relatives. Each piece of cloth was to be accom-*panied *by a donation of one penny, and the resulting funds were to be given to the Church.*

The class member who had the most pieces of cloth incorporated in her quilt block was to receive all of the quilt blocks, and could use them to make a quilt for herself.

I had completed my quilt block with 269 pieces of cloth and was awarded the other sixteen blocks, making a total of seventeen. However eighteen blocks were required, so I made one additional block and completed the quilt top. With the assistance of my mother, Mrs. Mary Walker, we completed the quilt in February of 1940. The quilt measures eight feet one inch long and six feet four inches wide.

Mrs. Hazel Barnard was the teacher of the 26 members of the Priscilla Class . . .

Hallady, who has also lived in Ubly and Detroit, Michigan, began quilting at ten years of age. She quilted with her mother and was a member of the Ubly Ladies Aid quilting group.

Sylvia Arnold Doty
Courtesy of Terry Doty Keiser

150. Sylvia Arnold Doty (1900–1955). Postage Stamp made 1934, Rochester, Oakland County, Michigan. Terry Doty Keiser, lender. Cotton with cotton filling, 64″ x 77″, MQP 86.1181.

According to Terry Keiser, the owner of this Postage Stamp quilt made by her grandmother Sylvia Arnold Doty, the 5,628-piece textile was made by Doty while in a sanitorium recovering from tuberculosis. Carl, Doty's son, from whom she was separated during that time, believes that the fabrics in the quilt did not come from the family but were donated to the sanitorium for use by the patients.

151. Anne Hartzell (1882–1970). Autumn Leaves (*Anne's Quilt*) made 1934–1935, Fremont, Newaygo County, Michigan. Milly Splitstone, lender. Cotton with cotton filling, 80″ x 85″, MQP 86.515.

Anne Hartzell was considered the best quilter in Fremont, Michigan, according to the owner of *Anne's Quilt*. In 1939 Hartzell introduced the then 13-year-old Milly Splitstone to quilts and quiltmaking. She preferred to use cotton fabric because, as she once said, "It quilts nice." This particular Autumn Leaves quilt was a favorite with Splitstone, and she describes its significance to her this way:

Anne made this quilt in 1934–35 after going to the '33 World's Fair and viewing the

Sears Contest winner in this pattern. She made upwards of 40 quilts and I personally saw 25 including this one on an August afternoon in 1939—the first time I ever saw a quilted quilt. Her collection, materials and frame were all stolen after she was put in a hospital in her failing years. Nobody knows where any are and I feel fortunate, indeed, to have had the chance to buy this one in 1975 for $75.00 from another neighbor.

The leaves were made from scraps of colorful cotton prints appliquéd onto a white muslin background. Rose-colored sashes separate the vines and central medallion. Hartzell used only a single quilting technique, elbow quilting, to complete this textile.

152. Laura May Clarke, appliquér; **Bozena Vilhemina Clarke** (b. 1871–?), quilter. Antique Urn made 1935–1939, Detroit, Wayne County, Michigan. Collection of Michigan State University Museum (acc. 6119), gift of Dr. Harriet M. Clarke and George Clarke. Cotton with cotton filling, 85″ x 95″, MQP 85.2140.

This appliquéd quilt was one of three made by Bozena Vilhemina Clarke to enter in the *Detroit News* Quilt Show in 1940. Clarke, born in Detroit in 1871, was a tailor before her marriage in 1896. At the age of 50, Bozena learned to quilt from members of the Rebecca Jane Circle, the quilt group that met at her church. Her

Bozena V. Clarke
Courtesy of Dr. Harriet Clarke

Laura M. Clarke
Courtesy of Dr. Harriet Clarke

expertise with thread and needle was then passed on to her daughter Laura May Clarke and daughter-in-law Emilie Clarke. Bozena was adept not only in quilting, but in crocheting, rug making, and gardening as well. Together with Laura and Emilie, Bozena made many of her own templates and patterns, and between the years 1926 and 1946 they completed over 40 quilts. Harriet Clarke, granddaughter of Bozena, remembers of her grandmother,

[Her] custom was to piece quilts in the warmer months as these could be carried in a

basket or box and taken by car to the family summer cottage. My grandmother would set the basket by her rocking chair and "piece" until everyone was up for breakfast. [She] quilted in the winter months usually, after Christmas, about two or three hours each afternoon until spring, or until the quilt or quilts . . . were done.

The Clarke quilt collection, along with all of the quilters' scrapbooks, templates, patterns, pattern books, and handwritten inventories of their work, were recently given to the Michigan State University Museum.

153. Elsa McEwan Pelton
(1892–1960). Radiant Star variation with Strawberry Vine Border made 1937, Comstock Park, Kent County, Michigan. Mrs. Betty L. Carpenter, lender. Cotton with cotton filling, 80.5″ x 100.25″, MQP 86.825.

Elsa McEwan Pelton
Courtesy of Mrs. Betty L. Carpenter

Elsa McEwan Pelton, daughter of John L. McEwan and Nellie Micham, learned to quilt in her late teens and was soon considered by some to be the best quilter in her home community of Comstock Park, Michigan, According to her descendants, it is estimated that she spent about 40 hours a week quilting until she was 58 years of age and made an estimated 20-25 quilts. She generally purchased her patterns and used cotton fabrics obtained at Lamoreaux's General Store. Her crude quilting frame consisted of two poles whose ends were placed over two wooden chair backs.

Pelton hand pieced and hand quilted this bedspread quilt for home use, incorporating appliqué and trapunto (the strawberries in the border are stuffed) techniques. Family history reports that Mrs. Ann Nicholson, a friend of the quilter, made a quilt in this same pattern. It also reports that when the quilts needed cleaning, the quilter's husband washed them on a board and rinsed them in a tub.

Made in 1937, this quilt was passed down to Pelton's daughter, Clarice Pelton Carpenter, and then to her grandson, David H. Carpenter and his wife, Betty.

154. Members of Hughes Missionary Baptist Church Missionary Society. Snail's Trail made 1937, Hughes, Arkansas. Mary Brown Holmes, lender. Cotton with cotton filling, 62″ x 86″, MQP 86.43.

Members of the Missionary Baptist Church Missionary Society of Hughes, Arkansas, produced this quilt in 1937 as a wedding gift for Muskegon, Michigan resident Mary Holmes. Using cheesecloth patterns, the women pieced together a quilt in the Snail's Trail pattern. The pattern is misshapen in many places because, rather than piecing the quilt block by block, the quilters used the strip method. As a result, some of the pieces don't quite match, and several of the tails are turned in the wrong direction. The quilt is visually striking, as each "mistake" adds an interesting twist to the traditional pattern. The cotton fabric, now rather thin from wear, is handwoven, and lumps of field cotton with seeds are visible through the back of the quilt.

*Thomasine Flaherty Gardner,
ca. 1930-1940
Courtesy of Ann Davis Irwin*

**155. Thomasine Flaherty
Gardner** (1862–1944). Flower
Basket made ca. 1938, California,
brought to Michigan ca. 1938.
Ann Davis Irwin, lender. Cotton
with cotton filling, 84″ x 87″,
MQP 85.1732.

The top of this summer quilt
consists of 20 white square
blocks of cotton, each containing
a basket pieced from tan triangles
and filled with appliquéd flowers
and leaves in various shapes and
colors. The entire arrangement is
separated from the wide outer
border by a row of tan triangles
that repeat the color and forms of
the baskets. Quilted scallops and

leaf designs, sewn by hand, fasten
the top to the white cotton back.

The Flower Basket quilt was
made in 1938 by Thomasine Flaherty Gardner, who was born at
Iron Mountain, Michigan, to Irish
immigrants Thomas and Nancy
Ann Ford Flaherty. Her mother's
brother, William Ford, was the father of Henry Ford, thereby making Henry and Thomasine first
cousins. Her granddaughter, Ann
Davis Irwin, relates that,

*in the 1870s, when Thomasine
was a young girl, she frequently traveled from her home
in Marquette, Michigan, on a
freighter to visit her Ford cou-*

*sins, William, Margaret, and
Jane. She stayed at the Ford
farm in Dearborn, Michigan,
in the summertime and helped
with the harvesting. It was during one of these visits that
Thomasine met James Gardner,
son of pioneer Richard
Gardner, who built his farm-
house in the early Scotch Settlement, Dearborn, Michigan, in
1832. James Gardner and
Thomasine Flaherty were married in 1885. In 1898 James
was elected supervisor of the
Village of Dearborn. James and
Thomasine had two children:
Russell and my mother who*

*was born Esther Gardner in
1894.*

Esther Gardner Davis's birthplace, the old Gardner family
home, was moved by Henry Ford
to Greenfield Village in the
1930s, "because it was put together with large dowel pins and
huge beam rafters, and made a
perfect example of Pioneer
Settlers in Michigan." Ann Davis
Irwin recalls that her grandmother, Thomasine Gardner, was
an imposing woman.

*She had white hair that was
marcelled in waves flat against
her head. Her figure was large.
She came from stout pioneer
stock, and in adult life grew
into a big boned, portly
woman. Thomasine designed
and made this quilt just for me
when I was a young girl 10
years old, in 1938. I very well
remember receiving the package. It was wrapped in brown
paper, and came through the
mail all the way from California. It remained on my bed for
many years. Then in the 1960s
when I had a family of my
own, it covered my own daughter, Clare Gardner Irwin's, bed.
Four generations have loved
that quilt, and we all know and
appreciate that family heirlooms have wonderful stories to
tell. A unique history lesson for
everyone.*

156. U. Florine Folks Plumb
(b. 1899), piecer; **unknown Amish woman** from near Toledo, Indiana, quilter. New York Beauty made 1938, Jackson, Jackson County, Michigan. U. Florine Folks Plumb, lender. Cotton with cotton filling, 76″ x 76″, MQP 84.35.

The following, written by the quilter, U. Florine Folks Plumb, aptly describes her thoughts on quilting:

In 1902 at the age of three I became conscious of some kind of artistry. Later I learned that the specific name was quilting. My mother had quilting gatherings. I would crawl under the quilt frame where I played with my dolls.

I always was fascinated with the contents of my mother's sewing basket. I really was mischievous. One day mother talked to me about a needle. She said "It is a very tiny useful thing. It also can be very dangerous." She proceeded to prick me. Then she smiled and said, "Well, if you insist on using the needle I will help you." On a piece of white cloth she drew some lines. Then she threaded a

large needle with red thread which was double and was secured by a knot. She carefully showed me how to hold the needle and how to make my first large stitch. Since I was an only child my mother had a lot of time to devote to me. At the age of five I started my first quilt which I still have. It was a single large pattern known as the postal card.

As time has passed, I have made 40 quilts. Some of them were given as wedding presents or gifts for a new baby. The names of some of the quilts were Around the World, Rob Peter to Pay Paul, Flower Garden, Ocean Wave, Four Patch, Double Wedding Ring, Dresden Plate, and New York Beauty.

Now at the age of 85 I still find the making of a quilt an enjoyable thing to do. Some one has said the art of making a quilt gives one a sense of comfort and strength. For me that is true.

And of this New York Beauty quilt she writes:

The first time that I saw a quilt like this was at the World's Fair in Chicago in 1933.

It was judged as the best pieced quilt at the exposition. It was auctioned off and sold for $1,000. This was a huge sum for a quilt at the time of the Depression.

After I returned home I immediately secured the pattern for the New York Beauty from a cotton batten company known as Mountain Mist. It took me four years to fashion the quilt and put it all together.

U. Florine Folks Plumb
Courtesy of U. Florine Folks Plumb

The quilting was done by a much more skilled quilter than I. She charged $1.00 per spool of thread. She used 20 spools of thread. At this time percale, a kind of cloth, cost ten cents per yard.

Plumb was also a member of 4-H clubs in her youth and later taught science at Concord, Vandecook Lake, and Lake Orion, Michigan. Now living with her daughter, she continues to quilt.

158. Hannah Higby Eisenhart
(1879–1978). Tulip variation
(Tulip Quilt) made ca. 1940, Columbus, Ohio. Anne Menard,
lender. Cotton, 83″ x 88″, MQP
86.382.

Although quilter Hannah Higby
Eisenhart was a life-long resident
of Ohio and Indiana, her *Tulip
Quilt* is the prized possession of
her granddaughter, Anne Menard
of Saginaw, Michigan, also a
quilter. The quilt was owned by
Eisenhart's daughter Maribel
Eisenhart Dozer before Menard
inherited it, and it has appeared
in the 1984 quilt exhibition at the
Saginaw County Historical
Museum.

The unusual diagonal orientation of this design may be the
maker's variation of a traditional

Hannah Higby Eisenhart, 1958
Courtesy of Anne Menard

pattern. Executed in a color
scheme of orange and white, with
green accents, this striking example of appliqué displays five separate quilting patterns. In addition to the outlining of the tulips
and their triangular pots, there
are diagonal squares in the two
borders, floral designs in the
corners, elongated figure eights
in the pots, and elaborate feather
stitching in the white sashing.

157. Lillie Jennings Nelson
(d. 1962). Wreath variation made
1939, Lawton, Van Buren County,
Michigan. Marian Nelson Root
Love, lender. Cotton, 77″ x
97.75″, MQP 85.1909.

Recognized by a Lawton area
newspaper as "Lawton's veteran
quilter," Lillie Jennings Nelson is
known to have made more than
50 quilts in her lifetime. Like
many traditional quilters, she
learned to quilt at a young age.
When she was eight years old she
helped her mother and grandmother quilt an Album quilt. During her life she pieced and
quilted five quilts for her three
daughters and four for her grandchildren. She made quilts of the
following patterns: Grandmother's Flower Garden, The Iris, Irish
Chain, Bride's Bouquet, Wreath of

*Lillie Jennings Nelson with her
daughter, 1893*
Courtesy of Marian Nelson Root Love

Leaves, Daisies, Dresden Plate, Autumn Leaves, and Tulip. The local
newspaper account noted that
"Mrs. Nelson enjoys the work and
can scarcely keep busy at her
general housework because of
her desire to quilt."

159. Ellen Deborah Havers Runyan Cox

(1882–1970). Crazy (*Crazy Stars*) made ca. 1940–1950, Flint, Genesee County, Michigan. Bernice Doughty, lender. Silk and velvet, MQP 85.1694.

Scraps of silk have been stitched together to create the 12 four-pointed stars that give this quilt its name. Between the stars are diamond-shaped velvet pieces that contain a variety of embroidered designs, especially flowers and birds. The quilt-maker, Ellen Deborah Havers Runyan Cox, made her Crazy quilt between 1940 and 1950, while living in Flint, Michigan. She based its pattern on a quilt that she remembered her grandmother making. For the stars, she used silk ties belonging to her son-in-law, a Mr. Doughty.

The ninth of 12 children, Cox was born in Flint to George J. Havers and Harriette Cudney Havers. Her father was a carpenter and farmer. In 1889, following the deaths of the two youngest children, the family moved to a farm near Corunna, Ontario, where Havers bought a store and meat market. The following year, they returned to a farm near Flint. While still a child, Cox learned how to quilt from her mother and from observing her grandmother, Ellen Hayloch Havers.

In 1910 Cox married her first husband, Bernard Runyan, an evangelist with several children from a previous marriage. Runyan had founded his own church, the Volunteers of America, at Flint. Working at home at a floor frame, Cox made at least six quilts. After she and her husband moved to Florida to homestead 160 acres near Samville (now Bay Shore), they used her quilts as room dividers while they finished building their house. Eventually the couple had two children of their own, Bernard and Bernice Doughty. The Runyans later sold their property and became active in the Salvation Army organization. They were first assigned to manage a men's home near New Orleans and then sent to conduct services at the Angola Prison Farm. Cox's Crazy quilt was made much later in her life, when she was living once again at Flint.

160. Dellia Obidiah Moody

(1915–1980). String Star made 1940s, Alabama. Sherri L. Long, lender. Cotton with cotton filling, 66" x 72", MQP 85.194.

Sherri Long treasures this String Star quilt made by her grandmother Dellia Obidiah Moody in the 1940s, at her home in Alabama. This was one of two quilts given to Long at the time of her marriage. Moody used whatever fabrics she could find, including scraps from a local sewing factory as well as feed sacks, flour sacks, and floral seed sacks. The use of solid black fabric in this quilt provides a sharp contrast to the small, printed, cotton pieces that constitute each block. It is not known why the quilt was cut off at one end, leaving a ragged edge.

Marion Fields
Courtesy of Marion Fields

161. Phyllis Ashcroft, piecer; **Marion Fields** (b. 1937), quilter. Original design: Little Girl made 1940–1979, Decker, Sanilac County, Michigan. Marion Fields, lender. Cotton with polyester filling, 48″ x 74″, MQP 85.1479.

More than 30 years passed during the making of this quilt. The top was pieced in the 1940s by Phyllis Ashcroft of Decker, Michigan. Ashcroft then gave her unfinished quilt to a friend, Julia Hayward, who eventually gave it to

her daughter, Marion Fields. Fields, a quiltmaker, undertook the quilting of the top and completed it in 1979. The top consists of 24 square blocks separated by white sashes. Each block has been pieced with plain and patterned cotton fabrics to suggest the silhouette of a young girl with outstretched arms, giving the quilt pattern its name, Little Girl. Fields used straight lines and outlines in her hand quilting. The quilt was displayed in a quilt show at the Marlette Presbyterian Church in 1985.

Marion Fields, the quilter, was born at Decker, Michigan, in 1937 to Russell and Julia Sherman Hayward. She is married to Robert Fields, who manages a grain elevator. They have three daughters and a son. Fields, who began quilting in 1979, learned to quilt by reading books on the subject. Working alone at home, she has made three other quilts, including a Double Wedding Ring, a Sunshine Sue, and a Pink Dogwood. Her other interests include sewing, knitting, and her activities in the Lamotte Township Firefighters Ladies Auxiliary.

162. Mabel Miel. Cross Within a Cross made ca. 1946, East St. Louis, Missouri. Mymia Large, lender. Cotton/polyester, 60″ x 80″, MQP 86.40.

This quilt pattern called Cross Within a Cross was pieced with the strip method on the diagonal.

The blocks of the resulting product do not meet precisely at the corners, and the diagonal rows of blocks in each strip are slightly skewed. A variety of interesting prints combined with strong geometric shapes makes this a striking example of Afro-American quiltmaking. The quilt is currently owned by Mymia Large of Muskegon, Michigan.

Dora Gardner with family members
Courtesy of Blanche F. Cox

163. Dora Gardner (b. 1891). Bow Tie made ca. 1950s, probably Muskegon, Muskegon County, Michigan. Blanche F. Cox, lender. Cotton with cotton filling, 66″ x 88″, MQP 86.34.

Two traditional Afro-American quilting techniques, strip piecing and the Clamshell quilting pattern, were employed in the making of this vivid quilt, one of "at least 500" made by Dora Gardner of Muskegon, Michigan. A rich color combination and striking geometric forms combine with the unusual off-center design to make it an excellent example of Afro-American quiltmaking.

Gardner, who was born in Hinds County, Mississippi, learned to quilt from her grandmother at the age of 20. The first thing she ever pieced was a "britches quilt," made from pieces of boys' pants. Gardner, who worked as a seamstress, continued to quilt throughout her life until blindness prevented her from continuing with her pastime. She has taught quilting to many of her 11 children and carries on a tradition of giving away quilts as wedding gifts.

Gardner prefers bright cotton or wool fabrics for quilting, but never mixes the two. Her filling of choice is pure ginned cotton. She has always used homemade or borrowed rather than commercially made patterns, although she used to enjoy looking at them in the Sears catalog. Gardner's favorite quilting memories include going to "October quilting bees" where there were enough women to make a quilt in a day. This she remembers being a "story telling time."

164. Nancy Johnson. String made 1950, Columbus, Mississippi. Dorothy Lester, lender. Cotton/polyester with cotton filling, 64″ x 82″, MQP 86.38.

Nancy Johnson combined two traditional Afro-American techniques, "string" and strip piecing, to make this quilt. The String quilt pattern, specifically designed to use scraps, combines variously shaped short "strings" of fabric to make each block. With the use of the strip method of quilting, the blocks were then sewn into strips that were pieced together to form the top. The irregularly pieced border, the use of the String quilt pattern, and the uneven alignment of the strips suggest that this quilt was made with utility, as well as beauty, in mind.

Muskegon, Michigan resident Dorothy Lester, a relative of the quilter, now owns the quilt, which serves as a reminder of Lester's heritage.

165. Christena Graves (b. 1910). Sawtooth made 1950, Deckerville, Sanilac County, Michigan. Mrs. Christena Graves, lender. Cotton with cotton filling, 72″ x 90″, MQP 85.43.

This Sawtooth pattern quilt, made around 1950, is a copy of a quilt made by Christena Graves's great-grandmother for her father. The original quilt was made in St. Mary's, Ontario, Canada and was passed through the sons in the family to the present generation. Because Graves was a girl, her family expected her to make her own quilts. Using pink and white fabrics she fashioned this quilt, which she still owns.

Graves has made more than 2,000 quilts, and has kept a record of each pattern, purchaser, and price. She has been making and selling quilts since 1955, when she

. . . went out to look for a job in a factory . . . & they told me I

was too old so Mrs. Melvin Swoffer ask me if I could make her 5 quilts. I bought unbleached cotton, pieced 5 nine-block quilts & quilted them for $5 each. Then different ones wanted quilts done until now I have quilts in almost every state in the Union including Alaska.

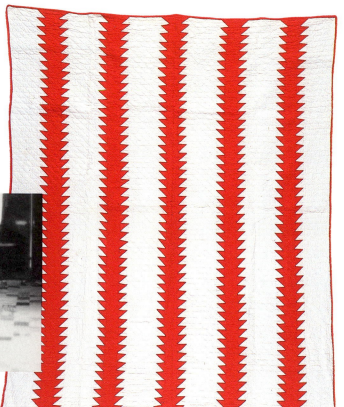

Christena Graves, 1986
Courtesy of Michigan State University Museum

166. Mary Berlincourt Walsh (1865–1961). Flower Garden variation made 1950–1951, Vermontville, Eaton County, Michigan. Harold and Edith Benedict, lenders. Cotton and some homemade materials, 78″ x 83″, MQP 86.1283.

Mary Berlincourt Walsh with her husband, John, and children Ethel, Etta, and Frank
Courtesy of Harold and Edith Benedict

Mary Berlincourt Walsh made her home in Vermontville, Michigan, with her husband, Eaton County farmer John Walsh. She made a quilt for each of her three children. This quilt is the one she made for her daughter, Etta Walsh Benedict, who was also an active quilter and is thought to have helped her mother do the quilting. Although the Flower Garden pattern is a common one, this version is a little different because the blocks are joined together by small, green, diamond-shaped pieces of fabric. A sawtooth edge and peach backing finish off the fully hand-pieced and hand-quilted work.

The quilt has been passed down from Etta Walsh Benedict to its present owner, Edith E. Benedict of Vermontville. It was once on public display at the home of Edith's daughter, Iris Benedict Wion, when the Vermontville community held a tour of local homes.

167. Clifton E. Cornell (d. 1983). Four-Patch variation made ca. 1960s, Walton Township, Eaton County, Michigan. Joan Cornell Shumaker, lender. Cotton, 65″ x 80″, MQP 85.1765.

A Walton Township farmer, Clifton E. Cornell, was part of a family of quilters that included his daughter and mother. He learned to make this quilt while recuperating from a childhood illness at the age of 8 or 10. His mother, Mi-

Clifton Cornell as a young boy, taken by Beardsley of Charlotte, Michigan
Courtesy of Joan Cornell Shumaker

nerva Fast Cornell, had run out of activities for him to try, so she taught him how to piece a quilt. Cornell's colorful cotton-print creation is referred to as a "comforter" by family members. It is not known whether he made other quilts.

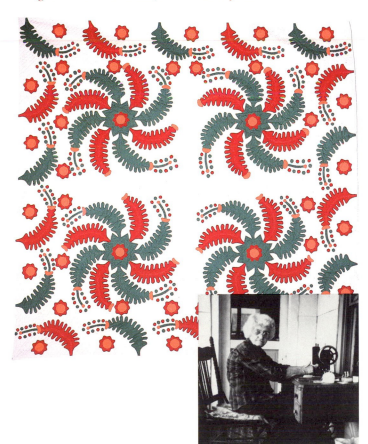

Ruby Wyman
Courtesy of MSU Museum

168. Ruby Wyman (b. 1900). Queen's Feather made ca. 1960s, St. Johns, Gratiot County, Michigan. Lucile Haas, lender. Cotton with cotton filling, 91″ x 94″, MQP 85.1443.

Surely one of Michigan's most prolific quiltmakers has been Ruby Wyman of St. Johns. Wyman has made more than 400 quilts since she began quilting in 1930, averaging more than 7 quilts per year. She was born in 1900 at Carson City, Michigan, to James and Estella Spangler Drew. Her father was a drayer, the driver of a cart used for hauling. Her mother, a homemaker, made quilts and wove carpets. Wyman was married in 1923 to Norman Wyman, a farmer, and has two daughters, Dorothy Wyman Husted and Lucile Wyman Haas.

A self-taught quilter, Wyman is still quilting even though her eyesight is failing. Her first quilt, a Drunkard's Path, was followed by quilts in many patterns, including

several Flower Garden quilts. She works on her porch in the summer and in her living room in winter, using handmade cardboard or purchased templates, mostly cotton materials and batts, and a pencil to mark her patterns. Although she recalls attending one quilting party years ago, Wyman never belonged to a quilting group and has done all of her quilting alone. She has sold numerous quilts, many of which were made with the colors requested by the purchasers. Other quilts have been given to her children, grandchildren, and great-grandchildren as graduation and wedding gifts. Asked why she has made quilts, Wyman answered that she has enjoyed both the work and the extra income. In addition to quilting, she has done sewing and been an active member of the Salem United Methodist Church. Wyman's fame as a quilter led some years ago to her appearance on a Grand Rapids television program.

169. Marie Fisher (1892–1971).

Baltimore Bride's Quilt made ca. 1960s, Detroit, Wayne County, Michigan. Lynne Charlet and Mary Lee Charlet, lenders. Cotton, 80″ x 87″, MQP 86.88.

The maker of this Baltimore Bride's Quilt, Marie Fisher, was born in 1892 to Russell and Maude Haynes Bradley. With her husband, Arthur Fisher, she had six children. During her recovery from diptheria and heart trouble, she became interested in the *Detroit News* Quilt Club Program on radio station WWJ in Detroit. She began quilting in 1931 and, only two years later, won the Grand Prize in the *Detroit News* quilt exhibition of 1933. When Fisher's picture appeared in the newspaper, she was recognized by her sister, Frances Janet Galton, from whom she had been separated through adoption 33 years earlier. After they were reunited, Fisher and Galton, also a quilter, became known as the Quilt Club Sisters. Fisher's great-granddaughter, Lynne Charlet of Royal Oak, Michigan, recalls that her great-grandmother

Marie Fisher
Courtesy of Lynne Charlet and Mary Lee Charlet

enjoyed the company of the Club as well as the quilting. Then in late 1933 when she won and was reunited with her sister, she had the added joy of quilting with her long-lost sister. Marie was sick from about 1930 until she died in 1971, so quilting and sewing were what she was able to do, and she did it all well.

170. Deborah Jane Small (b. 1955).

Original design *(Boobs and Bellybuttons)* made 1974–1976, Kalamazoo, Kalamazoo County, Michigan. Mr. and Mrs. Hamish Small, lenders. Cotton, cotton/polyester, and velvet with polyester filling, 78″ x 118″, MQP 86.479.

English-born Deborah Jane Small learned to quilt at age 16, a pupil of her mother, professional embroiderer and designer Beryl Small. She was an art student at Western Michigan University working on her Bachelor of Arts degree when she created *Boobs and Bellybuttons*. The only product of her whimsical foray into quilting was hung in the student art show in the Mid-Michigan Art Show of 1978 at the Midland Center for the Arts. Although Small is now a California art teacher and museum administrator, her unusual quilted wall hanging remains in Michigan, the possession of her parents.

Boobs and Bellybuttons is executed in shades of peach and tan, with painted and embroidered areas. Although far from tradi-tional in appearance, this soft-sculpture wall hanging can be considered an extension or modernization of traditional quilting methods. In addition to hand piecing and quilting techniques, Small uses appliqué and trapunto. As the title states, the dominant images in the quilt are anatomical details. Nipples and navels are delineated within abstracted torsos. Even though the peaches and tans call to mind the tones of flesh, anatomy is not faithfully reproduced. Rather, Small's approach to her topic seems playful, even comical. In some of the blocks the bellybuttons, for example, occupy the usual anatomical position but have the characteristic form of a common coat button.

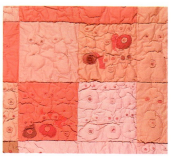

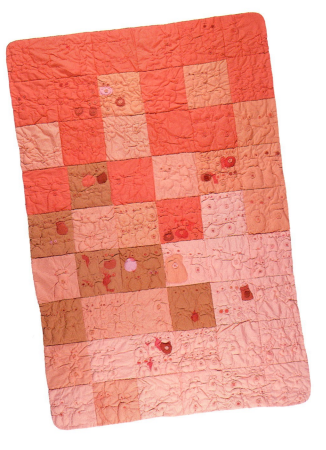

171. Women of Chandler Township. Pictorial Blocks *(Chandler Township Bicentennial Quilt)* made 1974–1976, Chandler Township, Charlevoix County, Michigan. The Women of Chandler Township, lenders. Cotton/polyester, 106″ x 106″, MQP 85.1164.

The history of land ownership in Chandler Township, Charlevoix County, Michigan, is recorded in this colorful quilt, made in 1974–76 by 40 Chandler Township women to commemorate the nation's bicentennial. Its design is based on a township plat map, with the top constructed of 36 solid-green cotton/polyester squares to represent the 36 640-acre sections of the township. Within the squares are appliquéd images of hills, trees, animals, homes, barns, schools, hand plows, a train, logging symbols, furniture, and various other artifacts, together with more than 800 embroidered family names of those who have owned land in the township for five years or more, ever since the first land transaction in 1871. All of these images were made from fabric scraps. Several motifs have special meanings, such as the hand plows, which hold the names of homesteaders; the train and logging emblems, which represent

the Grand Rapids and Indiana Railroad and the Cobbs and Mitchell Lumber Company, both large landowners at one time; and the maps of Michigan, which symbolize state-owned land, now about 80 percent of the township. One block, Section 2 (the second block from the top right), depicts the town of Springvale, the only town that has ever existed in Chandler Township. Belle Oldhame, who made this section by working from photographs of Springvale taken between 1920 and 1926, included every detail, even the flames in the gas lamps.

The quiltmakers recall that,

as we worked, we not only learned stitchery (only three or four of the women had made a quilt before) but also our local history. Many times, if the woman sewing the section knew the family she was working with, she would put in something that typified that family. Needless to say, we had lots of laughs and really enjoyed "doing our thing" for the bicentennial.

The *Chandler Township Bicentennial Quilt* has been displayed at the University of Southern Illinois and has won awards at the Cheboygan, Emmett, and Otsego County Fairs.

172. Members of the Birmingham-Bloomfield Art Association. Pictorial Block *(Birmingham Bicentennial Quilt)* made 1974–1976, Birmingham, Oakland County, Michigan. City of Birmingham, lender. Chintz, wool, linen, silk, velvet, and polyester, 90″ x 120″, MQP 85.845.

From the fall of 1974 until the spring of 1976, a group of members of the Birmingham-Bloomfield Art Association (BBAA) collaborated on the production of this bicentennial community history quilt, which they presented to the city of Birmingham. It took the 41 women and one man ten four-hour sessions at the BBAA plus many hours spent individually at home to produce the 42 blocks needed for the king-size spread. Aided by chairman of the board of the Historical Commission of Birmingham, Jervis McMechan, Rosemary Squires, coordinator of the *Birmingham Bicentennial Quilt,* and Jo Ewald, the designer of the quilt, selected scenes and/or buildings with historical significance in Birmingham to be represented on the quilt. After the quilt was completed, the BBAA circulated it to community organizations who wanted a chance to display it.

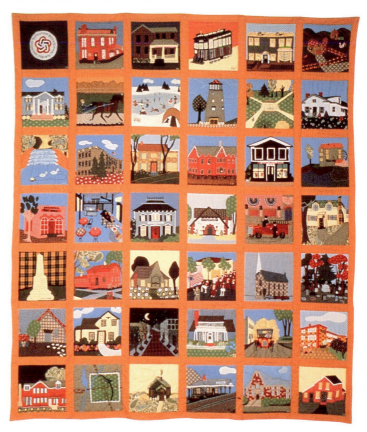

173. Mary Lee Kennedy (b. 1931). *Vegetable Garden* made 1975, Cadillac, Wexford County, Michigan. Mary Keirnan, lender. Cotton with cotton filling, 76″ x 96″, MQP 84.20.

The *Vegetable Garden* quilt is a fitting gift for an avid gardener such as Mary Keirnan, the owner of this quilt. Made by her daughter, Mary Lee Kennedy, the quilt is composed of blocks depicting vegetable or flower plots making up a garden. Kennedy made use of every available moment, embroidering the blocks at the beach while she waited for her children to take their swimming lessons.

174. Lillian Hill Komsie (b. 1911). Original design *(City Quilt, Wakefield, Michigan)* made 1975-1976, Wakefield, Gogebic County, Michigan. Lillian Hill Komsie, lender. Silk, velvet, and polyester with sheet filling, 96" x 110", MQP 85.840.

On October 22, 1911, Finnish-Americans Axel and Hilma Hill became the parents of Lillian, who later married another Finnish-American, Toivo Komsie. One of Komsie's quilts traces her Finnish family roots back to 1866. This quilt, one of ten she completed, was made for the nation's bicentennial celebration. In a letter to the Michigan Quilt Project staff, Komsie provided an explanation of her design and the quilt's contents:

First when looking at the quilt they'd think it was nothing but a jumble of names and places on it, so I'll try and explain how to read it. From the left hand side from the top to the bottom and across the bottom in a "L" shape (the L stands for Lillian), I started with business places . . . [the second row] are the stores and more businesses. Third row—bank, laundromats, correspondents. Fourth—newsstand, insurance, catering, etc., Fifth—churches, Sixth—Streets in Wakefield.

Lillian Komsie
Courtesy of Lillian Komsie

Ninth—Sunday Lake. 10—railroads, physicians, "sauna," public steam bath. 11—churches. 12—dinettes, pasty shop, lodges. 13—motels. 14—beauty and barber shops. It's not such a mess after you know how to read it!

Komsie gathered most of her information for this quilt while working in the tourist information center. For templates she used pieces of discarded sardine cans. All of the materials used in this quilt were scraps from various sources, and Komsie used only old drape material for the centers. In 1976 this quilt won a Blue Ribbon at the Gogebic County Fair.

Most of Komsie's quilting was done at the Wakefield bus station, which she owned and operated for 25 years. She says that quilting helped her to pass the time.

175. Sister Mary Albert Lenaway (1908-1986), piecer; **Ada Miller**, quilter. Original design *(Susan's Favorite)* made 1975-1978, Adrian, Lenawee County, Michigan. Susan Kelly Arnold, lender. Cotton with polyester filling, 88" x 105.5", MQP 86.475.

Born Eva Lenaway, at Hewleton, Michigan, Sister Mary Albert Lenaway possessed remarkable abilities both as an educator and as an artist. After joining the Dominican Sisters in Adrian in 1927, she earned several academic degrees, including a Ph.D. in education. She taught at all levels and was recognized as a superb teacher. Her many teaching appointments included positions at the Visitation Elementary School in Detroit and Siena Heights College in Adrian. Lenaway served the majority of her career as an administrator at colleges in Florida, Puerto Rico, and Massachusetts.

A tribute given at her death in 1986 states:

When she reached the age of 65, she retired from academic activity and began another career. She learned to quilt, and made quilting an art and a profession. . . . When she cast her skills and energy into quilting, she made it an art form, and remained a professional teacher. Through workshops and classes she brought new circles of friends into her life. Moreover, she found time to make more than a hundred colorful lap robes and head pillows for the sisters at Maria Health Care Center, and

Sister Mary Albert Lenaway, ca. 1985
Courtesy of Susan Kelly Arnold

brought them with affection to the sisters.

Susan's Favorite, one of the 40 quilts made by Lenaway, was made especially for her niece, Susan Kelly Arnold, and was named in her honor. Lenaway used a traditional quilt pattern for the central medallion and the blocks which form the pieced border. She also made quilts for her six brothers and sisters, nieces and nephews, and grandnieces and grandnephews as wedding and christening gifts. Lenaway worked in her 57-by-20 foot studio, using tag-board templates that she destroyed after one use.

At her death it was said:

We called her a perfectionist. She aimed for nothing less than excellence. She gave it herself, and insisted that others do likewise. God had lavished gifts upon her; she did not hoard them. She knew that to whom much is given much is expected and she gave with grandeur until "life with no end," October 9, 1986.

176. Lena C. McK____y. Tumbling Blocks or Hexagonal Star *(Bicentennial Quilt)* made 1976, Charlestown, West Virginia. Collection of Gerald R. Ford Library and Museum, Grand Rapids, Michigan. Cotton with polyester filling, 71″ x 77.5″, MQP 85.1605.

This pieced mosaic quilt, made in 1975-76 for the nation's bicentennial, is a remarkable record of many events that occurred during the first 200 years of our country's history. Using a pattern known as Tumbling Blocks or Hexagonal Star, the quiltmaker stitched together red, white, and blue diamond-shaped cotton pieces to form the top. In each of the white diamonds, she embroidered historical names, dates, and events. Among the names are those of the signers of the Decla-

ration of Independence and the nation's presidents. Maps of the states and dates of their admission to the Union fill 50 of the diamonds. Other white pieces document political events, inventions, and developments in medicine. The designs of the hand quilting include stars, stripes, and outlining. Unfortunately, even though the quiltmaker embroidered her signature and the date on the top of her quilt, her name is only partially legible as "Lena C. McK____y." However, it is known that she was living at Charlestown, West Virginia, when she presented her quilt to President Gerald Ford during the U.S. bicentennial year. The quilt is now in the collection of the Ford Library and Museum at Grand Rapids, Michigan.

Lois Nugent, 1987
Courtesy of The Mellus/News Herald
Newspapers of Wyandotte, Michigan

177. Lois Nugent. *World Without End* made 1976, Southgate, Wayne County, Michigan. Lois E. Nugent, lender. Cotton and cotton/polyester with polyester filling, 72″ x 103″, MQP 86.1799.

In 1976, Lois Nugent began a quilting project that celebrated the bicentennial of the American Revolution. She copied an 1876 "old piece of a quilt which had been used as a mattress pad" and had been in the family for years.

Nugent named her quilt *World Without End.* Executed in the patriotic color scheme of red, white, and blue with outline and feather wreath quilting, this was one of her first quilting efforts. "From it," she says, "I learned patience, perseverance, and perplexity!"

178. Lois Nugent. *Snowflakes* ▲ made 1977, Southgate, Wayne County, Michigan. Lois E. Nugent, lender. Cotton/polyester with polyester filling, 83″ x 104″, MQP 86.1798.

Snowflakes was among the first of Lois Nugent's ventures into quiltmaking. She asked 32 of her family members, friends, and neighbors to cut her a snowflake

from white fabric. Each snowflake was appliquéd onto a blue background, and the 32 pattern blocks were set with plain white blocks to build the quilt top. Nugent added a dark blue and a white border and used diamond and star quilting designs across the entire quilt. Like real snowflakes, each design in Nugent's quilt is unique.

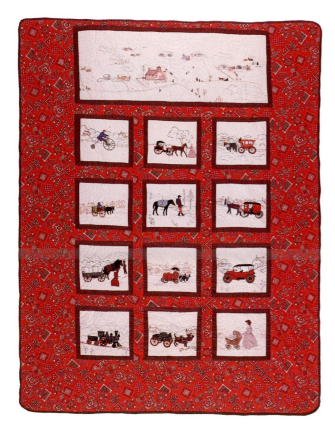

Dorothy Mork, ca. 1980
Courtesy of Dorothy Mork

179. Dorothy Mork (b. 1906). Pictorial Blocks *(Transportation)* made 1976-1977, Sutton's Bay, Leelanau County, Michigan. Jon W. Kellogg, lender. Cotton, cotton/polyester, and polyester knit with polyester filling, 77″ x 101″, MQP 86.454.

Dorothy Mork was 72 years old when she was selected as a Michigan finalist in the 1978 Great Quilts of America competition sponsored by *Good Housekeeping*, the United States Historical Society, and the Museum of American Folk Art.

A quilt of original design, *Transportation* was Mork's 1975 Christmas gift to her grandson Jon Kellogg. The design is her pictorial response to what she describes as "a small grandson asking about how we got around in the early 1900s." Among the modes of transportation Mork chose to picture are a steam locomotive, an early automobile, a baby carriage, a velocipede, and a number of animal-drawn conveyances.

Mork was born to Norwegian parents on October 16, 1906 in Sutton's Bay, Michigan, where she still lives. A painter and seamstress, Mork has made 20 quilts since she began quilting in 1970. She says she learned to quilt by watching other quilters.

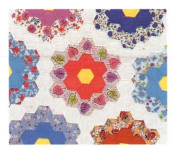

180. Mary Keller (b. 1911). Grandmother's Flower Garden made 1976-1978, Bentley, Bay County, Michigan. Mary Keller, lender. Cotton with polyester filling, 90″ x 110″, MQP 86.265.

Detroit-born Mary Hutek Keller, a homemaker since her 1938 marriage to Charles Keller, lives in Bentley, Michigan. A gardener whose interests include crocheting and embroidery, Keller is the only member of her family who quilts. She began her first quilting project when she was nearly 40 years old and has made more than 60 quilts since 1950. Keller quilts seasonally, spending more time on her quilts in the winter months than in the summer. She uses hand sewing for both piecing and quilting and sometimes pieces blocks by machine. She favors traditional patterns, although, as Keller herself explains, "I put them together differently sometimes." Keller says she prefers to use cotton fabrics because they are easy to work with, and she obtains her own patterns from magazines. Even though Keller recently suffered a stroke, she is relearning to use her hand for both writing and quilting and has begun another quilt.

A Blue-Ribbon winner at the 1978 Saginaw County Fair, this quilt was patterned by Keller after a Grandmother's Flower Garden quilt that she found in an issue of *Quilter's Newsletter Magazine*. Each of the 196 blocks has a single yellow hexagon for its center, an inner ring of solid-color hexagonal pieces, and an outer ring of a print fabric in a coordinating color. The flowers are separated by rows of white hexagons, and the entire collection of blocks is framed by a border of solid-color hexagonal shapes. Keller reinforced the hexagonal shapes by using outline stitching.

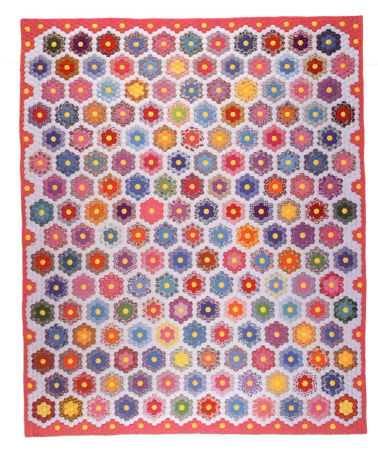

181. Mary Keller (b. 1911). Little Basket made ca. 1980 (before 1982), Bentley, Bay County, Michigan. Mary Keller, lender. Cotton with polyester filling, 93″ x 100″, MQP 86.268.

One of Mary Keller's Little Basket quilts, this predominantly white-and-gold quilt was awarded Best of Show at the 1982 Saginaw County Fair. Keller uses the arrangement of pieced blocks set with gold triangles to showcase both her piecing expertise and her facility with a quilting needle. At the center of this quilt is a single, large, white rectangle containing an elaborately quilted vase of flowers on a diamond-quilted background. Around this central medallion bands of Little Basket blocks alternate with wide, plain, fabric sashes. Two narrow gray-and-gold borders complete the design. The diamond quilting of the center medallion is repeated in the bands of little baskets, which are also outline quilted. The two white bands are quilted with flowers on leafy vines, and the two borders are cable quilted.

182. Mary Keller (b. 1911). Little Basket made 1982–1983, Bentley, Bay County, Michigan. Mary Keller, lender. Cotton with polyester filling, 90″ x 100″, MQP 86.266.

Another of Mary Keller's Little Basket quilts, this textile was awarded Best of Show at the 1983 Saginaw County Fair. As did many of Keller's patterns, the Little Basket design came from a magazine illustration. The 72 multicolored basket blocks are joined by light-blue sashes to an equal number of plain white blocks set in diamonds.

The plain blocks and the double border allow Keller to use a number of quilting designs with outline quilting. Various quilting motifs, mostly floral designs, adorn the plain white blocks, while the sashes connecting the blocks feature interlocked cable quilting. Keller uses quilted diamonds in the outer border and another cable in the narrow, gray, inner border.

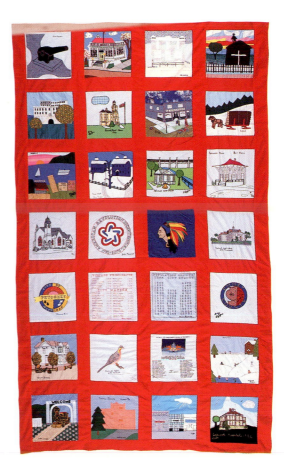

183. Mary Keller (b. 1911). Dresden Plate made 1983–1984, Bentley, Bay County, Michigan. Mary Keller, lender. Cotton with polyester filling, 88″ x 102″, MQP 86.270.

Mary Keller's variation on the traditional Dresden Plate pattern, this quilt won for Keller her third county fair award in as many years—the Saginaw Fair Sweepstakes for 1984. Keller, who found the Dresden Plate pattern in an issue of *Quilter's Newsletter Magazine,* describes her variation on the pattern: "I made regular size Dresden Plate and made small ones where the squares meet, then quilted a feather circle around the small ones." Although the plates are made from various multicolored prints, each

Mary Keller, September 1973, in her garden
Courtesy of Mary Keller

contains a center circle and four "spokes" of the same dark brown fabric, the spokes arranged in a cross or compass-like form.

184. Women of Petoskey, Michigan. Pictorial Block (*The Petoskey Bicentennial Quilt*) made 1976–1981, Petoskey, Emmet County, Michigan. Little Traverse Historical Society of Petoskey, Michigan, lender. Cotton, cotton/polyester, velvet, silk, 76″ x 128″, MQP 85.1167.

This bright quilt, a project for the nation's bicentennial, was made between 1976 and 1981 by a local quilting group in Petoskey, Michigan. Mostly white, 28 square blocks are separated by four-inch-wide solid-red strips to form the top. A four-inch red border frames the entire ensemble. Strong blue accents complete the patriotic color scheme. The blocks have been appliquéd, embroidered, or batiked with various original designs, including landscapes and buildings as they appeared around 1900, emblems, the profile of an Indian, and lists of information pertaining to the history of the Petoskey area. The

fabrics used include cotton, cotton/polyester, velvet, and silk, and the piecing and appliqué have been done by both hand and machine. The top has been tacked directly to a blue backing, without the use of a filling.

The blocks contain the signatures of the quiltmakers, who include Margaret Loodeen, Betty Munson, Carol Hinkley, Arlene Murphy, Carol Leiber, Daisy Sigafus, Charabelle Thompson, Edith Schmit, Doris Cox, Fran Tousain, Mary and Laurie Hall, Iva Ward, Julia MacDonell, Florence Bain, Clara Nasson, Laura Treadwell, Edwina Burgess, Catherine Schwartzfisher, Edith Fahl, and Cathy Cole. Shirley Greenwell helped to design several of the blocks. *The Petoskey Bicentennial Quilt,* presented to the Little Traverse Historical Society in memory of Joan M. Treadwell, has been exhibited at the Emmet County Fair and at many community events.

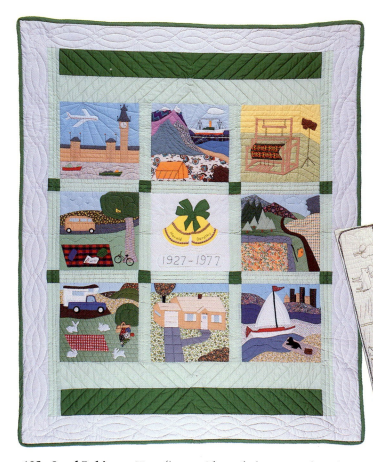

185. Carol Robinson Hare (b. 1929). Pictorial Block *(The Anniversary Quilt)* made 1977, Saginaw, Saginaw County, Michigan. Dorothy Webb Robinson, lender. Cotton and cotton/polyester with polyester filling, 78″ x 96″, MQP 86.428.

Carol Hare learned to piece quilts from her grandmother, Bertha Woodman Webb, at the age of 9, and began quilting at 45. She is a member of the Piecemakers Quilt Guild of Saginaw, Michigan.

Hare designed and sewed *The Anniversary Quilt* as a gift for her parents, Dorothy Webb and Harold L. Robinson, to celebrate their 50th wedding anniversary.

The quilt documents the Robinson's marriage and their personal accomplishments. The center block displays their names and the date of their marriage. Immediately beneath that is a quilted representation of the Robinsons' last home. Their hobbies, weaving and photography, are represented as well as their love of travel. Five blocks refer to the five Robinson children and their families, whose names are embroidered in these blocks. Hare enhances the pictorial blocks with three different quilting motifs, including outline quilting, cables, and diagonal lines. (See also no. 251 for another quilt by Hare.)

Stella Vanderburgh Strye
Courtesy of Stella Vanderburgh Strye

186. Stella Vanderburgh Strye (b. 1913). Original design *(History of Farmington)* made 1978, Farmington Hills, Oakland County, Michigan. City of Farmington Hills, lender. Cotton with cotton/polyester filling, 69″ x 96″, MQP 85.834.

Stella Strye, a resident of the Farmington area since 1921 and member of the Farmington Historical Commission, spent 11 months and 1,200 hours to make this quilt. Each of the blocks shows a building or scene that was important in the history of Farmington Hills and Farmington. Included are Farmington's first schoolhouse, a home that was used as an underground railroad shelter for slaves running to Canada, Minnow Pond, Warner Mansion (home of former Michigan governor Fred Warner), the Universalist Church (oldest Universalist Church in Michigan), and Botsford Inn. Other designs in the quilt represent local transportation, a Potawatomi legend, and the 1973 incorporation of Farmington Hills as a city. To complete the quilt, Strye added a border that depicts every kind of leaf found in the area, based on a collection she made in 1978. Strye presented the quilt to the city on June 18, 1978. (See also no. 147 for a quilt by Strye's mother.)

120

187. Emma Newswanger.
Whole cloth made 1978, Oden, Emmet County, Michigan. Mrs. George Oniu, lender. Satin with home-sheared and carded wool filling, 81″ x 90″, MQP 85.1102.

Although this quilted comforter was made recently, its filling has a special family history, as owner Veronica Oniu explains:

About 1933–34 my father brought home bushels of sheepskins, washed them, and cut off the wool. Father, sister and I pulled the wool, father made a carder and carded wool, then set up a homemade frame on 4 kitchen chairs. Top was lavender satin, bottom green satin. The pattern of mostly lines was put on the satin with carpenter's chalk. Father showed us how to bring the needle up and straight down. Father made two such quilts . . . in 1967 I found a box of rewashed, recarded wool in father's closet. I kept the wool until Mrs. Newswanger made a comforter for me.

The pink satin comforter is quilted in diamond and water lily quilting designs.

Helen Hoskins
Courtesy of Helen Hoskins

188. Helen Hoskins (b. 1926).
Sampler made 1978–1980, Hubbardston, Ionia County, Michigan. Peg Rasey, lender. Cotton with polyester filling, 55″ x 82″, MQP 85.1549.

An arrangement of 15 alternating appliquéd and plain blocks fills the top of this quilt. Each of the seven white squares holds a different appliquéd design, pieced from scraps of calico in an assortment of colors. Between these squares are solid-gold-colored squares, quilted with various designs. Solid-blue sashes separate the blocks and an appliquéd border frames the entire top. Each block was quilted to a different colored backing before the blocks and sashes were assembled. As a result, the back also contains 15 blocks of assorted colors. Begun in 1978 and completed in 1980, this Sampler quilt won First Prize at the Ionia County Fair of that year.

The quiltmaker, Helen Hoskins, now of Durango, Colorado, was living in Hubbardston, Michigan, when she made her prize quilt. She recalls that she took her designs from different sources, such as the *Quilter's Newsletter Magazine* and several books. She sold her quilt to a friend, Peg Rasey, who has said that she would never part with it.

Hoskins was born in 1926 to Ernest and Louise Smith Holm. Both her mother and grandmother were quilters. Married first to Harry Bollinger and then to Remine Hoskins, she has seven children. In 1971 Hoskins learned to quilt from her mother's neighbor, Mary Goodman of Pewamo, Michigan. After her husband's death in 1976, she enrolled at Michigan State University, where she majored in anthropology. Today Hoskins is the director of the Ute Cultural Tribal Center in Colorado. In addition to quilting and archaeology, her activities have included oil painting, antique furniture restoration, weaving, and playing the bass fiddle in her own band, Home Grown Grass, which has cut two albums of Bluegrass music.

189. Suzanne K. Ramsey (b. 1949). Original design *(Sock Quilt)* made 1978–1982, Sturgis, Ionia County, Michigan. Suzanne K. Ramsey, lender. Cotton and knit sock tops with polyester filling, 40″ x 65″, MQP 85.819.

The October 1984 issue of *Ladies Circle* magazine featured an article on this quilt, which is made entirely out of sock tops. Quiltmaker Suzanne Ramsey says, "The idea for the sock quilt came from saving old socks and not being able to mend them like my Grandma did. I had to do SOMETHING with all those socks!" In addition to this clever method of recycling worn clothing, Ramsey also uses old blankets as liners for some of her quilts. Recently Ramsey's father was the recipient of a quilt made in the tradition of church members' marking a special event in the life of their church leaders. To celebrate his 30th anniversary as a Lutheran minister, the Ladies' Group at Zion Lutheran Church of Columbus, Ohio, presented him with a Friendship quilt. At her own church in Michigan, Ramsey participates in a women's group that makes quilts to send to rest homes and refugee camps. Of their activity Ramsey says, "It's great to know we are needed."

190. Jenny Lamoreaux (b. 1942). Sampler *(Lamoreaux Wedding Quilt)* made 1978–1985, Shelbyville, Barry County, Michigan. Jenny L. Lamoreaux, lender. Linen, cotton, cotton/polyester with synthetic filling, 85″ x 85″, MQP 86.1528.

Jenny Lamoreaux, who hails from a long line of quiltmakers, recalls that

great-grandmother Nancy Ann Tyler McGinnis told of quilting with a candlestick on the quilt next to each quilter. . . . Great grandmother McGinnis said she had eight tops done and her wedding top pieced ready when she was married. . . . Great grandfather McGinnis made little stools for the group that came to quilt so they could prop their elbows on their knees under the quilt. . . . grandfather Brown helped design and piece a Double Wedding Ring during the Depression when he had no work. . . . Mother traded scraps with neighbors in 1930s to piece three tops.

According to Lamoreaux,

During childhood's illnesses I amused myself studying great grandmother's tattered quilts. Grandmother died young leaving seven children. Her quilts were either burned while saving the house on the day of the barn fire or worn out. The quilts lost saving the house (they were spread on the roof and soaked with river water from the Kankakee) were replaced in the next day or two by neighbors. Everyone tried to keep a spare quilt or comforter in case of need. All made tops in the winter and saved at least one or two for a spring quilting party when wagons could move on the roads and frames could be set outside. Some were completed in family quilting bees in the evening after supper and chores.

Later I found Mother's three tops, unfinished in the cupboard. Her mother died when she was 13 and as the last child she replaced her mother in the work schedule of the farm plus her previous chores. The tops were stored and left for her daughters to finish. Melissa has finished one, a pointed-petal daisy, I have finished the Ocean Wave top and will finish the third for my other sister, Cheri, for Christmas, 1986 or 1987. The third is a rounded-petal daisy. Mother waited to give us the tops until we had established our homes. Her business has taken the time others spend quilting especially since Father died (1978).

Lamoreaux began quilting during the eighth grade and has completed 30 comforters and 15 quilts, many of which she has given away as gifts for Christmas, weddings, births, or anniversaries. The *Lamoreaux Wedding Quilt* was made as a celebration of her marriage June 8, 1963 to Calvin G. Lamoreaux. According to Lamoreaux, its production was delayed until 1978 because she was busy completing college degrees and "working to pay off loans for college, house and land, cars, etc."

191. Mary C. Thorpe. Whole Cloth, original design *(Wedding Quilt)* made 1979, Portage, Kalamazoo County, Michigan. James and Deborah Stowe, lenders. Cotton/polyester with synthetic filling, 101″ x 101″, MQP 85.1745.

An original design made of tufted, appliquéd, and quilted motifs fills the top of this all-white quilt made in 1978–79. Mary Thorpe of Portage, Michigan, designed the quilt as a wedding gift for her friends James and Deborah Stowe, incorporating motifs with special significance for the couple. In the center medallion, a bride and groom are silhouetted against a background of clamshell stitches encircled by ribbons and bows. The bride's dress is identical to the wedding dress worn by Deborah Stowe. Surrounding the medallion are images of the roses, wedding rings, and bells used at the marriage ceremony. The wedding date of the Stowes is quilted within a banner, and musical notes represent their wedding song. The four seasons depicted in the four corners symbolize the year during which the Stowes

dated before their marriage. Along the edges, six hearts, quilted with the initials of family members, are linked by a chain to suggest the uniting of the two families. The *Wedding Quilt* won First Place at the Kalamazoo County Fair in 1979; Best of Show at the Blueberry Festival at South Haven, Michigan; and First Prize for original design at the Michigan State Fair in 1982.

Mary Thorpe is employed at The Upjohn Company, Kalamazoo, Michigan. Long involved with needlework, she began quilting in 1976 by making a quilt for her son's bed. The *Wedding Quilt,* completed in ten months, was only her second endeavor. Each week she holds an informal class in her home for other Upjohn employees who have become interested in quilting. Confessing that what she calls a hobby her husband calls her obsession, Thorpe keeps two quilts in progress at once, one on a hoop and the other on a frame. She says, "I like to spend an hour a night quilting. It's very relaxing, the way watching television or jogging is relaxing to other people."

192. Jane Ann McCarthy (b. 1935). Snowflake made 1979–1980, Highland, Oakland County, Michigan. Jane Ann McCarthy, lender. Cotton/polyester with blanket filling, 80.5″ x 82″, MQP 85.491.

Jane Ann McCarthy started quilting when she was 44 years old and has made five quilts. She

now estimates she spends about two hours a day at her quilting. Members of McCarthy's family participated in this quilt by contributing cut-out versions of their ideas of snowflakes. McCarthy appliquéd the resulting 35 white cotton snowflakes onto a light-blue backing, then outlined each snowflake in a simple line of quilting.

193. Letha Lundquist (b. 1903). Original design *(An Humble Hearth)* made 1979–1980, Port Sanilac, Sanilac County, Michigan. Andrew Willis, lender. Cotton with synthetic filling, 86″ x 102″, MQP 84.39.

At the age of ten Lundquist began quilting under the instruction of her mother, Mary Ann McKay Smith, and her grandmother, Christina McKay. As a child Lundquist quilted with older church members, but she now works alone in her home.

She has made ten pictorial quilts for members of her family, who regard them as treasured possessions. Three examples of her handwork are represented by quilts 193–95.

Lundquist writes of her quest to learn about pictorial quilts:

I read about the pictorial quilts made by pioneer women. I wanted one if I could find one and looked at museums, and antique shops, but couldn't find one. So I decided to try making one. After that I con-

tinued making pictorials as I got ideas. Children and grandchildren wanted one, so I have filled the demand as well as I can—but still work on pictorial quilts . . . for heirlooms.

Lundquist continues to make pictorial quilts and has just completed one for one of her grandsons. She lovingly assembles these gifts, sometimes using as many as four different needlework techniques including piecing, appliqué, crewel embroidery, and trapunto.

Grandson Andrew Willis is the proud owner of this quilt, titled *An Humble Hearth.* Lundquist incorporated the owner's log home into the quilt, as well as some of his interests. The log cabin assumes a prominent position in the center of the quilt and is surrounded by an outer border of blocks of the Pine Tree pattern. The quilt was "made especially for Andrew . . . as a keepsake to remember gramma."

194. Letha Lundquist (b. 1903). Original design *(An Ancient Cupboard)* made 1984, Port Sanilac, Sanilac County, Michigan. Rachel Jean Willis, lender. Cotton with synthetic filling, 88″ x 103″, MQP 84.40.

The quilter's collection of antique dishes served as the inspiration for this quilt made for her granddaughter, Rachel Jean Willis. Using appliqué, embroidery, and trapunto, Lundquist has fashioned a quilt full of memories for Willis. The diamond cross-hatching in the quilting serves to accent the pieces contained within the cupboard, and the outline quilting in the border highlights the flowering vines encircling the cupboard. The quilt has been exhibited only once, at a special mother-daughter banquet at the quilter's church.

195. Letha Lundquist (b. 1903). Original design *(A Village Street)* made 1979, Port Sanilac, Sanilac County, Michigan. Letha Lundquist, lender. Cotton with cotton filling, 78″ x 100″, MQP 84.42.

This quilt made by Letha Lundquist is unusual because it was not made as a gift for a family member. Used as a spread on her own antique canopy bed, *A Village Street* illustrates scenes from Lundquist's childhood.

Letha Lundquist
Courtesy of Letha Lundquist

196. Donna Rae Maki (b. 1947). Original design *(Alex Haley's "Roots" Quilt)* made 1979–1981, Holt, Ingham County, Michigan. Donna Rae Maki, lender. Cotton and cotton/polyester with synthetic filling, 72″ x 86″, MQP 86.857.

Donna Rae Maki was inspired to create this quilt after viewing the television program *Roots,* based on the book of the same name by Alex Haley. It took all her spare time for two years to complete this wall hanging which includes 13 scenes depicting key characters and events in Haley's book. For the development of her designs, Maki relied on illustrations from his book and from a calendar made to advertise his publication.

Although Maki learned the basics of quilting in a class in junior high school, she didn't become seriously interested in quilting until 1978 when she took a class from Pepper Cory. It was during the course of making the *"Roots"* quilt that she learned how to do appliqué. Maki says of the quilt, "It was a fun experience proving a quilt is like a painting and almost any design can be made into a quilt." It has been on ex-

Donna Rae Maki
Courtesy of Donna Rae Maki

hibit not only in the Lansing area, but also at the 1983 World of Quilts exhibit at Meadow Brook Hall in Rochester, Michigan, and at the 1981 Great Lakes Quilt Show in Mt. Clemens, Michigan, where it won two Blue Ribbons.

When Maki began this quilt in 1979, she was a member of the Lansing area Capitol Cutters quilt group. Now she is active in the Capitol City Quilt Guild and is a volunteer for the Michigan Quilt Project. Married and the mother of two, Maki resides with her family in Holt.

197. Grace Mary Stinton (b. 1922). Original design *(Easter Egg Quilt)* made 1980, Auburn, Bay County, Michigan. Grace Stinton, lender. Cotton and cotton/polyester with polyester filling, 92″ x 86″, MQP 86.840.

Born and raised in New England, Grace Mary Stinton moved to Michigan in her mid twenties, worked as a public school teacher, raised nine children, and began quilting in the process. Stinton learned to quilt in a class she took at Delta Community College when she was 45 years old and also received help with her quilting from her mother-in-law, Ella McCoig of Chatham, Ontario, who quilted until she was 90 years old. Over the years Stinton has used ideas for her original designs from quilt books, greeting cards, coloring books, and travel experiences.

Stinton shares her talent with others, both in her home in Midland and in Chatham with McCoig. She has taught quilting,

in particular the appliqué procedure, and has used some unusual materials such as men's ties in the refurbishing of an antique Crazy quilt. According to Stinton, each of her quilts is designated in advance as a gift for one of her daughters, daughters-in-law, or granddaughters.

On the *Easter Egg Quilt,* each of the four appliquéd "eggs" contains an elaborately embroidered picture, framed all around with a quilted border. The designs for these pictures were copied from five Hallmark Easter cards. A patterned sheet was used for the background. Stinton used diamond-shape quilting on the background, and outline quilting on the border designs. The back is of one piece—a pink cotton/polyester fabric. The quilt has been on public display at the Material Mart in Midland and at the White Pine Chapter of the Embroiderers Guild of America in Bay City.

198. Grace Mary Stinton (b. 1922). Pumpkins *(Pumpkin Quilt or Autumn Harvest)* made 1980–1981, Auburn, Bay County, Michigan. Grace Stinton, lender. Cotton and cotton/polyester with polyester filling, 99″ x 122″, MQP 86.836.

According to quiltmaker Grace Mary Stinton, the area around Auburn, Michigan "has beautiful pumpkin fields in October." Stinton wanted to design a quilt "to look like her neighbor's field of pumpkins." In what Stinton calls her *Pumpkin Quilt,* she has used a deep-brown-colored cotton sheet for the background to represent the soil for the pumpkins. Orange, mustard-yellow, and earth-toned fabrics were used in the appliquéd pieces to portray an autumn pumpkin field.

Stinton made this quilt in 1980 to be used as a spread on a carved Victorian bed. It was displayed at the Material Mart in Midland and at the Studio 23 Art Gallery in Bay City. In the 1981 *Women's Day* Quilt Contest, it won an Honorable Mention. Following that, it was pictured in the 1982 issue of *Woman's Day Prize-Winning Quilts, Coverlets, and Afghans,* which printed the pattern and renamed the quilt *Autumn Harvest.* Whichever name is used, the quilt is particularly representative of Michigan in the fall. ▼

199. Grace Mary Stinton (b. ▲ 1922). Hawaiian Pineapple *(Hawaiian Medallion)* made 1984–1985, Auburn, Bay County, Michigan. Grace Stinton, lender. Cotton/polyester with polyester filling, 88″ x 88″, MQP 86.837.

Grace Stinton enlisted the help of Sarah Deasy of Saline, Michigan, in making the central square of this medallion quilt done in the Hawaiian style. According to Stinton, Deasy teaches a unique way of Hawaiian quilting. The central square displays a Hawaiian Pineapple design and so do the the four corner squares. The inner border that surrounds the central square is pieced in the pineapple design. This very bold and stiking textile has been on public display at the Material Mart in Midland and at the White Pine Chapter of the Embroiderers Guild of America in Bay City.

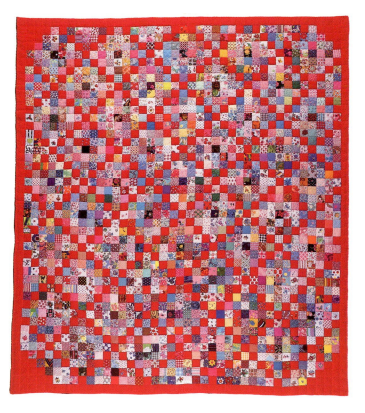

Ruby Strange, 1985
Courtesy of Ruby Strange

200. Ruby Strange (b. 1911). Irish Chain variation *(Scrap Quilt)* made 1980–1982, Sandusky, Sanilac County, Michigan. Ruby Strange, lender. Cotton, 82″ x 91″, MQP 85.1482.

The maker of this patchwork quilt calls it her *Scrap Quilt* because it was pieced with scraps of material left over from the countless aprons she has made and sold. There are 1,886 squares of cotton in the top, made in a variation of the Irish Chain pattern. Except for the red squares set in diagonal rows to create a diamond effect, there are no duplicate squares. The edges are finished with a red border and binding, and the hand quilting follows the shape of each square.

Ruby Strange of Sandusky, Michigan, made her *Scrap Quilt* in 1980–82 to serve as a "memory quilt" that would help her recall the many aprons she has made for her customers. She uses the quilt on her own bed. Strange was born in 1911 to James W. and Alice Minard. Her mother taught her how to quilt when she was only nine years old. Later she married James E. Strange, a metal finisher. Strange has made a total of 30 quilts, including the Dahlia, Irish Chain, Maple Leaf, Poppy, Daffodil, Roman Stripe, Pansy, an appliquéd quilt of relatives' hands, and a necktie quilt made from her husband's ties. She works alone at home, using a homemade frame. In addition to her quilting and apron making, Strange enjoys tending her garden and house plants and her activities in the Rebekah Lodge.

Ruby Pinner
Courtesy of Ruby Pinner

Lola Choinski
Courtesy of Lola Choinski

201. Lola Choinski, (b. 1938), designer; **Ruby Pinner** (b. 1920), and **members of Silver Threads and Golden Needles Quilt Club,** quilters. Holly and Berries *(Ruby's Christmas Quilt)* made 1981–1982, Utica, Macomb County, Michigan. Ruby Pinner, lender. MQP 87.168.

This quilt, designed "especially for Ruby Pinner" by her friend Lola Choinski, is a beautiful example of a "red and green" appliquéd quilt. Ruby Pinner's statement that "the only thing I never had was a red and green quilt to set on my bed" inspired Choinski to design the quilt. Many women, including members of the Silver Threads and Golden Needles Quilt Club, had a hand in completing the quilt.

Choinski has designed more than 200 quilt patterns and serves as a quilting judge every year at the Michigan State Fair. Pinner not only executed this quilt, but has made many others for members of her family. Each of her grandchildren receives a quilt when they graduate and get married. Pinner has been quilting for 40 years, and loves sharing her knowledge of quilts with others. She designed the Cranberry hoop and stand now marketed through Heritage Woodcrafts of Fremont, Michigan.

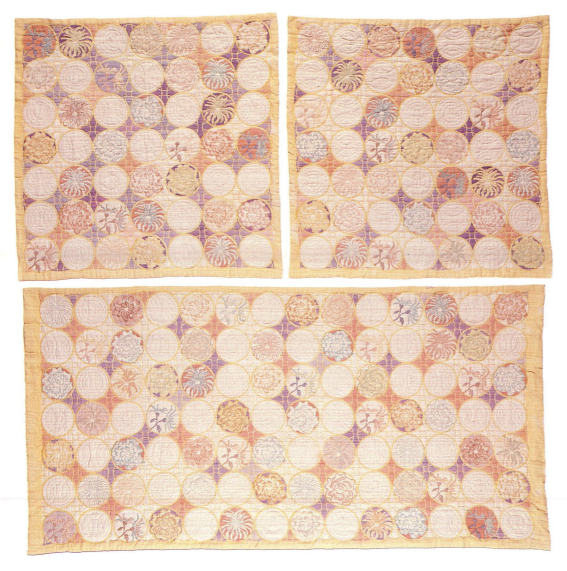

Marion Melody, 1985
Courtesy of Marion Melody

202. Marion Melody, designer; **Lizzy Kurtz** and **Effice Herschberger,** quilters. Original design *(Rondo of Life)* made 1981-1983, Riverview, Wayne County, Michigan. Marion Melody, lender. Dyed Thai silk with synthetic filling, 72″ x 72″, MQP 85.1697.

This wall quilt, once intended for a church altar, is an original design that has been influenced by Oriental sources. It combines silk screen and batik techniques in the raw silk top, which is in three sections to suggest a triptych. Tufting and outline quilting, done by hand with silk twist thread, highlight the major images and secure the top to the blue-purple dyed Thai silk backing. Marion Melody, the designer and artist who silkscreened and batiked the quilt, says that it "tells us about life in a very so-phisticated, subtle way with recurring circles, bridged with arcs connecting quiet and joyous times in our lives."

Entitled *Rondo of Life,* the wall quilt was made in 1981–83 by its designer, Marion Melody of Riverview, Michigan, and quilters Lizzy Kurtz and Effice Herschberger of rural Millersburgh, Ohio. Kurtz and Herschberger are Amish women who quilt for Amanda Miller's quilting and yard goods shop in Charm, Ohio. Melody, whose parents were Otto and Mary Palus Charvat, has several academic degrees, including a Master of Fine Arts in Studio Art from Wayne State University. Her first lessons in quilting were from Lola Choinski. She has completed three quilts and begun a fourth, all original designs silkscreened onto fabric. She plans to give each of her three children a quilt when they marry. Melody states:

I am a fiber artist (employed as a teacher) who hopefully will retire within five years. I have a studio (finally in the past year). After making several kinds of fiber art, I have found the most satisfaction by using my imagery for quilts. So far they are wall quilts. I enjoy the stitched line delineating and complementing the silk-screen and dyed imagery. Quilts are wonderful because they soften our hard, modern plastic surroundings, even though some of the designs may not be soft or comforting. I enjoy what fabric does as you work with it. I think there are many feelings that can be evoked with color, line (stitched), and texture. It's a wonderful way to express your feelings and ideas.

Rondo of Life has been exhibited at the Stitchery International '83 Show at Pittsburgh, Pennsylvania, in 1983; the Master of Fine Arts Exhibition at Wayne State University in Detroit, Michigan, in 1984; the Religious Art Show at Cincinnati, Ohio, in 1984; the Great Lakes Biennial Quilt Show at Mt. Clemens, Michigan, in 1984; the Quilt National '85 at Athens, Ohio, in 1985; the Annual Quilt Show of the American Quilters' Society at Paducah, Kentucky, in 1985; the Quilts = Art = Quilts Show at Auburn, New York, in 1985; and a one-woman show at Mt. Pleasant, Michigan, in 1986.

203. Sandra Zimmer (b. 1940). Original design *(Bag Quilt)* begun 1981 and finished 1983, Charlotte, Eaton County, Michigan. Sandra Robson Zimmer, lender. Cotton sacking (flour bags) with cotton filling, 90″ x 99″, MQP 85.1938.

Historically quilters frequently resorted to using feedbags and other commercially produced containers as backing for quilts. In this contemporary quilt, Sandra Zimmer has carefully arranged a collection of feedbags as the quilt top. According to Zimmer, "Chet (a friend) bought a box of feedbags at an auction and asked me to help his wife make a quilt with them and I could have enough for one myself." Zimmer is a self-taught quilter who now is a member of the Maple Leaf Quilters of Charlotte.

204. Marie McDonald (b. 1953). Sampler *(Fan Sampler Quilt)* made 1981–1983, Jenison, Ottawa County, Michigan. Marie McDonald, lender. Cotton with polyester filling, 75.75″ x 88.5″, MQP 86.564.

Born in Flint, Michigan, 34-year-old Marie McDonald has been a quilter for the past 11 years. Although her paternal grandmother was a quilter, she taught herself to quilt from reading books on the subject. Mother of a four-year-old, McDonald has completed at least one quilt a year since her first effort in 1976. She belongs to three quilt guilds in western Michigan and spends approximately 20 hours per week on her quilting.

The 20 rust, blue, and tan blocks in McDonald's Sampler quilt are variations of fans. With the exception of three blocks, all the fans' centers are located in the lower left corners of the blocks. In two of the blocks, however, there are two fans, radiating from the upper right and lower left corners. In a third block is a fully opened fan rather than the traditional partially opened shape. McDonald used both outline and scalloped quilting to complete her design.

205. Marie Combs (b. 1930). Original design *(Broken Sidewalk, 711 South St.)* made 1982, Kalamazoo, Kalamazoo County, Michigan. Marie Combs, lender. Cotton and cotton blends with synthetic filling, 83″ x 103″, MQP 85.340.

Machine-pieced and quilted by Marie Combs, this textile vividly depicts the destruction caused by a tornado on May 13, 1980 in her

Marie Combs
Courtesy of Marie Combs

hometown of Kalamazoo. Combs provided photographs and this description of the scenes she encountered in the aftermath of a tornado, which became the inspiration for the colors and shapes used in this quilt:

> *Lilac bushes in Bronson Park were undamaged by the tornado, this was taken the next morning. Sky directly after the tornado was a bright, brilliant blue—newly washed. Park department had planted pale yellow marigolds just the week previous to the storm.*

Combs is a prolific quilter who consciously attempts to explore the artistic possibilities of this traditional medium. She has won many awards for her quilts and has been in major juried shows throughout the United States, including the prestigious Quilt National. *Broken Sidewalk* was done with support from a 1982 Michigan Council for the Arts Individual Artist Grant.

206. Marquette County Quilters. Pictorial Blocks *(A Michigan Upper Peninsula Regional Quilt)* made 1982, Marquette, Marquette County, Michigan. WLUC-TV 6/ Marquette County Quilters, lenders. Cotton, cotton/polyester, and wool, 65″ x 54″, MQP 85.838.

In 1982 the Marquette County Quilters organized a quilt block contest to highlight the local television station's campaign to increase local interest in the region's resources. Participants in the contest were asked to create their impressions of upper Michigan history. Completed blocks were assembled into a wall hanging by the Marquette County Quilters, and the piece now hangs in the offices of WLUC-TV 6 in Marquette.

Blocks depict the following images: (1) Lady's Slipper flower; (2) cabin or "'camp" in pine forest; (3) eight-pointed star with

daisy center; (4) *distelfink*—Pennsylvania Dutch design; (5) recipe for pasty with a steaming trapunto pasty; (6) sailboat; (7) priest—Father Jacques Marquette; (8) milk bottle building—Asselin's dairy; (9) trillium flower; (10) black pine trees with moon

behind them; (11) the men, women, and children of the Upper Peninsula; and (12) lumberjack riding a log on a log run. The quilt carries the inscription "Upper Michigan, Someplace Special—by the people of Upper Michigan and the Marquette County Quilters—1982."

207. Mary Lee Kennedy (b. 1931). *Stained Glass Window* made 1982, Cadillac, Wexford County, Michigan. Mary Lee Kennedy, lender. Cotton and cotton/polyester with synthetic filling, 42″ x 47″, MQP 85.505.

In the last ten years a series of how-to books on making quilts in styles mimicking stained glass windows has prompted interest in this type of quilt. During the snowstorms of January 1982 Kennedy made this quilt to cover

a bathroom window "to keep the breezes out" in the winter months. Since then the quilt has been on display at the 1982 Great Lakes Quilt Show in Mt. Clemens where it was awarded Third Place and at the 1984 Traverse City Quilt Show. Kennedy is an avid quilter, teaches quiltmaking to a variety of individuals and groups (including 4-H'ers), and helps organize quilting shows in northwestern Michigan. ▶

208. LaDonna Fulton Jolliff (b. 1938). Original design *(Ribbon Quilt)* made 1982, Tipton, Lenawee County, Michigan. Brenda Jolliff Kendrick, lender. Satin 4-H award ribbons, 60″ x 78″, MQP 85.198.

As a youth, Brenda Jolliff Kendrick was an avid participant in 4-H horse shows and won numerous ribbons for her skills. Her mother, LaDonna Fulton Jolliff, used these ribbons to fashion two quilts for Kendrick. Kendrick used one as a wall hanging and the other on her bed in her college dorm room. The quilts now hang in Kendrick's apartment. ▶

Judith Alban
Courtesy of Judith Alban

◀ **209. Judith Kressbach Alban** (b. 1932). Eight-Pointed Star begun 1982, finished 1983, East Lansing, Ingham County, Michigan. Mildred (Mrs. Carl C. F.) Kressbach, lender. Cotton with polyester filling, 75″ x 85″, MQP 85.245.

Judith Kressbach Alban made this quilt as a Christmas gift for her stepmother. Although the pattern is a common one, the quiltmaker chose "all of the materials to look like flower beds and baths in a geometric garden."

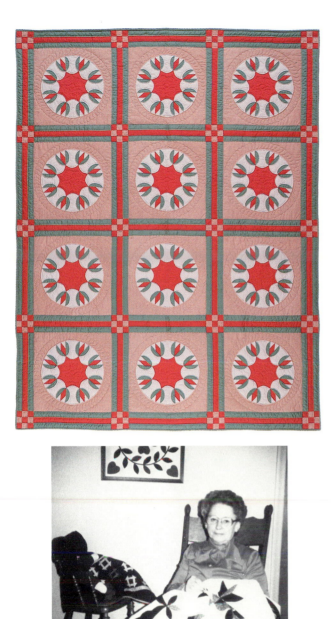

210. Doris Angell Dunlap (b. 1917). Cottage Tulips made 1982–1983, Saginaw, Saginaw County, Michigan. Doris Angell Dunlap, lender. Cotton/polyester with synthetic filling, 78″ x 102″, MQP 86.4.

Today many quilters often choose to copy traditional patterns they first encounter while visiting local quilt shows or sales. Such was the case for Doris Angell Dunlap of Saginaw, Michigan, who set out to replicate an antique quilt that she had viewed at a local quilt show. Employing the pattern called Cottage Tulips, Dunlap pieced 12 identical square blocks out of solid red, green, white, and beige cotton/polyester fabrics. Her color scheme differed from the original quilt only in her use of beige rather than yellow for the background of each square. The motif repeated in every block features a central eight-pointed hub, from which radiate eight stylized tulips. The blocks are separated by narrow red-and-green sashes with small Nine-Patch blocks in red and beige at the points of intersection. A triple border repeats the colors of the sashes. The hand quilting includes outline, feather wreath, and flower designs. Like the quilt that inspired it, the Cottage Tulips quilt has also been exhibited, winning Best of Show at the Farwell Methodist Church Quilt Show in 1984.

Dunlap was born at Saginaw in 1917 to Benjamin and Eva Hathaway Angell. She and her husband, Arthur W. Dunlap, have two sons and a daughter. She began making quilts in 1975 and, after completing two tops, enrolled in an adult education quilting class, taught by Victoria Williams at Saginaw's Arthur Hill High School. Since then, Dunlap has completed 17 full-size quilts and 8 crib quilts, including one pieced from scraps of clothing she had made for her daughter from the time of her daughter's birth until she was in college. Dunlap has given her quilts as gifts for birthdays, weddings, or "just because." She works at home, pinning the entire top together on a homemade frame and then lap-quilting it. Her favorite materials are cotton or cotton/polyester, polyester fillings, and all-purpose waxed thread.

Dunlap helped organize the Piecemaker's Quilt Guild, serving as its first president for two years, and has been involved in the month-long annual quilt shows at the Saginaw Historical Museum, giving workshops and lectures. Also fond of sewing and boating, Dunlap says she is motivated to make quilts by

a love of the history and stories of the pioneer quilters and their reasons for the designs and colors [and] the pleasure of creating something that will justify my having been here.

Doris A. Dunlap
Courtesy of Doris A. Dunlap

211. Doris Angell Dunlap (b. 1917). Diamond in a Square made 1983, Saginaw, Saginaw County, Michigan. Doris Angell Dunlap, lender. Cotton and cotton/polyester with polyester filling, 63″ x 70″, MQP 86.101.

As do many Amish and non-Amish quilters, Doris Dunlap purchased her fabric for this Amish-style Diamond in a Square wall hanging from Yoder's store in Shipshewana, Indiana. She took the pattern, a common Amish design, from books on Amish quilts. While the overall choice of color and geometric composition may be the most recognizable characteristics of traditional Amish quilts, the actual quilting work is equally significant. Dunlap says, "I like the geometrics of the Amish quilt designs and the space to fill with many different quilting designs." Among the quilting designs employed by Dunlap are the cable, basket, running vine, pumpkin seed, feather, and feather wreath. Her wall hanging was exhibited at the Piecemaker's Quilt Guild show "From Cabin to Cabin," held at the Saginaw Historical Museum in 1984.

133

212. Doris Angell Dunlap (b. 1917). Amish Lily made 1984–1985, Saginaw, Saginaw County, Michigan. Doris Angell Dunlap, lender. Cotton/polyester with synthetic filling, 86″ x 106″, MQP 86.7.

Doris Angell Dunlap's Amish Lily quilt was based on a wall hanging with a single motif. Dunlap's quilt contains 12 pieced blocks, set diagonally between 6 plain blocks and surrounded by plain half blocks and quarter blocks. Wanting to avoid the predominantly black color scheme she had used for an earlier Amish-style quilt, she chose a medium gray background for the pastel and deeper hues of the lilies in the pieced blocks. Black stems, pots, and border provide an interesting contrast to the colorful designs. Dunlap's hand-quilted designs include feather swags, tulips, wreaths, vines, outlines, and a large basket in each corner. Completed in 1985, the Amish Lily quilt was exhibited at the Saginaw Historical Museum that same year. Dunlap's favorite comment about the quilt came from a nonquilter who exclaimed, "It's just as good as if it were bought from a store!" ▶

213. Kay O'Connor (b. 1954). ▲ Nine-Patch begun 1982, finished 1983, Esmand, North Dakota, brought to Michigan in 1983. Becky Grossman, lender. Cotton, 68″ x 72″, MQP 85.200.

Kay O'Connor finished this quilt in 1983 in time to present it as a graduation present to her sister Becky Grossman who lives in Clinton, Michigan. Using five basic colors of fabrics for the backgrounds of the 50 Nine-Patch blocks and 50 setting blocks, the artist has created an unusual rainbow design in this otherwise simple tied quilt. Born April 17, 1954, married to John O'Connor, and now the mother of three children, O'Connor plans to make a quilt for her mother someday.

214. Kay O'Connor (b. 1954). ▲ Texas Purple made 1979–1980, Grand Forks, North Dakota, brought to Michigan in 1980. Tom M. Grossman, lender. Cotton, denim, and flannel, 66″ x 68.5″, MQP 85.201.

After making this quilt out of old blue jeans and other "odds and ends of materials," Kay O'Connor decided that these materials were too hard to sew on and that she wouldn't try one like this again. The quilt was made as a graduation present for her brother, Tom Grossman, and it was later repaired by her mother, Donna May Grossman.

Kay O'Connor
Courtesy of Kay O'Connor

215. Velma L. Bancroft (b. 1914). Broken Star made 1982–1983, Maple Rapids, Clinton County, Michigan. Wilbur D. Bancroft, lender. Cotton/polyester with polyester filling, 89″ x 93″, MQP 85.1350.

The interesting look of this quilt comes from the arrangement and vibrant, contrasting colors of diamond-shaped cotton pieces, joined to form an 8-pointed star within a larger 16-pointed star-shaped halo, both of which seem to radiate outward in ever-expanding rings. The effect is heightened by the color scheme, described by the quiltmaker as "deep shades of Aztec colors." Hand quilting outlines the diamond-shaped pieces. Large quilted medallions decorate each of the white blocks that separate the inner and outer stars, and quilted feather designs fill the corner blocks. The quilt is signed with an embroidered inscription, "To Wilbur from Velma," and is dated "Feb. 19, 1983."

The Broken Star quilt was made in 1982–83 by Velma L. Bancroft of Maple Rapids, Michigan, as a gift for her husband, Wilbur

D. Bancroft, a salesman. Velma Bancroft was born in 1914 at Ionia, Michigan, to Adelbert and Cora Bell Murphy Groves. The Bancrofts were married in 1934 and have three sons, James, Steven, and Kurt. A self-taught quilter, Bancroft began quilting when she was 16. Since then she has made 20 quilts and always has one in progress, usually working in her living room or on the back porch. She makes her own templates from cardboard, sandpaper, or plastic, and uses chalk or quilter's pencil to mark her quilting patterns. Her favorite colors are earth tones and green and pink, and her preferred material is cotton/polyester. Recently she made a quilt for the Michigan sesquicentennial.

Bancroft says she makes quilts "because I enjoy making them and giving them to my family and special friends." She gives quilts to her grandchildren as graduation, marriage, or Christmas gifts. In addition to quilting, Bancroft enjoys painting and knitting. She has been employed as a nurse's aid and as a postmaster. Her sister, Reva Bell of Maple Rapids, also is a quiltmaker.

Velma L. Bancroft, 1987
Courtesy of Velma L. Bancroft

216. Dorothy Sluder (b. 1924). Storm at Sea made 1982–1983, Adrian, Lenawee County, Michigan. Dorothy Sluder, lender. Cotton with synthetic filling, 83″ x 96″, MQP 85.170.

When quilter Dorothy Sluder drafted the pattern for this Storm at Sea quilt from a picture, she said it took several days to get it just right. She made the quilt to fit her king-size bed. Sluder learned quilting from her mother, Sadie Harrison, at the age of 50, and has now completed 20 quilts. She has also taught one of her two daughters, Patricia Yeutter, to quilt.

217. Lynne Davidson (b. 1946). Amish Bars begun 1982, finished 1984, San Francisco, California. Lynne Davidson, lender. Cotton and glazed cotton with polyester filling, 53.5″ x 56″, MQP 85.1903.

The growing appreciation for Amish quilting and quilt patterns has prompted non-Amish quilters to explore Amish patterns and color combinations. Lynne Davidson began quilting in 1976 by enrolling in a quilting class. After quilting as many as 20-30 hours a week she continued to take classes. In 1982 she began this

Amish Bars pattern quilt which she finished in 1984. The quilt, made with a traditional Amish pattern, has an unusual potatoe-vine border. According to Davidson,

The Potatoe Vine border is very unusual for a Lancaster County (Pennsylvania) pattern quilt. But after many hours of tedious work doing the center grid, I felt the need to loosen up—and the vine pattern felt right to me. I have only found one other Amish Bar quilt with this border.

218. Aileen R. Stannis (b. 1926). Seven Sisters made 1982–1984, Berkley, Oakland County, Michigan. Aileen R. Stannis, lender. Cotton with synthetic filling, 85″ x 108.5″, MQP 86.94.

Each composed of 7 hexagonal stars, 28 hexagonal blocks have been set together with triangles to form the top of this Seven Sisters quilt. Different printed cottons were used for each of the 168 outer stars in the blocks with the same green print for all of the center stars. Outline quilting defines each piece of the quilt, and quilted feather designs in the border conceal the maker's initials in each corner. Made by Aileen R. Stannis of Berkley, Michi-

gan, the quilt won a First-Place Blue Ribbon in patchwork and Best of Show in 1984 at the 4th Biennial Great Lakes Quilt Contest in Mount Clemens, Michigan. It was also displayed in 1985 alongside an antique Seven Sisters quilt at Quilts: An American Romance, a show held at the Somerset Mall, Troy, Michigan. Like many of today's quilters who prefer old, traditional patterns to new ones, Stannis faithfully recreated the familiar pattern, which she found in *Lady's Circle Patchwork Quilts*. She calls it her "favorite quilt."

219. Loma Viola Darling Tippin (b. 1921). *First Ladies Bi-Centennial Quilt* made 1982–1984, Harrison, Clare County, Michigan. Loma Viola Darling Tippin, lender. Cotton/polyester with polyester filling, 70″ x 80″, MQP 85.151.

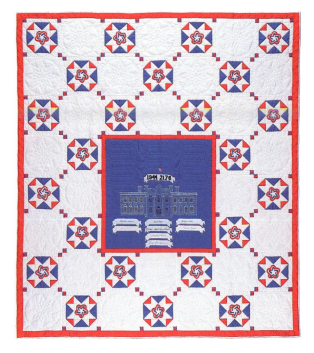

Loma Viola Darling Tippin comes from a family of many quilters, including her great-grandmother, Sarah E. White Whitney (the quilter of *Grandmother's Snow Flake Quilt,* no. 114 in this volume of quilts) and her sister, Sibyl Darling Mizer. Tippin writes of the *First Ladies* quilt:

I made this quilt to honor the first ladies, and also as a companion to the bi-centennial quilt, I finished in 1976, honoring the presidents of our country.

The bi-centennial quilt pattern designed by Mountain Mist was used as the background. I deleted the center blocks, and used a center of my own design.

It features the White House embroidered with white, gray blue, and black silk thread. Around the building are quilted spaces for future first ladies. Eight spaces have already been filled with first ladies' autographs, beginning with Bess Truman and Mamie Eisenhower, Jackie Kennedy, Lady Bird Johnson, Pat Nixon, Betty Ford, Rosalynn Carter, and Nancy Reagan.

The top took two years to assemble the fabrics, transpose the design (this is not a kit), write for autographs, appliqué

the star design and embroider the center portion. The quilt is completely hand done.

I completed the quilting in 140 hours, it took 27 days, on May 14, 1984.

The quilt is dated 1944, when Bess Truman was first in the White House, and 2176, when our country will be 400 years old.

People ask how I will finish this project, I tell them when I am 70 years old, I will leave the quilt with instructions to complete, to a family member or museum, and hope they will carry on the tradition.

If they don't co-operate, I will come back and tap them on the shoulder from time to time to motivate them. If that doesn't work, I have all bases covered and will be reincarnated and do it myself.

The quilt was awarded First Place and Best of Show at the Home Silk Contest in Los Angeles and was featured in the *Los Angeles Times Sunday Magazine* in November 1984.

220. Maple City Quilt Club, piecers; **Mary Jean Baker,** quilter. Sampler *(Me and My Friends)* made 1982–1986, Charlotte, Eaton County, Michigan. Mary Jean Baker, lender. Cotton and cotton/polyester with polyester filling, 78″ x 103″, MQP 86.115.

Members of the Maple City Quilt Club of Charlotte, Michigan, each contributed a 12-inch square block for this quilt and presented them to another member, Mary Jean Baker of Charlotte. Although each of the 16 blocks features a different pattern, all are made with the same color scheme of green, gold, rust, and white and signed with the makers' names. The center block holding an appliquéd pineapple design was made by Baker, who also did the shadow and outline quilting with rust-colored thread. In the course of one year, the Maple City Quilt Club created blocks for a Friendship Birthday Quilt for each of its 16 members,

Mary Jean Baker
Courtesy of Mary Jean Baker

using colors "of the birthday person's choice." Those who signed their names on the top of Baker's quilt include M. Latchaw, N. Conn, C. Chubner, T. Johnson, Corky, De Leauuw, C. Harter, Sandy Zimmer, L. Bockheim, ROD, J. Klingshirn, L. Klaiss, M C, S. Powers, Fay Voight, and S. Penrod.

221. Leila Brehmer Bahle (b. 1923). Cane Work made 1983, Leelanau, Leelanau County, Michigan. Leila Brehmer Bahle, lender. Cotton/polyester with polyester filling, 47.25″ x 50.5″, MQP 86.441.

A granddaughter of Swedish immigrants, Leila Brehmer Bahle is a self-taught quilter who shares her interest in quiltmaking with her sister, Ethel Rushmore. Bahle has been making quilts since her late twenties. She says that her favorite colors for quilts are "reds, rusts, blues," and she has no particular favorites among patterns. Two of these color groups are represented in this Cane Work quilt, made for her daughter, Lois Cole. This work has been on display in the windows of the family-owned Sutton's Bay store, where the quiltmaker purchased the fabrics for her quilt.

Leila Brehmer Bahle
Courtesy of Leila Brehmer Bahle

Milly Splitstone, ca. 1980
Courtesy of Milly Splitstone

222. Milly LaFever Splitstone (b. 1926). Sampler *(Michigan Winter)* made 1983, Fremont, Newaygo County, Michigan. Milly Splitstone, lender. Cotton with polyester filling, 64″ x 80″, MQP 86.518.

After her introduction to quilts at age 13, Milly Splitstone worked for a little over a year at learning to quilt, until the obligations of school work caused her to abandon quiltmaking. After school came her marriage and family, so Splitstone did not take up needle and quilting hoop again until after 1970. She prefers to work with cotton because, as she notes, "it behaves." Since her second beginning as a quilter, Splitstone has become a member of nine quilt guilds, including the National Quilting Association, the American Quilter's Society, a quilters' guild in Missouri, and three California guilds. With her friend and writing partner Betty Boyink, Splitstone has co-written *Michigan Quilters and Their Designs. Michigan Winter* was made specifically to be the cover illustration for that book, and it contains numerous patterns that either are specifically related to Michigan or, as she expresses it, "said 'Michigan' to me."

Betty Boyink
Courtesy of Betty Boyink

223. Betty Boyink (b. 1942). Sampler (*Michigan Summer*) made 1983, Grand Haven, Ottawa County, Michigan. Betty Boyink, lender. Cotton with polyester filling, 71″ x 90″, MQP 86.520.

Michigan Summer, made by Betty Boyink, is a companion quilt to *Michigan Winter* created by her partner, Milly Splitstone. Boyink prefers to use traditional patterns with her own variations. The wave-like border, chosen because it reminded her of "living along lakes," is a Boyink variation of Wheel of Fortune in which half blocks are alternated around the edge of the quilt. Boyink also created an original block design for this quilt, the center medallion of Michigan apple blossom and state map. That apple blossom design is repeated in the quilting.

224. Betty Boyink (b. 1942). *Baltimore Friendship* made 1979-1981, Grand Haven, Ottawa County, Michigan. Betty Boyink, lender. Cotton with polyester filling, 90″ x 104″, MQP 86.526.

A native Virginian who has lived in Michigan's Ottawa County for more than 20 years, quilter Betty Boyink gained national recognition in 1975 when, only a few years after she began to make quilts, she presented a U.S. bicentennial quilt to President Gerald Ford. In addition to designing and making quilts, Boyink creates quilt block patterns, writes and publishes books and articles on quilting, and presents workshops on quiltmaking. Among her contributions to quilting is the design for special 12-inch tablets of graph paper to aid quilters in drawing their pattern blocks. Boyink is a member of both the National Quilting Association and the American Quilter's Society. "I make quilts," Boyink says, "to learn, to check out patterns, colors, to use to illustrate quilt books and patterns I publish, [and] as teaching aids."

Of the 20 blocks in Betty Boyink's *Baltimore Friendship* quilt, 12 were made for her by members of her Tuesday Quilters

group as part of a year-long program in which members made one block a month for each other, so that at the end of the year each member had 12 blocks. The remaining 8 blocks came from friends in 7 states, *all the way from top prize winning quilters to one friend's* *first attempt at appliqué. One lady has an 1800s original Baltimore quilt so she copied one of those blocks for her design.* Boyink appliquéd the border and quilted the top. A work that has been shown at numerous Michigan quilt exhibits, *Baltimore Friendship* is, in Betty Boyink's words, "truly one of the treasures in my quilt collection."

225. Caron L. Mosey (b. 1956). Pine Tree, Mariner's Compass, and original design *(From the Woods to the Water)* made 1983, Flushing, Genesee County, Michigan. Robert Hayes Covert, lender. Cotton with polyester filling, 82" x 82", MQP 84.12.

A daughter's love for her parents is embodied in this quilt of original design by Caron L. Mosey. Titled *From the Woods to the Water* and presented to her parents on their retirement and move to their new home in Charlevoix, Michigan, the quilt is a unique combination of the traditional patterns Pine Tree and Mariner's Compass. The four pine trees in the corners of the central medallion signify the woods of the family's hometown, Flushing, and the mariner's compass in the center represents the water of Charlevoix.

This quilt has also appeared in *Contemporary Quilts from Traditional Designs* by Caron L. Mosey.

226. Caron L. Mosey (b. 1956). Original design *(Country Barns)* made 1981–1982, Flushing, Genesee County, Michigan. Sean Kempton Mosey, lender. Cotton and cotton blends with polyester filling, 52" x 52", MQP 84.11.

Caron L. Mosey made this bright pictorial quilt for her son, Sean K. Mosey, on his fifth birthday. Sean had requested a quilt that represented his favorite memories of his great-grandmother's farm in Montrose, Michigan. According to the quilter,

The barns stand for the barn at the farm, the chicken wire and the eggs rolling around the outer border in the quilting represent the chickens that should be at the farm but aren't, and the carrots and radishes . . . stand for the vegetable garden Sean and his Grampa Mosey plant each year.

The *Country Barns* quilt has received several awards, including a First-Place Blue Ribbon at the Michigan State Fair in 1982 and a special award at the International Quilt Festival in California, in 1983.

227. Sina R. Phillips (b. 1901). Crow Foot in the Mud made 1983, Muskegon, Muskegon County, Michigan. Collection of Michigan State University Museum. Cotton and polyester, 72″ x 80″, MQP 87.167.

Quilter Sina Phillips's contention that "any colors look good together" is proven in this quilt top that she calls Crow Foot in the Mud. The blocks are pieced entirely of a variety of colored polyester-knit fabrics, which the quilter finds to be "best to stitch." The variety of colors put together in a bold pattern, rather than fine or detailed stitching, is what makes this top "good."

Born in 1901 in Demopolis, Alabama, Phillips learned the art of "making covers" from her mother, Ida Jones, at the age of ten. She has since made quilting a lifetime hobby, producing more than 50 quilts in all. Phillips belongs to a quilting group in Muskegon which meets to exchange patterns and quilt together. To raise money the group puts on chicken dinners. The real heyday of quilting, Phillips noted, was before 1925 when many women would meet for a quilting bee, bring food, and spend the day quilting. Today, says Phillips, when young women get together to quilt, all they do is eat.

228. Sina Phillips (b. 1901). Shirley Pine made 1983, Muskegon, Muskegon County, Michigan. Sina R. Phillips, lender. Polyester, 66″ x 82″, MQP 86.45.

Sina Phillips made this quilt as a gift for her daughter. The pattern is one of her favorites because it reminds her of nature, which she loves. Her goal is to make a Shirley Pine quilt for every member of her family.

A friend of the quilter's lent her a block to copy in making the quilt, which is how she gets most of her quilting ideas. In fact, after 70 years of quilting, Sina Phillips has yet to buy a pattern. The quilt top is made primarily from polyester-knit fabrics, and the back is pieced together from a used embroidered sheet.

Sina Phillips, 1986
Courtesy of Michigan State
University Museum

229. Donna Loudenbeck.
Churn Dash made 1983, Fowler, Clinton County, Michigan. Donna Loudenbeck, lender. Cotton with polyester filling, 76″ x 92″, MQP 85.1374.

The top of this patchwork quilt contains 49 pieced blocks set in a diamond arrangement and separated by solid-blue cotton sashes. Each block is put together with patterned and plain cotton triangles and squares in various colors, to form a design resembling the dash of a butter churn against a white background. Three sides of the quilt are trimmed with a saw-tooth border. Within the pieced blocks, the quilting follows the shape of each square and triangle. The sashes have been quilted with intersecting curvilinear lines.

Using a pattern she had seen in a publication, Donna Loudenbeck of Middleton, Michigan, made the Churn Dash quilt in 1983 while living at Fowler, Michigan, as a gift for her daughter-in-law, Barb Loudenbeck, also of Fowler.

Donna Loudenbeck, 1987
Courtesy of Barb Loudenbeck

230. Helen L. Strong (b. 1914). Baltimore quilt made 1983–1984, Ithaca, Gratiot County, Michigan. Helen Kellogg Strong, lender. Cotton with polyester filling, 78″ x 87″, MQP 85.1419.

Twelve different designs, made from solid and patterned cottons and appliquéd onto squares of unbleached cotton muslin, classify this quilt as a Sampler. Several of the tree designs are similar except for the fruits that they bear. Many portions are three-dimensional, because of the way the fabric has been gathered into folds. Embroidery highlights the details of the designs, and an appliquéd border frames the arrangement of varied motifs. The quiltmaker, Helen Strong of Ithaca, Michigan, created original designs for about half of her blocks and took other designs from a pattern published in *Good Housekeeping* magazine in 1972. Because these latter designs had come from an antique quilt found in Baltimore, Strong calls her quilt a Baltimore quilt. In describing her color scheme, she explains that,

sage green and turkey red are used in every block to some degree and also in the border. Other colors are introduced to lend variety to the other blocks.

Strong recalls that the designs were difficult to execute and that the "most difficult took 6 weeks to complete." To secure her appliquéd top to the unbleached mus-lin back, she "quilted a shadowy design duplicating the complicated vines and leaves or flowers of each block." When she finished her quilt in 1984, Strong embroidered her name and the year on its top. The Baltimore quilt was displayed at the Gratiot County Agricultural Fair of that same year. It received several awards, including a Blue Ribbon, Trophy Ribbon, and trophy for best needlework.

Helen L. Strong was born in 1914 at Jackson, Michigan, to Keith and Harriet Eicher Kellogg. Her father was a farmer. She attended Alma College for four years and in 1936 married Delbert W. Strong, also a farmer. They have three sons: Robert, James, and Thomas. Although both her mother and grandmother made quilts, Strong is a self-taught quilter who has not stopped quilting since she began in 1954. She quilts about 20 hours each week, working on either a lap frame or large frame, and has completed 12 quilts. Strong prefers old-fashioned patterns; colors such as red, green, blue, and white; and 100 per cent cotton, since she thinks its colors "age better than synthetics." She has given a quilt to each of her grandchildren "when a wedding occurs." Helen Strong says that she makes quilts,

because I enjoy creating something useful and beautiful that will be in use long after I am gone from this world. I do not like kits, and I enjoy picking out my own colors and choosing or adapting a pattern from a picture. I find it a soothing, tranquilizing pastime and I hope to do it for many years.

231. Members of Little Quilt Group, piecers; **Katie Wilson,** quilter. Pine Tree *(Cardinal in the Pines)* made 1983–1984, Oscoda, Iosco County, Michigan. Jane VanDenburg, lender. Cotton with polyester filling, 86″ x 103.5″, MQP 86.979.

At Wurtsmith Air Force Base in Oscoda, Michigan, several women belong to the Little Quilt Group and have a tradition of making a quilt top for each member of their group.

This *Cardinal in the Pines* quilt top was pieced by the group for fellow member Jane VanDenburg. The Pine Tree pattern was found in Ruby McKim's *101 Patchwork Patterns* and was modified to include a small red triangle to represent a cardinal. The quilt group hoped this specially designed pattern would help VanDenburg

remember the cardinals in the pine trees she saw from her Oscoda kitchen window. One member, however, thought that the pieced "pine trees" were B-52s, since VanDenburg's husband flew this type of aircraft. VanDenburg pieced a second Pine Tree quilt top for her friend and fellow group member Katie Wilson. In exchange, Wilson did the quilting on this quilt for VanDenburg.

The 23-block textile was machine pieced and hand quilted. The scattered positioning of the red "cardinal" pieces adds an unexpected splash of bright color to the overall green, brown, and white motif. The signatures of the makers—Jane VanDenburg, Katie Wilson, Martha Levardson, Mollie Writer, Megan Legas, Cyndy Swenk, Sharon Danielson, and Marilyn Shealy—were stitched into the quilting and serve to increase the personal significance of this Friendship quilt.

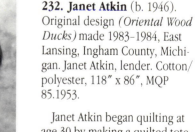

Janet Atkin
Courtesy of Janet Atkin

232. Janet Atkin (b. 1946). Original design *(Oriental Wood Ducks)* made 1983–1984, East Lansing, Ingham County, Michigan. Janet Atkin, lender. Cotton/polyester, 118″ x 86″, MQP 85.1953.

Janet Atkin began quilting at age 30 by making a quilted tote bag. After enrolling in a local quilt class she began exploring nontraditional patterns and creating her own designs. This quilt, entitled *Oriental Wood Ducks*, combines Oriental fabrics, Oriental words, and an Oriental design to create an original visual effect.

233. Deonna Todd Green and **Ione Todd.** Pictorial Blocks *(Todd Family Quilt)* made 1983–1985, Remus, Mecosta County, Michigan. Deonna Todd Green, lender. Painted cotton and cotton, 80″ x 80″, MQP 87.162.

In 1983, six Todd family women—Delores, Marion, and Ione Todd, Deonna and Diana Green, and Carol Norman—began a quilting project to commemorate their family history, at the suggestion of Ken Todd. The women documented with needle and thread significant family events along with the members of their family tree, beginning with their forefather Stephen Todd, who escaped from slavery in Kentucky.

Quilter Deonna Todd explains family history as depicted on the *Todd Family Quilt:*

It was made in 1983 for the Todd Family Reunion at Remus, Michigan. In the corners [is] the Todd Family Coat of Arms. [Starting from left to right] The house on block 12 is that of Stephen and Caroline Todd. Stephen Todd was born in Garrard County, Kentucky, where he escaped slavery. He ran to Indiana, where he met Caroline Kahler, born in Peppertown, Indiana. They ran to Port Huron, Michigan, where they crossed by river-raft, to Canada, where they were married. In 1875, Stephen and Caroline Todd came to Remus, Michigan, via covered wagon. The horse and cannon represent Stephen as "keeper of the horses," in the Civil War. The plots of land are places near Remus, Michigan,

where Stephen and Caroline lived, and raised their family. Around the heart [are] Stephen and Caroline's children, [showing] when they were born, who they married and when they died. Close to the children's blocks are their generations, by color code. Caroline's personal property consisted of twenty-four chickens and two cows. The letter to the Congressman was a request for a disability pension. Stephen and Caroline Todd are buried in Dye County Cemetery, Mecosta County, Michigan.

When the quilt was raffled off to a cousin at one of the Todd family reunions, Deonna Green and Ione Todd decided to make a duplicate for their immediate family to keep. The quilt is now put on temporary loan to close family

*Deonna Todd Green and Ione Todd, ca. 1985
Courtesy of Deonna Todd Green*

members so that they can enjoy looking at and learning from it. Occasionally, Green brings it to the annual Old Settler's Reunion held in Mecosta, Michigan, so that other family members and friends can see it.

234. Jane Akkala (b. 1918). Log Cabin made 1983–1985, Big Bay, Marquette County, Michigan. Jane L. Akkala, lender. Cotton with cotton filling, 87″ x 97.5″, MQP 86.973.

This reversible Log Cabin quilt was made over a two-year period by a woman for whom it holds deep personal significance. Jane L. Akkala explains that making this quilt helped carry her through an "emotion-laden period" in her life. She began working on it when her husband was quite ill and continued working on it through the period of his death and her adjustment that followed. When she met and married her present husband, he strongly encouraged her to complete it. Now that it is finished, she states simply, "I look at it lovingly."

Akkala began quilting in 1979 when she was working as a school principal in Japan, relying on booklets and magazines sent to her from the United States. She found that the Japanese do much patchwork but little quilting.

Akkala has made four quilts and is currently working on one using silk kimono fabric (most of it with gold designs) that she

Jane Akkala
Courtesy of Jane Akkala

bought in Japan. She has presented a quilt to each of her children's families; her goal is that eventually each grandchild will receive a quilt.

Akkala's reasons for quilting articulate what other quilters have come to appreciate about this timeless craft. She finds it relaxing and it gives her a sense of accomplishment as well as a creative outlet. Beyond that she affirms, "it passes on to my children some of our heritage and gives continuity to our family."

235. Gwen Marston and **Joe Cunningham** (b. 1952). Original design *(Coxcomb)* made 1983–1985, St. James, Beaver Island, Charlevoix County, Michigan. Gwen Marston and Joe Cunningham, lenders. Cotton with polyester filling, 72.5″ x 79″, MQP 85.1654.

Using traditional methods of paper cutting to create their pattern, the makers of this pieced and appliquéd quilt produced the original design resembling a coxcomb, which is repeated in the four main motifs of the top. Begun in 1983 and completed in 1985, the quilt was made at St. James on Beaver Island, Michigan, by Gwen Marston and Joe

Allen Cunningham. The coxcomb designs have been pieced out of red patterned cotton and appliquéd onto four, square, white blocks separated by white sashes. The green and red colors of the central medallion are repeated in a border of appliquéd scalloped swags. The quilting designs include diagonal lines, feathers, vines, squares, and outlining. The quilt was pictured in *Lady's Circle Patchwork Quilts* of November 1985.

Marston is a full-time quilter who is primarily self-taught, although she has had one year of instruction from Mennonite quilters. She credits her close friendship with quilter Mary Schafer as another source of her quilting

knowledge. Cunningham was born in 1952 at Flint, Michigan, to James L. and Janice Woodin Cunningham. His father is a retired General Motors employee, and his mother is a bus driver who makes tied quilts as gifts. In addition to being a quilter, Cunningham is a musician and writer. He began quilting at the age of 25 by making a Drunkard's Path wall hanging. Marston and Cunningham work on their quilts 40 to 60 hours each week in the second-floor studio of their home on Beaver Island, using an old-fashioned frame and hand-

made cardboard templates for their patterns, many of which are original designs. They prefer natural materials, such as 100 per cent cotton and 100 per cent raw silk. The couple has made more than 100 quilts, which are commissioned or sold through galleries. They also lecture and conduct quilting workshops throughout the country, including quilting seminars on Beaver Island. Cunningham says, "For five years, quilts have been my life" and adds that he even "built a house on an island to store and make quilts in."

146

Joe Cunningham
and Gwen Marston
Courtesy of Keva Photographics

236. Gwen Marston and **Joe Cunningham** (b. 1952). Lone Star made 1983–1985, St. James, Beaver Island, Charlevoix County, Michigan. Gwen Marston and Joe Cunningham, lenders. Cotton with polyester filling, 72.25″ x 77.5″, MQP 85.1655.

Inspired by an old crib quilt, Gwen Marston and Joe Cunningham made this appliquéd quilt in 1983–85. They describe it as "our attempt to make a rather garish Pennsylvania Dutch style quilt." The central medallion, an eight-pointed star, has been pieced from pink, rose, and green cotton fabrics and placed against a square white cotton background that is framed with rose-and-green sashes. Within the framed area, appliquéd tulips and a flowering vine surround the pieced star. A wide white border, appliquéd with a second, larger vine, completes the top, which is hand quilted with scallop, chain, flower, leaf, and outline designs. A photograph of Marston and Cunningham's Lone Star appliqué quilt appeared in the *Quilter's Newsletter Magazine* in the summer of 1984.

237. Karen Dorr, Linda Tergman, Sally Hatcher, Joyce Hubbard. Sampler, original designs made 1983–1985, Grass Lake, Jackson County, Michigan. G. Putnam and Caroline E. Dorr, lenders. Cotton with polyester filling, 94″ x 112″, MQP 85.191.

This Sampler quilt was made to commemorate G. Putnam and Caroline E. Dorr's 50th wedding anniversary. Each member of the family who collaborated on this project made a block and signed his or her name in the border. These blocks frame the family home, which is depicted in the center block.

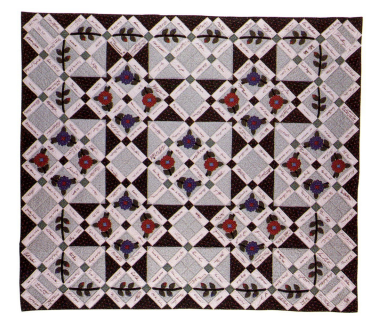

Mary Blandford and Ami Simms
Courtesy of Ami Simms

238. Mary E. Blandford (b. 1948). Original design *(Wild Rose Celebrity Quilt)* made 1983–1986, Otisville, Genesee County, Michigan. Mary E. Blandford, lender. Cotton, 78″ x 88″, MQP 85.32. See 239.

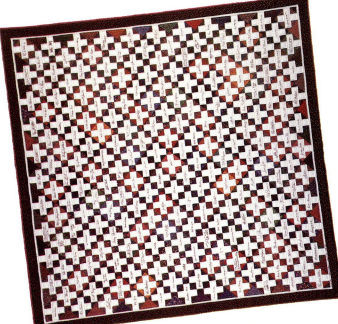

239. Ami Simms (b. 1954). Original design made 1983–1984, Flint, Genesee County, Michigan. Ami Simms, lender. Cotton with polyester filling, 89″ x 89″, MQP 85.46.

On October 17, 1971, an article appeared in the *Flint Journal* which told of Mrs. Harold J. Aurand of Clio, Michigan, who had collected signatures of famous people over a 35-year period and had fashioned several quilt tops from the fabrics signed. Inspired by the article, Mary Blandford and her friend Ami Simms, both of Flint, Michigan, spent nearly two years collecting signatures from politicians, movie and television stars, athletes, scientists, and others. They collected the signatures on strips of muslin, two and one-half inches wide by six and one-half inches long. The signatures were then embroidered by the quilters, and the pieces of cloth were used as part of the design in two Signature quilts.

Blandford's quilt, of original design, titled *Wild Rose Celebrity Quilt,* uses the signature blocks to frame appliquéd roses arranged in groups of four. Simms also designed the pattern used in her quilt, but has not given it a name. Simms used more than 30 different fabrics to represent the variety of backgrounds and accomplishments of those people included in her quilt.

The quilts include signatures from notables such as astronaut Bob Crippen, former Presidents Gerald Ford and Jimmy Carter, and popcorn king Orville Redenbacher. Blandford collected 228 names for her quilt, and Simms's quilt includes 221 signatures, including her own. Even though some of their requests were denied, the rejection letters are treasured by the two women almost as much as the autographs. The two quilters were turned down by President and Mrs. Ronald Reagan; Diana, Princess of Wales; and atheist Madalyn Murray O'Hare. O'Hare's reply, minus a signature, as reported in the *Flint Journal* of November 10, 1984, asks:

There is a matter of life and death in the human community in the build-up of nuclear weapons based on the Judeo-Christian concept of Armageddon and the destruction of Earth. Our president speaks in terms of that final holocaust— and you are making a quilt?!

240. Ami Simms (b. 1954), designer and piecer; **Polly Yoder,** quilter. Amish Center Diamond made 1985, Flint, Genesee County, Michigan. Ami Simms, lender. Cotton with polyester filling, 80″ x 80″, MQP 87.190.

Ami Simms's Amish Center Diamond quilt was inspired by the photograph on the cover of *A Gallery of Amish Quilts,* by Robert Bishop and Elizabeth Safanda. Simms drafted and pieced the quilt, which was quilted by Polly

Yoder of Middlebury, Indiana. Simms owns this quilt, while another identical quilt was a gift to her mother, Beebe Moss.

Simms lived with an Old Order Amish family in Middlebury, Indiana, when researching her thesis while a student at Kalamazoo College in Kalamazoo, Michigan. It was during this time that Simms took her first stitches in a quilt. Simms is now very active in organizing quilt shows and teaching quilting.

241. Annamae Kelly (b. 1915). Original design *(Fractured Iris)* made 1984, Royal Oak, Oakland County, Michigan. Frederick W. Arnold, D.D.S., lender. Hand-silk-screened cotton with polyester filling, 59″ x 59″, MQP 86.471.

The daughter of French-Canadian Americans, Annamae Lenaway Kelly began quilting at age 15 and shares her interest in the craft with her maternal grandmother, her sister Sr. Mary A. Lenaway (see no. 175), and her daughter Susan Arnold. Mother of eight, Kelly is a quilt designer, teacher, and lecturer. She studied art at the Center for Creative Studies, and by 1986 she had designed and made 182 quilts. Originally a painter, Kelly describes her transition to quilting this way:

In 1974 I turned in my paints temporarily and turned to fabrics as an art medium. That was the year I made my first quilt. Interestingly enough, I had used silk-screened squares combined with bright prints for my quilt which won a prize at the Bi-Centennial Quilt Show in Warren, Michigan.

Fractured Iris continues Kelly's use of silk screening as a quilting technique. Kelly silk screened the image of irises on fabric and then cut the fabric into pieces and rearranged them, "fracturing" the iris. She describes how she completed the design:

I thought the result [of rearranging the pieces of fabric] interesting but it left a blank space in the center which I then painted with a feather wreath.

Kelly quilted the wall hanging in straight-line stitching.

Kelly says:

Quilt designing and the actual sewing and quilting process is a very rewarding way for me to spend out the remainder of my time here on earth. I am now a widow, and what could have been long, lonely days are filled with a happy, fulfilling occupation. Each stitch becomes a prayer that I don't lose my eyesight or that my fingers don't get too stiff from this

Annamae Kelly, 1986
Courtesy of Annamae Kelly

pesky arthritis. All quilters know that a good quilter needs nimble fingers and good eyesight, and lots of imagination!

Vivian Gottlieb, ca. 1980
Courtesy of Vivian Gottlieb

242. Vivian Sosna Gottlieb (b. 1930). Original design *(Monkeys in the Jungle)* made 1984, Flint, Genesee County, Michigan. Vivian Sosna Gottlieb, lender. Cotton, silk, and polyester satin with polyester filling, 49″ x 66″, MQP 85.86.

A resident of Flint, Michigan, artist Vivian Gottlieb earned a Bachelor of Design degree from the University of Michigan in 1952 and has worked in oil and watercolor paint, ceramics, photography, collage, and drawing. Gottlieb added quilting to her list of artistic methods at the age of 30. She explains,

> *I make quilts as another facet of my artistic expression. In my life as an artist, I am now working in cloth and thread instead of paint, clay, wood or stone.*

Her work in cloth and thread has yielded more than 100 quilts to date and earned Gottlieb recognition through a one-woman quilt exhibition at the Flint Institute of Arts in 1974 and Honorable Mention in the Great Quilts of America competition in 1978. Although neither her quilts nor her methods are traditional, Gottlieb's practice of giving quilts to her children at marriage and the births of grandchildren is.

The blocks at the bottom of the quilt resemble a traditional patchwork pattern, while the top of the quilt contains two white monkeys with curling tails set against a blue area surrounded by leaves. Gottlieb describes this quilt as

> *designed as a way of using the monkey's tails as an abstract design. The leaves in the background are also part of the abstract design. The traditional quilt blocks in the lower half give the design stability. The quilting stitches accentuate the shapes and flow of the design.*

The abstract curvilinear quilting stitches actually serve two purposes. In the upper portion of the quilt, the curved quilting echoes the swirls of the monkeys' tails; at the bottom, the curves are a counterpoint to the horizontal and vertical orientation of the sewn blocks.

243. Emogean Morden (b. 1917), piecer; **Mrs. Ted Wilson,** quilter. Sampler made 1984, Clinton, Lenawee County, Michigan. Emogean Morden, lender. Cotton, 96″ x 106″, MQP 85.174.

Using a book of 12-inch quilt-block patterns, Emogean Morden selected and pieced the 30 different blocks in this Sampler quilt. The top was quilted by Mrs. Ted Wilson and was shown at the Mason Methodist Church quilt show in August 1984. Morden has also made a Sampler quilt of 16-inch blocks and a Christmas quilt. Morden, who began quilting at age 62, plans to make a quilt for each of her five children.

Emogean Morden
Courtesy of Emogean Morden

244. Laura Wierda (b. 1959). Rainbow Sherbet made 1984, Holland, Ottawa County, Michigan. Gregory Nelis, lender. Cotton with polyester filling, 42″ x 45″, MQP 85.64.

Laura Wierda presented this crib quilt to Kevin and Colleen Nelis upon the birth of their son Gregory. Machine pieced and hand appliquéd, with upside-down and right-side-up ice cream cones, the pattern was found in a spring/summer 1982 issue of *Quiltmaker*. Wierda's selection of pastel colored fabrics for the rainbow border and background was inspired by the colors of rainbow sherbet.

245. Katherine Anderson Mattson (b. 1940). Eight-Pointed Star made 1984, Marquette, Marquette County, Michigan. Katherine Anderson Mattson, lender. Cotton with polyester filling, 94″ x 94″, MQP 86.949.

Katherine Anderson Mattson sent out announcements to her close friends when her Eight-Pointed Star quilt was finished— "like a birth announcement" she says. This pieced quilt uses a red, white, and blue motif in alternating star blocks and solid red blocks. In addition to the Dresden Plate design on the red blocks, chain, line, and outline quilting have been used on the quilt.

Mattson was born of Finnish/ Swedish parents in Sagola, Michigan. She sews, does calligraphy, and is active in the Marquette County Quilters Association. Other quilters in her family are her mother, Mildren Wickman Anderson, and her sister, Susan Anderson of Iron Mountain, Michigan.

Mattson's Eight-Pointed Star quilt was displayed at the 1985 Marquette County Harvest Festival where it won a Blue Ribbon, Best-of-Show Rosette, and a Michigan State Fair Exhibitor's Award.

Katherine Anderson Mattson
Courtesy of Katherine Anderson Mattson

151

246. Wilma Rosevear (b. 1914). Pictorial Block *(Scottish Family Quilt)* made 1984, Clare, Clare County, Michigan. Wilma Rosevear, lender. Cotton with polyester filling, 80″ x 97″, MQP 85.135.

In this pictorial quilt Wilma Rosevear depicts the ethnic heritage of her ancestors, the Keyes family, who originated from the Key of Dundocket, Scotland. The tartan materials used in the quilt sashing and on the costumed figures and the embroidered thistles and heather serve to accent the Scottish character of the quilt.

Wilma Rosevear
Courtesy of Wilma Rosevear

247. Mary Lee Smith (b. 1940). Whig Rose made 1984–1985, Whitmore Lake, Washtenaw County, Michigan. Mary Lee Smith, lender. Cotton with cotton filling, 90″ x 90″, MQP 85.253.

A full-scale quilted version of a Whig Rose woven coverlet, this textile was made to be entered in the first American Quilter's Society quilt contest in Paducah, Kentucky, in April 1985. Quiltmaker Mary Lee Smith began the quilt when she was 32 years old. She hails from a family that includes quiltmakers on both her mother's and her father's side. Smith is active in the Heritage Quilters of Brighton, Michigan, and usually makes quilts for new babies of her nieces and nephews.

Mary Lee Smith
Courtesy of Mary Lee Smith

248. Linda Cragg Buzon (b.
1947). Original design (*Arizona Sunrise*) made 1984–1985, Saginaw, Saginaw County, Michigan. Linda Cragg Buzon, lender. Cotton with polyester filling, 42″ x 42″, MQP 86.128.

The original design of this Hawaiian-type appliquéd wall quilt evokes memories of her life in Arizona for the maker, Linda Cragg Buzon of Saginaw, Michigan. Buzon developed her design after attending a workshop on Hawaiian-style quilting taught by Caron Mosey in 1983 at the Saginaw Historical Museum. Completed in 1985, the wall quilt features a central gray ring composed of palm tree motifs and other foliage-like elements, silhouetted against an undulating gold background. A gray border, containing a gold sun in each corner, completes the design. The intricate quilting echoes the irregular shapes of the various forms. Buzon says that this is "the first and last Hawaiian quilt I'll make. It was fun to do—but too much quilting!"

Buzon was born in 1947 at Grosse Pointe Farms, Michigan, to Richard and Margaret Cragg. She received a bachelor's degree in medical technology from Wayne State University. Married

Linda Cragg Buzon
Courtesy of Linda Cragg Buzon

in 1970 to physician Gualberto Buzon, she and her husband have two daughters and a son.

When she was 31 years old, Buzon learned to quilt at a quilt store in Phoenix, Arizona, by making a quilted apple. Since then, using a roll-type frame made by her father, she has made ten quilts, some of which she has given as wedding and baby shower gifts. She prefers all-cotton fabrics, polyester fillings, and appliqué patterns. Buzon belongs to both the Saginaw Piecemakers Quilt Guild and the Arizona Quilters Guild. Three of her quilts have won prizes at the Great Lakes Quilt Contests of 1982 and 1984, held in Mount Clemens, Michigan.

249. Winifred L. Riddle (b. 1948). Original design: Mandala variation made 1984–1985, Cheboygan, Cheboygan County, Michigan. Winifred L. Riddle, lender. Cotton and polished cotton with fleece filling, 45″ x 45″, MQP 86.84.

This wall hanging, completed in 1985, was begun by Winifred Louise Riddle of Cheboygan, Michigan, as a study of the Mandala style of piecework. Riddle based her original design on an umbrella she had seen pictured in a magazine. Later, after seeing a book on Mandala quilts, she began her 45 inch wall hanging, using a compass and protracter to create her design, which is pieced from solid and patterned cotton fabrics in red, rust, aqua, and peach. Hand-quilted straight lines at quarter-inch intervals join the top to a filling and the peach polished-cotton back. The wall hanging was exhibited at the Rivertown Patchworkers Quilt Show held at Cheboygan, Michigan, in 1985.

Riddle was born in 1948 at Lansing, Michigan, to Albert E. and Vivian Bateman Powis, Jr. Married in 1969 to David C. Riddle, she has one son, Wesley. Riddle began making quilts in 1978 when she took a sampler class through the Manchester Art Guild. She says that her teacher, Sarah Deasey, "managed to pass along not only the knowledge to make a quilt but also the desire to have pride in my accomplishments." Since that time, Riddle has begun 14 quilts and completed 3, "working whenever and wherever possible." She belongs to the Rivertown Quilters of Cheboygan and the AuSable Quilt Guild of Grayling. Riddle adds,

Before quilting, I tried many types of handwork and enjoyed it all, but quilts and quilting have taken over all of my interest in handwork.

250. Winifred L. Riddle (b. 1948). Nancy's Fancy made 1979–1984, Grass Lake, Gaylord, Indian River, and Cheboygan, Michigan. Winifred L. Riddle, lender. Cotton with polyester filling, 75″ x 90″, MQP 86.85.

Winifred Riddle made this quilt between 1979 and 1984 while living successively in the Michigan towns of Grass Lake, Gaylord, Indian River, and Cheboygan. After seeing a picture of a quilt block in a quilting magazine, she drafted the pattern, which she calls Nancy's Fancy. Eight-pointed stars are set within interlocking squares to create an intricate and intriguing design. The use of two alternating schemes of bold, contrasting colors, placed against a white background heightens the visual impact of the pattern.

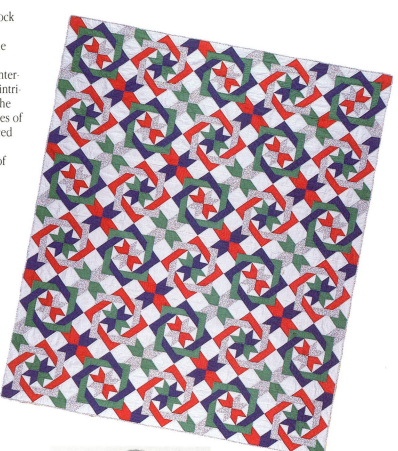

Winifred L. Riddle
Courtesy of Winifred L. Riddle

Carol Robinson Hare, 1985
Courtesy of Carol Robinson Hare

251. Carol Robinson Hare (b. 1929). *Star Shimmer* made 1985, Saginaw, Saginaw County, Michigan. Carol Robinson Hare, lender. Cotton and cotton blends with synthetic filling, 72″ x 86″, MQP 86.249.

Like quiltmakers of past centuries who used pattern books for design information and inspiration, Carol Hare found the design for her *Star Shimmer* in the fall/winter 1983 issue of *Quiltmaker* magazine. In 1984 Hare began work on *Star Shimmer*, adding her own design for the triple border to the magazine pattern. She finished the quilt in early 1985 and showed it in the Piecemaker's Quilt Show at the Saginaw County Historical Museum in March of that year.

The abstract jagged star forms of the pieced blocks have rays in various colors. The quilting matches the piecing in both complexity and design. Quilting stitches outline each pieced star and decorate both the background and the three borders. The contemporary star motif of the piecing is complemented by a more traditional eight-pointed star that is quilted repeatedly on the mottled-blue background and into the first navy-blue border. Smaller stars also appear in the quilting on the main body of the quilt. The outer navy-blue border is quilted with cables, while long- and short-link chain quilting completes the catalog of quilting stitches that Hare chose for her *Star Shimmer*. (See no. 185 for another quilt by Hare.)

252. Mrs. Walter A. McLean,
designer and embroiderer; **Roberta F. Stine,** quilter. *Martha's Birthday Quilt* made 1985, Cass City, Bay County, Michigan. Martha Anderton Campbell, lender. Cotton with cotton filling, 100″ x 150″, MQP 86.298.

Christmas 1985 was made memorable for Martha Campbell when she unwrapped her gift from long-time friend Willie Maie McLean and discovered this 12-and-a-half foot, hand-embroidered quilt. *Martha's Birthday Quilt* was conceived and designed by McLean, who did the embroidery. Assembled by Mrs. William Martin and Marjorie Ward, it was quilted by Roberta F. Stine. It is constructed of 150 embroidered navy-blue and white squares, of which 147 contain handprints, signatures, and birth-

Mrs. Walter A. McLean with Martha's Birthday Quilt, 1985
Courtesy of Mrs. Walter A. McLean and Martha Anderton Campbell

dates of Martha Campbell's family and friends. Embroidered on the back is the inscription "All for you, Martha, in gratitude for your friendship past, present and future, Willie Maie   1985."

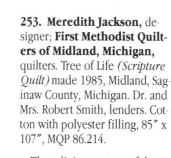

253. Meredith Jackson, designer; **First Methodist Quilters of Midland, Michigan,** quilters. Tree of Life *(Scripture Quilt)* made 1985, Midland, Saginaw County, Michigan. Dr. and Mrs. Robert Smith, lenders. Cotton with polyester filling, 85″ x 107″, MQP 86.214.

The religious nature of the various block patterns in this medallion quilt reflects the character of the group of women who jointly created this unusual piece over seven months in 1985. Members of the same church in Midland, Meredith Jackson and her friends Aleta Smith, Phyllis Syverud, Inarae Young, Lillian Richardson, Karen Gray, Alice Ralston, and Sally Roberson are known as the First United Methodist Quilters. They meet weekly, either in the church or at a member's home, to practice their craft. They make quilts both for home use or, as in

the case of *Scripture Quilt,* as fundraisers for their church.

Scripture Quilt is thematically organized; blocks of abstract designs representing both Old and New Testament topics are set diamond-fashion around the central rectangular medallion of the Tree of Life. Starting at the upper right corner and continuing clockwise around the perimeter of the quilt, the 14 blocks represent: Crown of Thorns, Joseph's Coat, Jacob's Ladder, Temple Court, Children of Israel, Dove in the Window, Cross within Cross, Job's Troubles, Steps to the Altar, Golgotha, World without End, Christmas Star, Star of Bethlehem, and Eye of God. Subdued grays, pinks, navy blues, and a strong burgundy in both print and solid-color cotton fabrics complete the color scheme of the 14 outer blocks and the Tree of Life medallion.

254. Jean Eitel (b. 1941). Tree of Life variation made 1985, Palm Beach, Florida. Jean Eitel, lender. Cotton with cotton filling, 60" x 66", MQP 85.1692.

Based on the traditional Tree of Life design, this quilt was created as a form of self-therapy while the quiltmaker was taking care of a sick relative. Jean Eitel, of North Palm Beach, Florida, began her quilt in December of 1984 and completed it in January of 1985. Her membership in the Episcopal Church and interest in theology give special significance to the design of her quilt. The tree that dominates the center of the top is made from cotton shapes appliquéd onto a white background. The birds, which Eitel found in a printed chintz panel, were cut out and appliquéd onto the tree. Other chintz birds appear in the vine design of the border. Eitel used feather and clam-shell designs, cross-hatching, and outlining to quilt the top to a cotton filling and back. Her quilt has been exhibited at the Barrington Folk Art Museum, Delray Beach, Florida, where it was judged Best of Show; the National Quilting Asso-

ciation Show, Sanford, Florida, where it won First Place among appliquéd quilts; and the American Quilter's Society Show, Paducah, Kentucky.

Eitel was born at Flint, Michigan, to Max H. and Ernestine Havers Wright, the owners of a restaurant business. She lived in Michigan until 1946, when her family moved to Florida. She is married to Fredrick G. Eitel, a design engineer, and has three children. Eitel majored in visual arts at Palm Beach Junior College

and was drawn to textile arts. She began quilting in 1979, learning her skills from Helen Van Epp and continuing a family tradition, since Eitel's grandmother, great-aunt, great-grandmother, and great-great-grandmother had all been quilters. Working at home about six hours each day, she has made a total of 24 quilts, including two Tree of Life quilts. A member of the National Quilt Association, the American Quilter's Society, and the American-International Quilt Association, Eitel also belongs to a quilting

group, the Sand Dollar Quilters of North Palm Beach. She sells many of her quilts through galleries and has given others as wedding gifts and to "celebrate a healing of a friend from cancer."

Eitel is the editor of *Quilt, Country Quilts,* and *Old Fashioned Patchwork* magazines. She has also written a book on quilting, *Creative Quiltmaking in the Mandala Tradition,* and has conducted many quilting workshops throughout the country. Eitel says that she makes quilts

because I have a compulsion to work with fabric, color, form and texture. Each finished quilt leads to a new idea, a new design. I just can't stop.

*Katherine Kay Vielmetti Peters
wearing her great-grandmother's
wedding dress*
*Courtesy of Katherine Kay
Vielmetti Peters*

255. Katherine Kay Vielmetti Peters

(b. 1938). Original design *(Sauna)* made 1985, Marquette, Marquette County, Michigan. Steven Clark Vielmetti, lender. Cotton and cotton/polyester with polyester filling, 65.5″ x 88.25″, MQP 86.961.

Katherine Kay Vielmetti Peters, a resident of Marquette, Michigan, made this quilt in 1985 as a Christmas present for her son Stephen. Peters, who used a photograph of the sauna Stephen had helped build as the source for her design, said she enjoyed working on this quilt and especially "liked quilting the smoke curls in the border." The quilt was on public display at the fall 1985 Marquette County Quilters Association Show.

Although quilting has long been a family tradition for Peters, she is the only family member who now quilts. Her great-grandmother was an avid quilter and made 15 quilts for her own dowry. Peters remarks that she's glad she didn't know about that custom or she'd "still be single!" Peters also remembers her aunt pulling family quilts from a hope chest:

> *Each was different . . . she saved them from use . . . I also remember sleeping under family quilts at my grandmother's home in Detroit. One had material with 1776-1876 dates.*

Peters is a member of the Marquette County Quilters Association, attends monthly meetings ("which are like parties"), and goes to quilt shows every other year. Since she began quilting in 1982, she has made three full-size quilts and has conducted workshops on quilted feathers. (See also no. 25 for a quilt by Peters's great-grandmother.)

256. Bonnie Bus.

Pickle Dish variation made 1985, Haslett, Ingham County, Michigan. Bonnie Bus, lender. Cotton, 81″ x 86.5″, MQP 87.19.

This quilt is a contemporary version of the traditional pattern called Pickle Dish. To make the quilt, the blocks from the original pattern were doubled in size and arranged in a bold geometric pattern. It won First Prize at the 1985 Great Lakes Biennial Quilt Show. Quiltmaker Bonnie Bus says that traditional patterns frequently provide the basis for her quilt designs. Her color selection reflects her love of nature. In this quilt, the colors were inspired by the summer sky.

257. Maryellen Hains (b. 1942), piecer; **Amish women of Centreville, Michigan,** quilters. Original design *(Black and White Series: Diptych I)* made 1985–1986, Kalamazoo, Kalamazoo County, Michigan. Maryellen Hains, lender. Cotton and cotton/ polyester with polyester filling, 91.5″ x 73.5″, MQP 86.617.

Brooklyn-born Maryellen Hains is Professor of English at Western Michigan University and a self-

taught quilt artist. She has been quilting since 1980, when she made a Michigan map quilt as her first project. A member of the Log Cabin Quilters, she spends as many as 40 hours weekly making quilts in her basement studio. All of Hains's quilt patterns are original designs, and she prefers to use cotton and cotton-blend fabrics with polyester filling. Hains sells her quilts through her company, Contemporary Quilts.

Diptych I is part of Hains's black-and-white series of quilted works, which she is currently completing with the support of a grant from the Michigan Council for the Arts. The quilt was on display in the 1986 Area Show at the Kalamazoo Institute of Arts.

Hains uses reds, greens, and blues sparingly here to accent the predominantly black-and-white pattern. She describes the combination of patterns in this two-

piece work as "checked top with 'fish eye' exaggeration, random blocks on lower section, plus 'kite' floats." The quilting on this contemporary abstract quilt outlines the various small pieces, including the "kite" forms, and covers the surface of the quilt in curves. Hains designed the quilting pattern so that her signature is incorporated into the stitching.

Henrietta Fausnaugh and her
two grandchildren, 1985
Courtesy of Henrietta Fausnaugh

258. Henrietta Fausnaugh (b. 1942). Star Sampler *(Star Medallion Sampler Quilt)* made 1985–1986, Freeland, Saginaw County, Michigan. Henrietta Fausnaugh, lender. Cotton/polyester with polyester filling, 104″ x 104″, MQP 86.255.

An 11-month sewing project for quilter Henrietta Fausnaugh, this king-sized Star Sampler quilt adorns her own bed during much of the year. Fausnaugh, who has been an active quilter since 1984, spends two to three hours daily on her quilting and is a member of both Piecemakers Quilt Club and Holy Spirit Quilt Club in her hometown of Saginaw, Michigan. Fausnaugh chose prints and solid colors in varying shades of her favorite blue and arranged them against white muslin to make up the different star pattern blocks. In addition to outlining the individual pieces in the star blocks with quilting, Fausnaugh used quilted leaves and flowers and straight-line quilting at one-inch intervals to complete her quilt.

259. Thelma Caruss. *Kaleidoscope* made 1986, Lansing, Eaton County, Michigan. Thelma Caruss, lender. Cotton, 69″ x 76″, MQP 87.163.

Thelma Caruss has lived on the same farm in Eaton County for more than 50 years. She learned to quilt from her mother, an excellent seamstress, who once helped to make Mrs. R.E. Olds's wedding dress, and who had quilted for as long as Caruss can remember. Of her mother she recalls,

In those days, the houses weren't very warm. We usually made quilts during the winter so we'd have them for the next winter. [My mother] sewed a lot so she always had a lot of scraps to use.

Caruss has made more than 60 quilts in the last 14 years and has given them all away. Each of her 6 children and 14 grandchildren, all of her sisters, and her 12 nieces and nephews have received at least a couple of her quilts as gifts. "I've never sold one," she says.

For 35 years, Caruss met once a week with a quilting group in Dimondale, Michigan. She remembers:

I'd pick up two or three ladies on the way and we took potluck dinner. It was a big hall and we had two quilts going at a time, one for quilting and one for tying, because some of the ladies couldn't quilt, their hands were so arthritic. . . . We didn't charge too much money, I think we got around $25.00 or $30.00 for quilting them for other people. The money all went for projects around Dimondale. We helped the Boy Scouts when they wanted to go to camp and needed tents. We always gave to the Red Cross . . . . We never kept any money.

Caruss remembers one special quilting project:

I had a friend who died of cancer . . . . She had a quilt almost made, almost quilted, when she died . . . . It was all little squares, a Double Irish Chain. A couple of us had offered to quilt it, [but] her husband said, "My wife said you're the only one who can quilt like she does." It took me 100 hours to finish that quilt.

Kaleidoscope, a medallion-style pieced quilt, uses a variety of interesting fabrics in an Oriental design that Caruss borrowed from a photo in a quilt calendar.

Thelma Caruss and her
husband, Byron
Courtesy of Michigan State
University Museum

260. JoAnn Shelby, designer; **Laestadian Church members,** quilters. Pictorial Blocks made 1986, Marquette, Marquette County, Michigan. Corinne Frederickson, lender. Cotton and cotton/polyester with polyester filling, 81″ x 97″, MQP 86.869.

When members of the Laestadian Church of Marquette, Michigan, decided to make a quilt to raffle as part of a fundraising effort, they turned to JoAnn Shelby, a member of the Marquette County Quilters Association. Shelby designed the blocks, and a group of church members made and put them together. Begun in February and completed in July 1986, the result of their effort is this pictorial quilt, which reflects Shelby's love of nature in Michigan's Upper Peninsula. Each of the pictorial sections depict wildlife scenes such as pileated wood-

peckers, a fish, trillium, jack-in-the-pulpits, chickadees, raccoons, and a moose. Appliqué, piecing, embroidery, and painting (on the fish) techniques are used in the pictorial blocks, which are framed in dark brown sashes. The present owner of the quilt, Corinne Frederickson of Minneapolis, Minnesota, won the quilt at the 1986 raffle.

The Marquette County Quilters Association has traditionally made quilts to raise funds for public buildings and various charity causes in the community. Shelby, a self-taught quilter who works in her home studio, has been very active in this group. Her quilting interests have often focused on wall hangings and clothing, in addition to regular full-size quilts.

---

261. Marcia Waara. Eight-Pointed Star *(Evening Star)* made 1986, Marquette, Marquette County, Michigan. Marcia Waara, lender. Cotton and muslin with polyester filling, 39.5″ x 54.5″, MQP 86.1027.

In *Evening Star* Marcia Waara uses subtle prints as stars on an off-white background. Although made in 1986, the quilt has an older appearance largely because of the fabrics that were chosen. Waara admits loving "old country stuff" and old quilts, so she made this quilt to "look old."

The pieced star blocks have been set alternately with solid off-white blocks quilted with a feathered circle design. Waara intended that this quilt would lie folded at the foot of her daughter's bed to complement the Log Cabin quilt already covering the bed. Waara has done other quilting for home use and display, including wall hangings.

Marcia Waara
Courtesy of Marcia Waara

262. Marcia Waara. *Hands to Work, Hearts to God,* made 1986, Marquette, Marquette County, Michigan. Marcia Waara, lender. Cotton, 35″ x 35″, MQP 87.189.

Inspired by a quilt she had seen in *The Quilt Digest,* Marcia Waara designed this wall hanging with traditional and original motifs that have special meaning for her. Waara describes the significance in this way:

It was fun because I incorporated special things from my life—squirrel on the roof,

baskets and quilts because I love to make them, my Cavalier King Charles Spaniel.

The Flying Geese, Bear Paw, and Pine Tree motifs signify the Waaras' home in the woods of Michigan's Upper Peninsula. The three stars represent Waara, her husband, and their daughter. The Heart in Hand symbol is borrowed from the Shakers. Waara adds, ". . . lately I find myself using antique fabrics and 'aging' my quilts to give a time-worn appearance."

263. Donna Esch (b. 1918). Kansas Sunflower made 1986, Mio, Oscoda County, Michigan. Donna Esch, lender. Cotton and cotton/polyester with polyester filling, 96″ x 104″, MQP 87.165.

Interviewed at her Fairview, Michigan, home in the summer of 1986, Donna Esch reported that her earliest recollections of quilt-related activities were her experiences of piecing and embroidering at age eight. She said that growing up in the Mio-Fairview Mennonite community "everybody in the community quilted—all had homemade bedding." She also recalled "quiltings" during the winter when quilters would begin around nine o'clock in the morning and quilt to, but not past, supper time.

Esch recounted several strong family quilt traditions in her area. She received her first quilt as a present for her hope chest and, thanks to gifts from various relatives, had 16 quilts on the day

she was married, including a Friendship quilt from Detroit, three from her grandmother, and "some" from her mother.

Esch regularly participates in the annual Mennonite Relief Sale held at the Oscoda County Fairgrounds and in 1986 made two crib quilts, one queen-size quilt, and one machine-made coverlet to be auctioned off. She also makes quilts for other Mennonite communities that have relief sales or fundraising efforts. For example, she recently made a Kansas Sunflower quilt of her own design for a quilt auction held by Heston College (a Mennonite college) in Kansas to raise scholarship money for students.

In addition to her quilting activities with family and fellow church members, Esch also shows her quilts in secular quilt shows. Her most recent venture has been a quilted recreation of the 26-star Michigan flag in honor of the state's sesquicentennial.

Donna Esch, 1986
Courtesy of Michigan State University Museum

161

Community Education program. The talent for design and craft she now shares with others is evident in this large, elaborate, pieced-cotton quilt made over a period of about 15 months. Aquino made it as a gift for her daughter, Abigail, for whom she named it, explaining, "because I love her."

The quilting patterns used in this quilt are (from the outside edge to the center): cable/heart (a border Aquino designed herself), clamshells, and hearts and flowers. The piecing was done both by machine and by hand, and the quilting fully by hand. The completed work was on public display at the West Michigan Quilt Guild show in April 1986 and again the following month at the Holland Tulip Festival.

Aquino, whose maternal grandmother, Marie Sellers Carroll, also quilted, was born in Lansing, Michigan, and now resides in Kentwood, Michigan, with her husband, Joel, and their three children.

264. Gale Ellen Aquino (b. 1952). Original design *(Abigail)* made 1986, Kentwood, Kent County, Michigan. Abigail and Gail Aquino, lenders. Cotton with polyester filling, 87.5" x 104", MQP 86.569.

Gail Ellen Aquino relied on a quilt book to teach herself how to quilt in 1975. The first quilt she completed was a memory quilt made as a wedding present for her brother David Evert. Now, only 11 years later, she has completed 8 quilts and teaches quilting through the Grand Rapids

265. Jacquelyn Faulkner (b. 1955). Original design *(Another Green World)* made 1986, East Lansing, Ingham County, Michigan. Jacquelyn Faulkner, lender. Linen, cotton, and silk, 68" x 44", MQP 86.2058.

Jacquelyn Faulkner combines nontraditional designs with excellent technique in an attempt to "challenge formalities and use the familiar in unfamiliar ways." Faulkner, a mammalian biologist, began to explore the art of quilting in 1980 as a creative outlet from her technical job.

While studying biology and ecology for eight years . . . I came to realize that most "right brain" functions were being suppressed either directly or indirectly. In an academic environment I was becoming calculated, whole-heartedly accepting the process in exchange for a license to practice scientific research. Recognizing a real need *to be emotional and imaginitive first, I turned to working with fabrics. Fabric is emotional. It's fragile, textured, tactile, highly changeable and transitory. It reaches to the very roots of our experience. We are born into it, we marry in it, and it surrounds us when we are buried.*

This recognition of the traditional role that fabrics play in people's lives is combined with nontraditional subject matter and nontraditional design methods in Faulkner's fiber arts.

Another Green World *comes from thoughts about accessing other space and time dimensions. These creatures are visiting worlds other than their own. They find themselves amidst intersections in time (pterodactyls, and the remains of primitive human civilizations) and in space (huge fingerprints quilted into the* background contrast with the apparent large size of these creatures wading through the vegetation). They are a vision of factual detachment akin to statues of Egyptian pharoahs overlooking expansive valleys of abundance and wealth.

Fabric scraps from a local clothing designer constitute the majority of materials in my quilts. They are often a source of inspiration; ideas to elaborate on. Another Green World *evolved in this way and the scraps can be seen intact in the quilt.*

Jacquelyn Faulkner
Courtesy of Jacquelyn Faulkner

In an 1889 issue of
Good Housekeeping, *Mrs. F.A.W. suggests*
the variety of quilt patterns available.

During our warm summer weather we had sewing classes, in which we taught our young girls how to sew and piece quilts. We found it one of the best ways of teaching our girls how to use a needle, and really an economical way too, for every household has more or less to spare, and the quilts are always saleable. Plain nine square is one of the best patterns for very new beginners; after that the road to California and back, of the wedding knot, or the haystack. Any of these pretty and easy to piece.

Start a sewing class or society. I do think there should be one in every community. It pays in a matter of economy, and pays parents to have their girls know how to sew. Now is a good time to commence one, before the long winter evenings. In these classes work is play, the girls become interested, compare their work, and quite naturally strive to excel. We have a nice variety of patterns in our class. If any one wants new patterns, send stamps to pay postage and I will send them to you. We have the road to California and back, king's crown, castle stairs, moon and stars, devil's puzzle, Dutchman's puzzle, old maid's puzzle (you see we favor puzzles) and robbing Peter to pay Paul, pincushion and cucumbers, Centennial, bear's paw, wheel of fortune, wedding knot, mother's fancy, hit and miss,—this uses pieces of all sorts and sizes,—also haystack, button string, toad in a puddle, Texas tears, Texas star, coffin star, maple leaf, box, Garfield's monument. This is a lovely pattern; the letter G in the center of the white monument, and that set on a dark ground makes a very pretty quilt. Then we also have the ocean wave, basket, northern star, sweet gum leaf, brick wall, broken dishes, double T, blind man's fancy, hearts and gizzards, monkey wrench, tangled garter, and sunflower; this last one makes quite a showy spread. You can send a stamp for postage on any one of these patterns I have mentioned, and if you wish I will make and send you a paper block with each pattern, so you can see just how they look before commencing one of them. I will also give five directions what colors to use, etc. where necessary.

By Mrs. F.A.W., East Saginaw, Michigan, *Good Housekeeping,* October 26, 1889, p. 311 quoted on p. 59 of Jeannette Lasansky, *In the Heart of Pennsylvania: 19th and 20th Century Quiltmaking Traditions* (Lewisburg, Pennsylvania: Oral Traditions Project of Union County Historical Society, 1985).

The Michigan Quilt Project

by Ruth D. Fitzgerald, Marsha MacDowell,
and C. Kurt Dewhurst

The Michigan Quilt Project, or MQP, began in 1984 as a sesquicentennial project of the Michigan Traditional Arts Program at the Michigan State University Museum. In collecting information on quilts and quilters, the MQP was very open in accepting what went into its inventory. Many of the restrictions—such as accepting only quilts made before a certain date or excluding ones made from commercial kits—imposed by planners of other state projects were not used here. The criterion for acceptance in the Michigan Quilt Project inventory was that the quilt or quiltmaker have some association with Michigan. A "Michigan quilt," then, was not necessarily one handmade in Michigan by a Michigan resident. Rather, the inventory included quilts brought to Michigan, quilts made from commercially available kits, quilts made before 1850, and quilts made as recently as last year. The MQP inventory also accepted information on quilts that were simply "in the collection of someone who was or is a Michigan resident." Thus we attempted to broaden the collection of data that would help in analyzing migration patterns, ethnic or regional variations in quiltmaking styles and patterns, variance in processes of learning quilting methods, and the influence of technological change and improved communication systems on quiltmaking.

Methodology

Five distinct methods were developed by MSU Museum staff to collect the data: (1) soliciting and cataloguing data sent in by individuals; (2) coordinating and implementing a series of public Michigan Quilt Project Quilt Discovery Days; (3) interviewing and photographing individual quiltmakers by MQP staff and volunteers; (4) archival and library research on selected quilt-related topics; and (5) developing a collection of quilts and quilt-related materials. A standardized inventory form was developed for use in each of these collection methods, and a system was set up for cataloguing all collected information. Since the availability of inventory forms was announced to the public in August of 1984, more than thirty-six Quilt Discovery Days have been held in communities around the state, and more than 5,000 quilts representing over 3,500 quilters have been registered. In addition, data have been extracted from the forms and entered into a computerized data base management program which has enabled staff to quickly access information for both research and public service uses.

The Michigan Quilt Project Inventory Form and Cataloguing System

The first step in the Michigan Quilt Project was to develop both a set of inventory forms to be used throughout the project and a method of cataloguing the data as they were collected and submitted. After reviewing sample questionnaires from other states and consulting with quiltmakers, folklorists, and oral historians, the MQP staff decided to adapt a questionnaire developed by quilt collector and historian Jonathan Holstein. With Holstein's permission, the first version of the Michigan Quilt Project inventory form was drafted and printed. The form was divided into three four-page sections labeled "Quilter Information," "Quilt History," and "Technical Information." Questions in the first section sought such

Collection of MSU Museum.

biographical information about the quilter as age, birthplace, occupation, ethnic background, organizational affiliations, names of family members, how the quilter learned his/her art, and participation in quilt-related activities. Questions in the second section pertained to why the quilt was made, what stories were associated with the quilt, who it had been made for, any damage or repair to the quilt, and who had owned it. The last section requested such technical information as materials, name and source of pattern, size, number of quilting stitches per inch, and date. In each section respondents were encouraged to provide information about the availability of other quilt-related information such as diaries, scrapbooks, photographs, and ribbons. In each case, questions were written in such a way that the form could be completed by a quilter, a quilt owner, or a person simply recording information on a quilter or quilt. The inventory form was used to record both historical and contemporary quilts or quiltmakers. After the first 100 questionnaires were sent out and returned, project staff made some minor changes to simplify the process of completing the form, and the revised version has been in use since.

Although it was recognized that many persons would not take the time to complete a twelve-page form, delineating all of the areas of information that would be important to have for future use was necessary. Because persons filling out the forms might not have all of the information requested of them, they were instructed to fill in what they could. Given the length of the form, the amount of time it takes to complete, and the lack of available information to answer many of the questions, it is not surprising that many of the forms are incomplete. Even so, minimal data have been secured on thousands of quilts and quiltmakers and, in numerous cases, the form was not only entirely completed but

also submitted with additional, unsolicited information.

As each form was returned to the MSU Museum, staff, students, and volunteers began the task of cataloguing the material. Each set of forms collected was assigned an MQP number. Every item relating to that form received an extension of that number. Thus slides, black-and-white photographs, Polaroid photographs, news clippings, tape-recorded interviews, and other materials pertaining to one MQP Inventory Form received the same number. Forms are stored in vertical files, photographic prints and paper materials placed in protective archival sleeves, and slides placed in binders. Next an Artist Data card and a Quilt Data card listing up to forty fields of information were filled out, and this information was then entered into a computerized data base management program on a micro-computer. The Artist Data and Quilt Data cards were then filed respectively in alphabetical and numerical sequence. Lastly, a thank you note bearing the MQP number was sent to the person who had completed and sent in the form.

Thus the files themselves and the computerized data base on quilts, quiltmakers, and quiltmaking traditions collected and catalogued through the Michigan Quilt Project Inventory Forms provide the basis for future research and educational use.

Michigan Quilt Project Discovery Days

During 1985 and 1986 thirty-six Michigan Quilt Project Quilt Discovery Days were held around the state. A Quilt Discovery Day (QDD) provided an opportunity for members of a community, who may or may not have been quilters, to bring their quilts to a central location and have them documented. Each QDD was co-sponsored by a local organization that worked with the MQP staff to plan and carry out the event. These groups included local historical societies, church groups, quilt guilds, museums, quilt shops, and Michigan State University Cooperative Extension Service county offices. Each of these groups was responsible for securing a place to hold the event, scheduling volunteers to inventory the quilts, and arranging for local publicity. A member of the MQP staff attended virtually every MQP Quilt Discovery Day. Before the event a packet of information was sent to the sponsoring organization. The packet contained detailed instructions on the arrangements and the number of volunteers needed to set up a Quilt Discovery Day, a compilation of suggestions from other groups that had already hosted Quilt Discovery Days, and a sample press release that said, in part:

> If you own a quilt, are a quilter, know a good story about a quilter or have quilt-related information, this event provides a good opportunity to share your special information. . . . Citizens are invited to bring in both new and old quilts that were either made in Michigan or

Sign announcing Quilt Discovery Day in Clinton, Michigan, March 1985.

have special significance to their families. At these official MQP sites, volunteers will photograph their quilts and will assist them in filling out inventory forms.

At each Quilt Discovery Day, the following generally took place: When a community member arrived with a quilt, a number was assigned to it, a tag bearing that number was attached to the quilt, and the number was recorded on a set of inventory forms. The person was then directed to a table where she or he was requested to begin filling out the forms for the quilt(s). In the meantime, the quilt was taken to an area set up for photography where it was hung or laid flat with its number visible so that the photographs could easily be matched to the forms at a later date. Five photographs were taken of each quilt and, where possible, a photograph was also taken of the quilter. These photos included a color polaroid print that was immediately attached to the set of forms and both a full view and close up using both color slide film and black-and-white print film. The color slides provide an accurate visual representation of the quilt, while the black-and-white prints, since they are less likely to fade with age, provide a more permanent archival image of the quilt for researchers.

After the quilt was photographed, it was taken to a table where technical information was recorded on the forms by volunteers. For every photography station used, two tables for measuring and recording the technical information were needed to keep the process flowing smoothly and quickly. Volunteers recorded information such as the overall measurements of the quilt, the number of quilting stitches per inch, the types of fabrics used in the quilt's construction, what kind of filling the quilt had, and how old the quilt was. After this process the quilt was returned to the owner and the forms and photographs were retained for the archive.

At several Quilt Discovery Days an area was set up where stories about quilts and quilters were recorded on tape. These areas worked best if they were set up near, but not within, the area used for inventorying the quilts. The information gathered

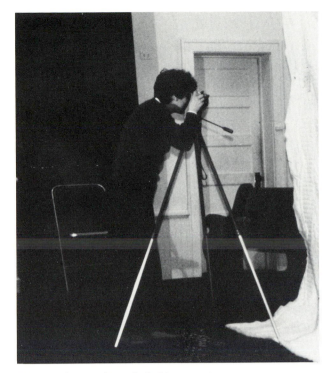

Photographing quilts at Quilt Discovery Day.

at these quilt story collection centers has provided valuable glimpses of the quilting traditions of both the past and present.

Discovery Days were held statewide from Detroit to Ironwood, Kalamazoo to Alpena, and Muskegon to Saginaw in an effort to represent the state both geographically and demographically. Because initially few quilts made by Upper Peninsula or Black quilters were registered, special series of Quilt Discovery Days were planned. In the summer of 1986 five such days were held in the Upper Peninsula to ensure that quilters from that region would be adequately represented in the resulting inventory. In addition, Quilt Discovery Days that targeted historically important or predominantly Black populations were held in Idlewild, Muskegon, Grand Rapids, and Detroit, in partnership with local county Michigan State University Cooperative Extension Service offices, Muskegon Community College, the Museum of African-American History in Detroit, the Detroit Historical Museum, and the Idlewild Crochet Club in Idlewild.

Oral History Interviewing and Photographic Documentation of Individual Quiltmakers and Quiltmaking Events

Data collected through the solicitation of complete MQP inventory forms and the Quilt Discovery Days were an important first step in the understanding of the role of quiltmaking in people's lives. However, the format of MQP methods did not allow more than a glimpse at the stories behind the quilts

Quilt story collection center set up at the March 1985 Quilt Discovery Day in Clinton, Michigan.

and their makers. Therefore, when and where possible, a follow-up visit was made by staff, Michigan State University students, and contracted folklorists to the homes of quiltmakers to conduct tape-recorded interviews and to photograph the quiltmakers at work in their own surroundings. Students and volunteers then assisted staff in transcribing the tapes and cataloguing the materials.

Archival and Library Research Projects

As data from the Michigan Quilt Project were submitted, the staff began to delineate a number of topics about which a body of quiltmaking-related data available in archives or libraries could be pursued for more in-depth research. The list included such topics as references to quilts in the *Pioneer Collections, Report of the Pioneer Society of the State of Michigan,* and the history of the *Detroit News Quilt Club.* With the assistance of undergraduate and graduate students at Michigan State University, a number of these topics were pursued. Most notable was the effort of one student in locating the records of premium winners in the quilt judging categories at the Michigan State Fair.

Development of the Michigan State University Museum Michigan Quilt Collections

As public interest in the documentation project has grown, the MSU Museum also became the recipient of numerous quilt and quilt-related donations. Two significant collections of quilts were received from George and Dr. Harriet Clarke and Merry and Albert J. Silber; individual quilts were received from donors all over Michigan and from across the country. Quilt-related donations included historical photographs of quiltmakers and quilts, patterns, pattern books, quiltmakers' scrapbooks, and news clippings. All of these accumulated materials, along with a contribution toward the establishment of a long-term endowment for the Michigan Quilt Project, have enabled the Michigan State Uni-

Collection of MSU Museum.

versity Museum to become a center for the study of quiltmaking in Michigan.

Implications for Future Research and Education Projects

The initial research phase of the Michigan Quilt Project has provided a sound foundation for future research. One of the underlying premises of the project is that quilts and quilters can be best understood through the application of precise methodology. The inventory and documentation effort has emphasized the collection of extensive data on the life of both the quilt and the quilter. The compilation of this information on a computerized data base system, the creation of a major photographic archival record of Michigan quilts, and the success of the Quilt Discovery Day format in sites throughout Michigan are examples of the efforts taken to date to strengthen the methodology used in quilt data collection. Attention to the application of a precise methodology to quilt study will be an ongoing goal of the emerging Michigan quilt study center at the Michigan State University Museum.

Among the in-depth research projects in process or under development by the Michigan Traditional Arts Program staff are more locally focused surveys and inventories of quilts and quilters, oral histories with Afro-American quiltmakers, studies of community and family history quilts, biographical studies of historical quiltmakers, and histories of quilt clubs.

The results of the research also provide a base on which the staff of the Michigan Traditional Arts Program can develop a variety of educational projects that will broaden the understanding of traditional art and artists. Among the educational projects in process or under development are exhibitions of Afro-American quiltmaking in Michigan, community and family history quilts, and the George and Dr. Harriet Clarke quilt collection; publications to accompany the exhibitions; an educator's handbook on quiltmaking in Michigan; a slide-tape program; and a quilt block exhibition designed to fit into a suitcase for traveling around the state.

Three areas are promising for future research and study:

1. **Quilts as Cultural Maps.** The extensive collection of computerized quilt data on quilts and quilters has begun to make it possible to map out visually the cultural regions of the state of Michigan. Patterns of settlement can be substantiated in the quilts that were brought to Michigan or made by both natives and settlers. Visible evidence of distinctive regional traditions can be found in these textile documents, whether their makers or owners hailed from upstate New York, European countries, or the upland South. The cultural fabric of Michigan has been woven steadily, with a distinctive pattern that reflects the cultural life of the people of Michigan.

2. **Tradition and Innovation in Michigan Quiltmaking.** The prevalence of particular quilt patterns, styles, techniques, and functions used and developed by Michigan quiltmakers deserves further investigation. Data collected to date indicate that certain quilt traditions appeared frequently, and the prevalence of these traditions can be correlated with other community cultural characteristics. In addition, there is evidence that such things as popular magazines, newspaper columns, and quilt shows contributed to brief periods of sometimes widespread popularity for selected "new" quilt patterns and techniques. Over the years, quiltmakers have demonstrated innovative quiltmaking that has resulted in unique quilt patterns. Most recently, the increased interplay between traditional arts and fine arts has yielded extremely innovative quiltmaking styles and techniques.

3. **The Quilter as Traditional Artist.** One of the most critical and yet fundamental premises of the study of material culture is that any object maker, such as a quiltmaker, invests in his/her creation an intended "message" or "sign." The traditional quilter has a wide array of traditional knowledge to impart in a quilt that often is not readily visible just by examining the quilt as artifact. Traditional quiltmakers quilt within a social system—a community context—whether it be a church-affiliated group, a family circle, or a network of quilting friends. To fully understand the message in any quilt one must seek to better understand the quiltmaker and those with whom the quiltmaker seeks to communicate. Through talking with the quiltmaker and those for whom the quilt was intended, we can better understand both the messages invested in individual quilts and in traditions.

Current and future educational applications of new knowledge about quiltmaking take four forms:

1. **Michigan Quilt Exhibits.** Currently, the Michigan Traditional Arts program staff is preparing two quilt exhibitions, one on Afro-American quiltmaking in Michigan and one on community history quilts in Michigan. These exhibits will be the first in a series on Michigan quiltmaking that will grow out of the quilt inventory and the in-depth research projects of the Michigan Quilt Project. The exhibits will originate at the MSU Museum, and many will travel to other Michigan museums, community centers, schools, and fair sites. MSU Museum staff will provide technical and program assistance to other museums interested in developing exhibits featuring Michigan quilts.

2. **Referral Services to Local and Regional Educational Programs.** As a result of the initial inventory effort, the Michigan Traditional Arts Program staff can now provide additional referral services by helping local organizations identify quilters in their communities for educational programs. The Michigan Traditional Arts Program will continue to provide the assistance in planning local and regional educational programs that present Michigan traditional arts and artists.

3. **Folk Artists in Schools Programs.** In recent years many school districts throughout Michigan featured Michigan traditional artists, such as quilters, as part of the Artists-in-Schools Program. The inclusion of such artists helps to strengthen the sense of pride in local culture and expand awareness of artistic traditions that are sometimes taken for granted by local residents. Increased appreciation for these local artists and their work is one of the objectives of the Michigan Traditional Arts Program.

4. **Folklife in Education Projects.** The potential for integrating an understanding of Michigan folklife in arts and social studies school curriculums is strong. Schools throughout Michigan have renewed their commitment to the study of Michigan during the state's sesquicentennial year (1987). The continued celebration of Michigan "living" traditions, passed on from generation to generation by Michigan people, can best be realized by incorporating folklife and folk arts, such as quiltmaking, in school programs.

It is clear from the research conducted by the Michigan Traditional Arts Program staff that the body of information on Michigan quiltmaking to be collected and analyzed is vast and the efforts to date have but scratched the surface. It is also clear that the current image of quiltmakers and quiltmaking in Michigan is varied and complex. Strong traditional quiltmaking practices do indeed exist in Michigan, but there are also many new influences on quilters such as national quilt magazines, professional instructors, workshops, and statewide quilting networks, guilds, and clubs. Together, the combination of new and old contributes to a lively and changing picture of Michigan quiltmaking—a picture that the Michigan Quilt Project hopes to bring into focus through the continued development of research and educational projects.

Michigan Quilt Project
Quilt Discovery Days and Local Sponsors

March 5, 1985	Clinton: Clinton Historical Society	**May 3, 1986**	Grand Rapids: Grand Rapids Public Museum
March 24, 1985	Caspian: Iron County Historical Society	**May 10, 1986**	Kalamazoo: Kalamazoo Public Museum, Kalamazoo Area Quilt Guild
April 12-13, 1985	Detroit: Michigan State Fair	**June 7, 14, 1986**	Detroit: Detroit Historical Museum, Museum of African-American History
April 26-27, 1985	St. Clair Shores: Quilt Guild of Metropolitan Detroit	**June 21, 1986**	Grand Rapids: Kent County Cooperative Extension Service
May 7, 1985	Marlette: Women's Association of the First Presbyterian Church of Marlette	**July 10-11, 1986**	Idlewild: Idlewild Crochet Club, Lake County Cooperative Extension Service
May 10-11, 1985	Dearborn: General Henry Dearborn Quilting Society		
May 23-24, 1985	Ionia: Ionia County Cooperative Extension Service	**August 14, 1986**	Baraga: Baraga County Cooperative Extension Service
June 1, 1985	Flint: Crossroads Village, Genesee County Parks and Recreation Commission	**August 23, 1986**	Ironwood: Gogebic County Cooperative Extension Service
		August 25, 1986	Houghton: Thimbleberry Quilters
June 19-20, 1985	Bay View: The Terrace Inn	**August 27, 1986**	Marquette: Marquette County Quilter's Association
July 11-14, 1985	Maple Rapids: Maple Rapids Sesquicentennial Commission	**August 28, 1986**	Stephenson: Menominee County Cooperative Extension Service
July 20, 1985	Cheboygan: Sally's Fabrics, Cheboygan Rivertown Quilters	**September 6, 1986**	St. Ignace: Mackinac County Cooperative Extension Service
October 19, 1985	Saranac: Saranac Public Library		
October 25, 1985	Traverse City: Con Foster Museum	**September 6-7, 1986**	Hastings: Historic Charlton Park, The Hastings Women's Club
October 26, 1985	Leland: Leelanau County Historical Museum	**October 18, 1986**	Centreville: St. Joseph County Cooperative Extension Service
October 26, 1985	Charlotte: Eaton County Historical Commission	**November 12, 1986**	Wyandotte: Wyandotte Museum Quilt Guild, Crosstown Patchers, Quilters of the First United Methodist Church of Wyandotte
November 16, 1985	East Lansing: MSU Museum, East Lansing Public Library, Capitol City Quilt Guild, East Lansing Fine Arts Commission		
December 7, 1985	Alpena: Jesse Besser Museum	**November 15, 1986**	Muskegon: Muskegon County Museum, Muskegon County Cooperative Extension Service
February 15, 1986	Muskegon: Muskegon County Cooperative Extension Service, Muskegon Community College	**November 25, 1986**	Mt. Pleasant: The Center for Cultural and Natural History, Central Michigan University
February 16, 1986	Lansing: Ingham County Cooperative Extension Service	**December 15-16, 1986**	Sterling Heights: Quilt 'n Friends
March 7-8, 1986	Saginaw: Piecemakers Quilt Guild		

SELECTED BIBLIOGRAPHY

Binney, Edwin, 3rd., and Binney-Winslow, Gail. *Homage to Amanda: Two Hundred Years of American Quilts.* San Francisco, CA: R K Press, 1984.

Buferd, Norma Bradley, and Cooper, Patricia. *The Quilters: Women and Domestic Art.* New York: Doubleday, 1977.

Chappel, Bernice M. *In the Palm of the Mitten: A Memory Book of the Early 1900's.* Brighton, MI: Great Lakes Books, 1981.

Dewhurst, C. Kurt; MacDowell, Betty; and MacDowell, Marsha. *Artists in Aprons: Folk Art by American Women.* New York: E. P. Dutton, 1979.

Dewhurst, C. Kurt; MacDowell, Betty; and MacDowell, Marsha. *Religious Folk Art in America: Reflections of Faith.* New York: E. P. Dutton, 1983.

Dewhurst, C. Kurt, and MacDowell, Marsha. *Michigan Folk Art: Its Beginnings to 1941.* East Lansing, MI: Michigan State University Museum, 1976.

Dewhurst, C. Kurt, and MacDowell, Marsha, eds. *Michigan Hmong Arts.* East Lansing, MI: Michigan State University Museum, 1984.

Frye, L. Thomas. *American Quilts: A Handmade Legacy.* Oakland, CA: Oakland Museum, 1981.

Green, John M. *Negroes in Michigan History.* Detroit, MI: Privately printed, 1985.

Hains, Maryellen. "Contemporary Quilting in the Great Lakes States." *The Great Lakes Review,* Vol. II, No. 2 (Fall 1985), pp. 37-47.

Hall, Carrie A., and Kretsinger, Rose G. *The Romance of the Patchwork Quilt in America.* New York: Bonanza Books, 1935.

Hamlin, Mrs. M. Carrie. "Old French Traditions." *Pioneer Collections, Report of the Pioneer Society of the State of Michigan,* Vol. IV. Lansing, MI: W. S. George and Company Printers and Binders, 1883.

Holstein, Jonathan. "Collecting Quilt Data: History from Statistics." *The Quilt Digest.* San Francisco, CA: Kiracofe and Kile, 1983, pp. 62-68.

Joyce, Rosemary O. *A Woman's Place: The Life History of a Rural Ohio Grandmother.* Columbus, OH: Ohio State University Press, 1983.

Kolter, Jane Bentley. *Forget Me Not: A Gallery of Album and Friendship Quilts.* Pittstown, NJ: Main Street Press, 1985.

Lasansky, Jeannette. *In the Heart of Pennsylvania: 19th and 20th Century Quiltmaking Traditions.* Lewisburg, PA: Oral Traditions Project of the Union County Historical Society, 1985.

Leech, Leslie; Polyak, Stephen; and Ritzenhaler, Robert. "Woodland Indian Ribbonwork," in *Art of the Great Lakes Indians.* Flint, MI: Flint Institute of Arts, 1973, pp. xxvii-xxix.

Lipsett, Linda Otto. *Remember Me: Women and Their Friendship Quilts.* San Francisco, CA: The Quilt Digest Press, 1985.

Malanyn, Margaret. "Fifteen Dearborn Quilts," *Uncoverings.* Vol. 3. Mill Valley, CA: American Quilt Study Group, 1982, pp. 87-100.

Manning, Susan. *Quilts and Coverlets in the Collection of the Ella Sharp Museum.* Jackson, MI: Ella Sharp Museum, 1973.

Marston, Gwen. *The Mary Schafer Quilt Collection.* Flint, MI: Privately printed, 1980.

McMorris, Penny. *Crazy Quilts.* New York: E. P. Dutton, Inc., 1984.

Meo, Lyndon. *National Bicentennial Quilt Exposition and Contest.* Warren, MI: Women's Association for Macomb County Community College and the Warren Historical Commission, 1976.

Roach, Susan. "The Kinship Quilt: An Ethnographic Semiotic Analysis of a Quilting Bee," in Rosan A. Jordan and Susan J. Kalcik, eds., *Women's Folklore, Women's Culture.* Philadelphia, PA: University of Pennsylvania Press, 1985.

Swan, Susan Barrows. *Plain and Fancy: American Women and Their Needlework, 1700-1850.* New York: Holt, Rinehart and Winston, 1977.

Van Buren, A. D. P. "Raisings and Bees Among Early Settlers." *Pioneer Collections, Report of the Pioneer Society of the State of Michigan,* Vol. V. Lansing, MI: W.S. George and Company Printers and Binders, 1883, p. 296.

Van Buren, A. D. P. "The Frolics of Forty-Five Years Ago." *Pioneer Collections, Report of the Pioneer Society of the State of Michigan,* Vol. V. Lansing, MI: W.S. George and Company Printers and Binders, 1883, p. 305.

Webster, Marie D. *Quilts: Their Story and How to Make Them.* New York: Doubleday, Page and Company, 1915.

Wilson, Benjamin, C., *The Rural Black Heritage Between Chicago and Detroit, 1850-1929: A Photograph Album and Random Thoughts.* Kalamazoo, MI: New Issues Press, 1985.

Tape-recorded interviews:
Sina Philipps
Donna Esch
Rosie Wilkins
Josephine Collins
Letha Lundquist
Christena Graves
Vivian Rybolt
Thelma Caruss
Margaret Thelen
Grace Field
MQP Discovery Day, Clinton, MI
MQP Discovery Day, Grand Rapids
MQP Discovery Day, Muskegon
MQP Discovery Day, Detroit
MQP Discovery Day, Idlewild
Archival papers: MSU accession numbers 6268, 6119, and 6275.

I N D E X E S

Index of Artists by Groups

References are to quilt numbers.

Index of Quilts by Title
(given by maker or owner)

References are to quilt numbers.

Signature Quilt, 13
Snowflakes, 178
Sock Quilt, 189
Spider Web Comforter, 135
The Sunflower Quilt, 136
Susan's Favorite, 175
Stained Glass Window, 207
Star Medallion Sampler Quilt, 258
Star Quilt, 149
Star Shimmer, 251
Stripes of Triangles, 108

Todd Family Quilt, 233
Tracy Miller Family Quilt, 143

Transportation, 179
Tree of Life, 254
Tulip Quilt, 158

Vegetable Garden, 173
A Village Street, 195

Wedding Quilt, 100
Wedding Quilt, 191
Wild Rose Celebrity Quilt, 238
World War I Quilt, 115
World without End, 177

Index of Pattern Names

References are to quilt numbers.

The following is taken from the
secretary's records of a womans' society of the Clinton [Michigan]
Methodist Episcopal Church, organized November 20th, 1868.

April 11 1883—Ladies Society entertained by Mrs. Levi Richmond, 25 present. Weather *quite windy.* Ladies working on their blocks, quite a number completed.

July 18th 1883—A month had passed and we gathered with Mrs. Wastell for the afternoon to commence joining our famous quilt over which the ladies were all getting discouraged. A "council of war" was held & a decision to "quit the job" was reversed. So now the work commences in good earnest. Mrs. Geo. Brown & Mrs. F. Muir offering to be purchasers at a five dollar bid, when completed if nothing better offered. Mrs. Wastell is a pleasant host and all moved off pleasantly, the guests enjoying it.

Pending this social & one advertised for next fortnight, the sickness of Wm. Gadd (in our President's family) so paralyzed us that we readily took a vacation of four weeks. Meanwhile the basement is being thoroughly painted & papered anew. Mrs. McIlwane was carried up to see Miss Audelia Allen by Mr. Wastell, and secured a gift of 35 bed quilt blocks to be used by the Ladies society for the benefit of their fund. The quilt was completed by aid of 14 new blocks set together and material furnished by Mrs. McIlwain who here leaves the record of a few stitches taken for love of the cause. Let us to the "littles," each of us, if we could keep our dear church.

Nov. 8th 1882—The Ladies were entertained by Mrs. & Mr. James Halladay at their pleasant home, there was a large attendance, and the ladies busied themselves in sewing for Mr. and Mrs. Hulit, whose house and goods were last consumed by fire. A number of sheets and pillow cases were made from cloth donated by "Freeze & Son," also a bed quilt was commenced.

Feb. 14th 1883—A Social was held at the house of Mrs. Wm. Gadd—the day proved to be one of the *most stormy* of the season, and many remained at home who fully intended to go. In the afternoon the ladies took into consideration the piecing of an "Antique Album" to raise a second "hundred dollars" towards the proposed "New Parsonage." The pastor asked for the Society's subscription, and after due consultation, the members present gave their President (Mrs. Wm. Gadd) instruction to subscribe for them $200....Also they decided to commence the quilt. 53 1/4 blocks were subscribed for at $1.20 each (The names of those given who had collected autographs and money for a block or more).

Feb. 28—An afternoon social was held at the church, with 34 persons present. By vote some Red Calico was purchased, for the quilt, and ladies began to cut them. 3 ladies had their quota of names. Mrs. Dr. Adams was selected to take charge of the work and of the money collected, and also write the names in each block.

Sept. 5th 1983—Quilting Social at the church all day. Dinner and supper served at 5 cents each for workers. Good attendance. Net receipts after paying for linings, thread, wadding, & table expenses—$2.70.

Sept. 26th 1883—Quilt Social at basement. Quilt sold to James Halladay for $5.50. Quite a good attendance, a good entertainment. A very good essay read by Mrs. McIlwain, giving a history of the quilt, etc. Money received for sale of the Allen quilt that was given to Mrs. McIlwain. $5.40

Jan. 16th 1884—The Social was held at the residence of G. R. Brown. Afternoon and evening, the weather was very pleasant and there was a large attendance. The quarterly report was read by the Sec. A vote was taken whether or no the ladies should prepare for a fair. It was decided in favor of the negative. The next question in order, that there was home missionary work to be attended to at present, rather than contributing all to the foreign missionary cause. The ladies time was occupied in the afternoon in piecing quilts to be sold at a later date, the next question was whether or no the proceeds of the Autograph Quilt, when sold, should be taken for the benefit of the new Parsonage, which was not decided.

Feb. 21st, 1884—The ladies of the M.E. Society met at the basement for the purpose of quilting the two quilts (then on hand).

Feb. 27th—One of them was the autograph quilt to be sold by casting lots at 5 cents a vote. The quilt was then presented to Mrs. J. M. Kerriage.

B*ernice Chappel, in this excerpt from her book* In the Palm of the Mitten: A Memory Book of the Early 1900's, *recalls a quilting bee to help the family of Reuben and Onie Camp.*

One winter [a neighbor woman] Onie became ill and was unable to work. Ma decided to hold a sewing and quilting bee to help the unfortunate family. Our parlor door was opened early the morning of the sewing bee so that the seldom used room would be warm. That afternoon a dozen neighbor women arrived armed with a quilt top, cotton batts and lining material as well as some of their daughters' outgrown clothing which would be repaired and made over to fit Margaret.

Pa blanketed and tied the horses while Ma took the women's "wraps" and laid them on the bed. As they settled down to work, some sat at the dining room table, others in the few rocking chairs and some on the narrow red plush backless couch in the parlor. Needles and tongues flew as the women exchanged recipes, chatted about their families or gossiped about an absent neighbor.

Rose Raymer and Bernice and George Thomas Finlan came with their mothers. We four listened and watched as we wandered from room to room. I'd seen these children a few times but we made no effort to play together, choosing instead to watch and listen...I wandered into the parlor followed by Rose, whose mother was one of several women gathered about the quilting frames. There wasn't much room so we squeezed against the wall at the end of the parlor organ. The quilting frames which consisted of two wooden cloth-covered poles the length of the donated hand-pieced quilt top were suspended on the tops of four straight chairs in the center of the room. The quilt lining had been basted to the quilting frames. The cotton batts were unrolled evenly on the lining and the quilt top was laid and secured over all. We watched as two or three women worked at each side "tying off" the quilt. Tying off was done by sewing a double threaded needle through the quilt at regular intervals and knotting the string securely on the right side before clipping it an inch from the knot. As the work progressed on each side, the frame was rolled over the completed work so that the next section toward the center could more easily be reached. Finally when the quilt was tied off, the edges were released from the quilting frame and rolled up and turned over the pieced top, then stitched down by hand to make a rolled hem on all four sides.

Bernice M. Chappel, *In the Palm of the Mitten: A Memory Book of the Early 1900's* (Brighton, Michigan: Great Lakes Books, 1981), pp. 124-25.